Date Due

Dynix

DEMCO

HOUSE
WITH A
HUNDRED
GATES

Snow College

Lucy A. Phillips Library

Ephraim, Utah

Presented by

MaVon Herring

Books by April Oursler Armstrong

House with a Hundred Gates
Water in the Wine
When Sorrow Comes,
    with Grace Perkins Oursler
The Greatest Faith Ever Known,
    completed for Fulton Oursler
Fatima: Pilgrimage to Peace
    with Martin Armstrong
Stories from the Life of Jesus
The Book of God
Ben and the Green Corduroy Angel
The Tales Christ Told

HOUSE
WITH A
HUNDRED
GATES

by April Oursler Armstrong

McGraw-Hill Book Company · New York · London · Toronto

To my daughter
Catherine Grace Armstrong
who helped prepare the manuscript,
this book is dedicated with love

Contents

HOUSE WITH A HUNDRED GATES: The Church is a house with a hundred gates: and no two men enter at exactly the same angle.

G. K. Chesterton

1

Amble and Preamble

I was born October 15, 1926 to Grace and Fulton Oursler.

I was born again, March 22, 1948 to grace, in the Catholic Church.

These are my lives, the second building on the first. Together they make an adventure of which I cannot guess the end.

They are distinct, these two lives, and so different that each puzzles those who know me only in the years of the other. When I try to tell my children what my young life was like, they do not easily believe me. Some of the older family friends who watched me grow up are baffled and saddened that I should have ended up where I am. I don't blame them. I myself would have been appalled as a child to know what I would be in my thirties.

Conversion is impossible to explain. I do not often speak of my own, any more than I analyze my love for my husband in public. Religious conversion is like falling in love, the beginning of a new life, quite personal.

11

Besides, my conversion lacks drama. I was never a drug addict, a notorious sinner, or anything glamorously sordid before I became a Catholic. I was just myself, and then: more than myself.

But it may help someone to know not only how it happened, and how it affected my life, but also how it gave me what I consider the touchstone to joy and freedom.

Conversion is not the end but the beginning. All is not halos and lilies. The life of a convert in the Catholic Church has its peculiar difficulties, stress and confusion, which people too seldom talk about. I talk about it, because I think it's important.

When I was younger I fought against the Catholic Church. If what I then believed about the Church were true, any sensible person would fight it. And today, within the Church, I, like so many others, still keep challenging whatever seems to me to mar her human structure.

When I was younger I also fought against believing in God. I fought belief in God, which I once had and then lost, because I was afraid, though I did not understand that then. I was afraid God was just too good to be true.

It's hard for a shy heart and an educated mind to believe not only that there is a creator running the universe, but that he personally loves each one of us beyond reason. It's the love part, and the shattering truth of personality in God that is so hard to dare to believe in.

In the days when I was too intelligent to believe in God, I assumed that people who did believe took the easy way out. I know now that willing to believe is not easy. You don't get swept into conversion on an emotional tide. You have to decide.

Having balked as long as I could, I willed to believe when I was twenty-one. It is understatement to say that decision changed my life. It formed me again, and is still forming me. It altered my career, shaped my marriage and my role as mother, made me new friends and new enemies, changed my ambitions. It made life much easier and also more difficult. It gave me more to think about, laugh about, cry about. It showed me infinite horizons and pinned me down. It made me disgustedly aware of my faults and convinced me that I was still, incredibly, lovable and loved.

The people who had great hopes for me as a child look at me now, stuck in what seems to them—and sometimes to me too—a dull suburban house-bound parish-bound existence, and in polite silence they assume the Church has ruined my life.

"You left the mainstream," one gentle friend of my parents' generation said. "You're out of everything. I would never have expected it. But I suppose you're happy."

I wish everyone were as happy.

Ours is a noisy cluttered home, a tangle of children and visiting priests and political arguments and manuscripts and friends, a far cry from what I dreamed of having. Yet I believe that in this din unnoticed emerges a meaningful pattern. To me it is certain that, with grace, life is suspenseful, beautiful, a drama of constant surprise. And without grace, even in the thick of ideas, cocktails and status, life has no meaning.

I am no Pollyana. I do not think my life is all fun. I have, frankly, a lot of heartaches and headaches. But I wouldn't trade with anyone.

And I can't wait to see what happens next. Some people take for granted that when you're in your thirties the pattern's set. I don't. You see, everything up to now has been so unexpected.

I knew, once, exactly what I wanted to make me happy. In almost every detail my life has turned out to be the exact opposite of what I hoped for and planned.

Yet today I am happy.

I consider that fact an example of grace, and of God's sense of humor.

I asked for a stone and, smiling behind his hand, God gave me bread.

2

The Happy Pagan

I've given up trying to tell my children what it was like when I was a child. Even after we passed the "olden days" barrier and I oriented them in time so they no longer thought their mother was raised before electric lights, we found little common ground.

When I was a child, I'd say, I once waited in an inn while the prince of the Jebel Druzes arranged the rescue of my baby brother from a gun battle on the road to Damascus. (My children know princes belong in fairy tales.)

I remember, I'd say, the time I had breakfast in bed with President Roosevelt in the White House. (This sometimes raises adult eyebrows till I explain I was only seven. My children dismiss the story as fiction because they know we're Republicans, and the only way I have been able to show them the inside of the White House is by turning on the television.)

I remember the sunny blue day when I stood in the spot where once the statue of Athena reigned in the Acropolis. Standing there was said to guarantee me wisdom. A few minutes later my father was running down the hill leaping from one pile of marble ruins to another, when he leaped to one which was not marble. It was wet lime—soft, clinging, burning. I laughed. Standing on Athena's pedestal does not guarantee wisdom.

Shall I tell my children of buying green lovebirds in the street where Christopher Columbus was born? Of the ruby necklace in the backroom of the Pushmahul Brothers' souvenir store in Cairo? Of the way I wept in Gethsemane? Can they believe I was there?

We do better talking of more homely things, such as the times I was a bad girl, when I broke Mother's expensive phonograph, or ate a whole box of Louis Sherry candy and denied it even though, when my parents woke me up, I had chocolate not only all over my face but all through my hair.

Did your mother ever spank you? my children ask. Only once. My governess usually did that. (Yes, dear, a governess is sort of like a babysitter). The one time my mother spanked me was when I refused to take my part in a French one-act play on the stage in the library of our home. I was to play opposite Mary Pickford, who was hiding from kidnappers at our house. Perhaps the police outside made Mother nervous, for she really knew I couldn't act, or memorize French, but she was afraid my refusal would offend Miss Pickford. I knew Miss Pickford couldn't care less, and she kissed me to prove it, after the spanking.

Mother was always hoping I'd acquire some ladylike distinction. She wasn't a pushy mother, but sometimes I made her rather desperate about my future as a woman. I looked exactly like my father, which was unfortunate for a little girl, and I liked to read what he liked to read, and I wasn't a cheerful or lacy child. Secretly Mother must have wondered if there was anything of her in me. There was, but it didn't show up then, which saddened me as much as it must have her. Anyway, when she saw I couldn't act, or sing, or wear dresses gracefully, and when I actually was asked to leave the Fokine ballet school because I couldn't even learn to skip, she pinned her hopes on the piano, poor thing.

Once an eminent pianist whom she deeply admired came to tea. Mother asked me to play for him. I demurred. She asked me again, smiling. I said I wasn't good enough, hadn't practiced that week, and really didn't want to play. She smiled again, and I understood that was it. So I played. The sweat made my fingers slippery and I did even worse than usual, but I really tried to do well.

When I finished, the pianist blinked, put down his tea, and said: "My child, I must compliment you highly. You displayed an admirable reluctance to play."

Which is why I vowed I'd never force my children to perform

for anyone. But they're not impressed. They're of a different ilk, and they know my problem as a mother is to keep them from performing endlessly for everyone.

Hopefully, my children try another conversational gambit. Did you collect things, like Dinky cars or baseball cards, when you were a child? I had a whole home-made museum of collections. I had a hank of hair and a lady's bone and pottery shards I dug up at Cuzco, Peru. The shells from Galilee, the water from the Jordan. A diabolo I learned to spin in China and a musky-smelling abacus. A stone I stole from the catacombs. Dolls from everywhere. Arrows and butterflies from Ecuador, and a carved ivory Key of Life from Egypt. In a glass jar a mouse's caecum which I dissected and pickled. My collection of brittle dry egg-cases of conch, skate and other seaside creatures. No baseball cards.

Did you play games, Mom? Of course. I was a witch at Parchesi, and learned to practice psychokinetic control of dice before Dr. Rhine did. I played Chinese checkers with the seventh son of the seventh son of the Prophet, who was really a writer named Achmed Abdullah. He cheated at Chinese checkers, but I never could catch him at it. Mostly I played make-believe games by myself on my bike, or down by the edge of Buzzards Bay.

Didn't you have any friends, Mom? Few. We lived far away from most people who had children, and I did not have the gift of making friends at school. One girl, Dot Burke, giggled with me. The others I had to make up.

Did you help your mother around the house? Yes. I helped her with hydroponic growth of tomatoes when she was hipped on that, and the making of scrapbooks, which was a full-time occupation in our home. And in the summer I arranged the forty-odd bowls of cut flowers from our garden, with special care for the exquisite roses Mother planted. My mother did not then cook or sew or clean or wash or iron. I didn't think she knew how.

Did you say your prayers every night? I did not say prayers.

No one spoke of God around our house when I was little. I went once to a Sunday school in Theosophy in Hollywood while my parents worked on movie scripts. All I remember is a drawing of a road which looked like a triangle and was The Way. That was the year we rented the house of movie star Jack Holt. And the year writer Frances Marion's son, Fred Thompson, whom I wanted to marry, told me there was no Santa Claus. At the same time I was reading about Pegasus, the winged horse, and a frightening tale of a man who sold his shadow, to the devil, I think. These made a much more lasting impression on me than Theosophy.

My children shake their heads and go about their business. They do not see what all these stories have to do with me. I am their mother and I pray and do housework and have friends and I do not live in a make-believe world of travel and servants. Like most children anyway, they cannot really believe their mother was a child. They are right.

I was never a child. Childish, yes. At times I am still childish. But childhood was not a golden value in my home. It was a necessary condition to be overcome. I do not say this resentfully. I wasn't a happy child, and for a time I took comfort in the fact that in many novels heroes and heroines have miserable youths, and many biographies take young unhappiness as an indication of genius. Of course, I've mostly gotten over that. Seriously, though I hope our children are happy, I can't see why anyone expects children as such to be happy. Being a child is painful when you want to be wise and strong and independent and able. Children are usually told that being a child is wonderful. And, being false, this kind of talk makes childhood harder to endure.

I was never treated as a child, except occasionally by my mother, who kept trying to think of me as her charming pretty baby even when that was patently unrealistic. My father expected me to think and to be sensible and imaginative too. From the earliest time I can remember, he treated me as a person rather than as a child. When I was stupid or unrewarding as a person, his attention left me, tactfully, till I should grow up some more. Everything from language lessons in the bathtub to trips abroad was focused on the time when, childhood survived, I would be what I was meant to be:

adult. Though I knew I was an ugly duckling, that wasn't so bad because I knew sometime somehow that must pass. Growing-up was what I was here for.

For better or worse, I was a bright child. I could read before I was four, which is how I entered second grade at five, which meant graduating from college at nineteen. Because I could read I always knew too much to play with dolls, or get along with my age group or my class group, and often I couldn't get along with myself. At nine and ten I was reading Dumas and Nancy Drew, Poe, Hugo, Shakespeare and *Mary Poppins*. I lived in my imagination, invented companions, knew the stirrings of *weltschmerz*. I wrote glibly and happily. I was taken seriously, at least at home, and took myself seriously because I didn't know what else to do.

It's not quite true that I never heard about God. I did, of course, and not just in Christmas carols. I had a Roman Catholic cousin, Bonnie Herman, who visited me summers. I had my Grandma Oursler, who was a Baptist. She ruined tomato soup for me. One Sunday she took me to church three times, and between afternoon and evening services, when we had supper at her house, she poured tomato soup. And as she poured she sang:

> " 'There is a fountain filled with blood
> Drawn from Emmanuel's veins . . .' "

I seldom visited her. My Grandma Oursler didn't approve much of my father's way of life. She had named him for a Baptist minister, the Rev. Charles Fulton, and wanted him to become a preacher. She had little use for writers, didn't like the seaside, and at the time I knew her wasn't very cheerful. So I wanted no part of her religion, which was unfair of me but understandable. Her hymns however I loved and kept, as they came to be transmitted by my father's voice singing through shaving soap. "When the Roll Is Called up Yonder" mingled happily with "Bye-Bye Blackbird."

Not until years later did I know that Mother's mother, Grandma Perkins, was a Catholic. She never mentioned religion to me. She remains in my memory only with sweet Peter Rabbit tea parties, exquisite afghans crocheted during her invalid years, and the strange smell I later learned belongs to cancer.

In place of God as an ideal I had the muse of poetry, the flair of drama, the hard-hewn ideals of reporters and scientists, and a vague abiding love for the sea as a mystic image. My parents, who practiced no religion and did not believe in God, were determined to let me choose for myself when I grew old enough.

Mother was a fallen-away Catholic. My father a fallen-away Baptist, who nearly drowned in immersion and had a neurotic fear of swimming the rest of his life. He had married in his teens, and that marriage ended in divorce. He believed in reincarnation, transmigration, the possibility of prophecy and spiritual sin, and no church at all. He considered Jesus Christ a good man misrepresented, misunderstood and maligned by organized religion.

None of that did I know. Until the age of eleven I remained a pagan with no trouble at all.

3

High, Handsome and Hectic

My mother, Grace Perkins Oursler, was half-Irish and all heart. She was one of three children of a Catholic beauty, Margaret Judge Perkins of Boston, and a non-Catholic father, Lamont Perkins of Maine. She had been raised a Catholic. When her father, a publisher, died while she was in her teens, she promptly left the Church. A beautiful, tall, compelling girl with large grey-green eyes and regal carriage, she found herself suddenly older and wiser than her own mother, and far more practical. She realized she must get out and help support her mother and her younger sister. So she went on the stage. Thanks to the help of such indomitables as

Minnie Dupree and Florence Reed, young Grace Perkins learned enough of the trade to do creditably on the Broadway stage and on the road. She had a long run in that famous old standby *Lightnin'*.

And, in the pattern that runs through our family on both sides, because this young woman had great energy and a great constant need for money, she took up half a dozen sidelines. She made ukulele arrangements of popular tunes for reprint houses. She composed original songs, such as "Mama, Take Me to the Zoo" and "Iffle Diffle Dumple Dee," which went into New York public school textbooks. As Daddy Dusk and as Jill Jackson she wrote fairy tales for newspapers, including a gem about "The Land of the Lost Pencils." And soon she wrote her first book, *Music Al*, a charming education in music in fairytale form, peopled with characters such as Grace Note and illustrated by her sister, Bobbie.

When she was twenty-four Grace Perkins, who was determined to succeed as a writer and wanted to get out of the theater, met Fulton Oursler who was already a successful writer and editor. She hoped to sell him a story about a girl named April, and Thyra Samter Winslow introduced her to him, and they fell in love. The next thing you know he was calling her April after her heroine, and that is how I got my name, two years later.

None of Mother's books, whether written under her maiden name or under her pen name of Dora Macy, made literary history. But she had a flair for the heart, and an irresistible breathless excitement in her writing. And her books made money. Magazines ate them up as serials. Hollywood made movies of such books as *Night Nurse, Personal Maid* and *No More Orchids*. Later, part of our basement, called the Ego Room, was papered at one end with theater posters featuring Clark Gable, Carole Lombard and the like in Mother's stories. She had more movies on her side than my father did on his.

And Mother, who never had illusions about being a great writer, and never learned to spell, and never could write anything short, kept writing because people she loved needed money. She would rather have been a musician. She had trained to be a serious singer, but her voice had broken when she was quite young. She had not her brother Ray's magnificent talent at the keyboard, but all her life her piano and her record collections filled our home with music. She was a woman of beauty and loneliness, extravagant with money and compassion and love. She was prodigal with life, and though at times life treated her miserably, she kept hoping.

My father was the only surviving child of a streetcar conductor in Baltimore. But Fulton Oursler had enough careers to make a family's worth. He was a skilled magician. His first professional income, after he flopped as a waterboy and as a student of law, was as a sleight-of-hand artist in Baltimore. He was a newspaperman, a silent poet, a thwarted actor, a self-made expert on music. His leap from a dual career in newspaperwork and free-lance writing in Baltimore to the New York big time came when he landed a job as editor of *Music Trades* magazine. He was, when I first became aware of him, editor-in-chief of all the Macfadden Publications magazines, and of the weekly *Liberty* in particular. He was also then a playwright, novelist, mystery story writer, and a popular lecturer on Americanism, personalities, current events and crime prevention. A self-educated man who never finished grade school, he still set courses of study for himself, and read the big dictionary for fun every night.

I was born in New York City on a kitchen table in a West Side apartment. Later my father bought a house at 217 West 70th Street on which there was soon both a first and second mortgage. He named the house Sandalwood. He had already written a novel called *Sandalwood*, which drew its title from the Chinese proverb: "The sandalwood tree imparts its fragrance even to the axe which hews it." That motto he kept before him all his life. The more the axe of life hewed him, the more determined he was to yield a sweet return.

In that brownstone Sandalwood I became aware of two teenagers, Helen and Bill, who were my brother and sister because they were my father's children, but who were not related to my mother. So I learned that my father had been married before, to Rose Karger, and had had these two children whom he loved tenderly. My father later suggested that if I wanted to know what that marriage was like I could, when I grew older, read his novels and study the first wife characters therein. I don't pretend to know if it was an unhappy marriage or not, because I wasn't there. But at any rate, my father had sought a divorce to marry my mother, and Rose declined to give it to him, so on advice of that fabulous lawyer Arthur Garfield Hays, he had gone to Mexico for the first of the Mexican divorces that are now rather commonplace. Mother, chaperoned by her mother, followed him on another ship. My Grandma Perkins, staunch soul, resigned to the heartache of seeing her daughter wed a divorced non-Catholic, insisted she would go all the way with her to be sure she was properly married by a Catholic priest even if it had to be in Yucatán, then went home to let them honeymoon alone. Eventually another divorce was obtained in New York, and Grace and Fulton settled down there to live their lives. Helen and Bill, the children of the first marriage, went to live with their mother, of course.

But then, for one reason or another, Helen and Bill left their mother and chose to come and live with mine.

According to those who remember those days, it seems I was always running around in a red kimono, looking cute. I don't remember the kimono or looking cute. I remember the floods of people flowing through our house. I remember my father's pet monkey who smeared ink all over manuscripts with his tail, and once perched on a chandelier throwing things exactly as monkeys do in old movie comedies. We didn't have the monkey long.

Reading my mother's diary of those years is an eye-opening experience because, being a child and therefore self-centered, I couldn't begin to understand then the enormous proposition it was to be my father's wife at that time. Here is a woman in her late twenties with a little girl, two teen-age stepchildren, her own mother suffering from cancer, and her husband's mother, who came for occasional stays, showing signs of deteriorating health. In her role as wife of an editor-writer she had to entertain and to be on tap to go to other people's homes and to the theater, lunches, dinners, afternoons, evenings and far into the night. In a four-month span of her diary there's not a single day when she was left to the privacy of her family, and the roster of names she wrote down to memorize who was who includes 197 personalities in the many fields in which my father was interested.

On top of all that, the Ourslers, living high, handsome and hectic, were just about broke all the time, so Mother was writing. She had contracts with Covici Friede and with Lowell Brentano for a total of nine books at one time. She was dictating on two serials at once, writing not only for Macfadden Publications, but for everything else that came to hand, and sweating it out while her red-headed agent got into fights with editors and payments were delayed while bills were not. Many a woman rather expects to find security when she marries. My mother, I'm sure, didn't expect it, which is a comforting thought, because she never did find it for more than a year at a stretch. Let me make it clear that I'm not accusing my father of being a poor provider. He worked even harder and drove himself even more than my mother did, and made good money. But it was never enough to go around for long.

How did they get so desperate financially? Well, there was alimony, substantial and constant. There were her mother and his mother needing support—his mother in her own house, her mother at home and later in an apartment—and both with medical bills. There were my governess and I, and if I hadn't had a governess my mother couldn't have worked. There was Helen and her dramatic school, and Bill with art lessons in New York and in New England, and his courses from a tutor. And mostly there was the fact that like others in that day and tribe of writers, the Ourslers had gotten on a treadmill from which they couldn't withdraw. Days and nights were so crowded with people essential to business, who all had to be given drinks and fed, that if anything personal was to be discussed it had to be discussed after midnight. Mother, recording an attempt to go for a walk alone with my father and encountering people, then seeking privacy with him for supper by choosing Childs' Restaurant and even there running into people to whom they couldn't afford to be rude, finally writes in her diary: "I'm so damn sick of meeting people wherever I turn that I could cry."

She did cry. More and more she became so tired that she couldn't sleep, and Daddy would give her sherry and a couple of aspirins to prevent insomnia. Her health was leaving her. She had hyperthyroid trouble, with all its excruciating nervous physical difficulties, and had an operation in 1930 that left a delicate necklace of scar around her throat. Those first years of her marriage were tough, and I conclude now, quite objectively, that to stick them out she had to be a woman of incredible stamina, and deeply in love.

Prime among her objectives was to be as good a mother as possible to Helen and Bill. And with Bill she forged a loving closeness in those early years. Again and again her diary notes how she would snatch time to have long talks with him in the fourth floor room he used as a studio. There's a charming passage where she describes the time Bill, the young art student, surprised her with a design for the jacket of her new book, *Promiscuous*. She liked it, urged him to send it to the publishers, and gallantly fought for its use even after it was turned down.

I remember understanding clearly by the time I was four that Bill was a great artist and a man of the world. And that Helen was going to be a great actress. I saw her in a maid's uniform on a real stage.

Unfortunately, Helen was unhappy with us. She never liked my mother, which made things hard for both of them. The differences between them were enormous. Helen moved out of our home when I was four or five. And life barreled on. I went to kindergarten at Eleanor Roosevelt's home, and tried to learn to handle scissors accurately, and to discover the meaning and relevance of that song about "Shoo Fly, Don't Bother Me." That song sure bothered me.

Soon we didn't live in New York any more. My father decided we had to get away from it all, and find a place to live and work where there would be peace and quiet. So we moved to Cape Cod, into a new Sandalwood, which, being roomier and more attractive, attracted and held more people and confusion than the New York brownstone ever could.

4

Sandalwood-by-the-Sea

The first appointment I ever made to see my father was in the summer of 1931 when, quite formally, I told him I wanted a sister or brother.

My father was never remote or unapproachable. I had with him always a rare, cherishable closeness. But there was, at all times, a delicate gradation of proper conversational material with him. All his life he worked from offices in our home. This meant that while he was working at home you were to live as if he were not there at all, and never intrude, any more than you would if he were physically away at an office. That was sometimes difficult, but, because he didn't commute out of the home, his every off-hour put him immediately in the family circle, and that was wonderful.

Early in the morning I could tiptoe into the bedroom to share his breakfast while the rest of the house slept, and there was no need for him to hurry because he wasn't going anywhere. We'd watch birds at his window-sill feeder, peer through binoculars at the ships in the Cape Cod Canal, whisper and laugh without waking my mother. Then he'd wash, dress and stroll into the library to start his workday.

Because he was home he could really use short breaks in the day for fresh air. He'd call to me to walk with him and the dogs. He'd wear his Sherlock Holmes hat and choose one cane from his exotic collection, and off we'd go. In fifteen minutes he'd be back with manuscripts and dictation, but meantime we'd seen how the wild blueberries were faring.

In evening moments I was his ready audience for magic tricks, or his forays into ventriloquism. He had two dummies, Ambrose Glutz, a curly-haired scamp, and the more sophisticated Sir Jasper Bedworthy, who really smoked cigarettes and leered. Ambrose and Sir Jasper were taken as members of our family, along with a group of invisible spirits, all distantly related to Aunt Arabella, who supposedly dwelt in our attics with her abominable niece, Sally Jones. Sally Jones often turned up at dinner table and could be heard telling my father what she had done that day. She had always done whatever I had done, only better and nastier. To complete the family roster, there was Profolingo, a minor devil, summoned by rubbing my father's elbow. Profolingo was an expert at removing the pain of skinned knees, or the heartache of a broken butterfly collection.

On special occasions we had what my father called "Private Dates," dress-up excursions into the world for a strawberry soda and the zoo, a matinée, a visit to the flea circus, or a prowl through a second-hand bookstore. The custom of Private Dates, a chance to be alone together as individuals rather than as parent and child, continued till I was married. I can think of no finer compliment to pay a child, no surer way to cement friendship between father and daughter, than to choose to spend a couple of hours in joint recreation every few months.

In off-hours you relaxed with my father and let him relax. But matters of some importance, such as report cards or requests for money, were handled in an official way. I would submit a memo to my father which would pass through the regular secretarial channels, reach the To-Be-Done folder in the Come-Up File, and be sent back to me with his inked scrawl, OKFO, penned in one flowing hieroglyph. That OKFO became so much a part of our lives that he had it reproduced in gold for Mother's charm bracelet and mine.

Matters of truly grave importance were not handled by memo. They were discussed adult fashion, with appropriate dignity and setting. Only by appointment could anyone except my mother intrude on his workday in the library.

Solemnly in 1931 I sat across from him at his desk and made my request for a sister or brother. I didn't, of course, know the precarious state of my mother's health after her operation. I didn't know then, at the age of five, where babies came from, or how. I assumed they could come rather well-grown, so I didn't think it necessary to explain that I wanted one five years old, so it could play with me.

He said he would take my request under advisement. As the months passed I rather gave up hope, and I didn't mention it again because I was trained never to nag.

Then, in June 1932, I was sent to Falmouth Theatre to the movies alone at night. This was a startling surprise to me. Mrs. Davis, who sold the tickets, and Mr. Davis who took the tickets, and everyone else smiled at me, and they knew why I was there that night even if I didn't. When I came home my father led me upstairs and showed me a red squalling infant he said was the little brother I had asked for. He grew up to be Tony, and after that first depressing encounter I never regretted asking for him.

In those days thirteen magazines selling a total of 15,000,000 copies a month emanated from our home on Cape Cod. Four secretaries worked full time in a room that had once been a porch. We had our own Western Union machine, and our own teletype to the New York Macfadden offices. Manuscripts and correspondence came and went in a daily bag on the train. The phone was the fourth string tying the Cape house to New York. Daddy wanted to live by the sea and make his work come to him, a man trying to hoard privacy as others hoard gold.

And Sandalwood-by-the-Sea was as unprivate as any other madhouse.

This, our real home, my father discovered when it was only a pup, a small summer cottage on a cliff overlooking Buzzards Bay. It was thoroughly impractical as an Oursler home. So he bought it. Over the years he had the walls pushed out, doubling the size of living room and master bedroom, and installed ungainly handsome picture windows framing the waves. He had a cellar dug and a furnace installed. He raised the roof and built a third floor for me and little Tony and Jane Paul, the wee Scottish governess we called Paul. He added four porches. He raised the garage roof and built an apartment for the help. Then he built a library, a two-story wing larger than the main house, with a stage for magic and amateur theatricals, acres of glassed-in bookcases, a walk-in fireplace, a private aerie of a writing room, and three more picture windows.

The result was the architectural monstrosity I still consider the most perfect house in the world. Gabled and sprawling, salt-silvered shingles covered with the rambling roses Mother loved, Sandalwood stood on the edge of a cliff rough with Scotch broom, heather and pine. The beach was a giant's rockyard. Across the road on another lot crops of three kinds of corn, asparagus and strawberries were guarded by a most elegant scarecrow: with a granite head sculpted by Arlene Wingate, and clothes cast off from Broadway musicals. Her name was Madeline. In a separate poison garden my father whimsically nurtured every deadly plant he could buy, borrow or steal.

When I grew up, I realized Sandalwood was typical of our life; its many-roomed personality mirrors ours. In its wild youth it was lavish, idiosyncratic, comfortable, busy and expensive, and like its inhabitants anything but elegant. I thought it was heaven, and I never perceived that it fell short of ordinary standards of fashion. We had inlaid ivory and wood game tables we'd brought home from Damascus, and two grand pianos. But there was no sterling or fine china. And not one drape for any window, because who would want to cut off the sight of the sea and sky? We did usually have a butler and cook and handymen. We did, for a time, raise mink in our woods. But the dining room wallpaper was faded, the staircase treads were uncarpeted and worn, and no one was permitted to run a carpet-sweeper or a lawnmower while my sensitive-eared father was at home.

Emperor Haile Selassie sent us a monkey rug from Addis

Ababa. Eleanor Roosevelt, until we became Republicans, sent us each year exquisite enameled chests of tea from Bubbling Well Road in Shanghai. And I remember the summer when former Kaiser Wilhelm sent us two blue and gold ashtrays with the imperial monogram of W and H (for his second wife, Hermione), because, being an ardent mystery fan, he reveled in German translations of the murder stories my father wrote under the name Anthony Abbot.

That was the same year that rodeo stars parked their prize saddles, glittering silver and gold, in our living room. Mother was doing a novel called *Riding High,* and steeping herself in research, so cowgirl Alice Greenough became my ideal for six weeks. And that was the year Neil Vanderbilt, Jr. parked his fancy trailer, Stardust, at our house before taking it to England to cover the coronation for *Liberty.* Emil Ludwig was writing something in the upstairs guest room, and indulging his hobby of imitating dogbarks. I remember that while he was there James Barrie died, and I was appalled to discover that a literary light, no matter how foreign, had never heard of Peter Pan.

John Erskine, whom I worshipped, was teaching little Tony to play the violin, because my parents thought Tony wanted to play one, and he was too polite to contradict them. Tom Dewey was singing arias at the piano with my mother, and discussing crime with my father.

The family learned to weave trails in and out of the transient excitements. Tony and I and Paul lived upstairs with what even then I recognized as luxurious privacy. The grownups may have wanted us out of the way, but not any more than we did. Downstairs the known and unknown could down highballs and stage skits, play The Game, argue, laugh, flirt, and compete, but upstairs we were safe. And, when it all got too much Daddy or Mother would sneak up to join us.

Mother's brother Ray, and her sister Bobbie, and their spouses, and to a degree Daddy's mother, were used to the confusion and didn't expect fuss when they came to stay. Even our guests had to rough it, which some thought delightfully bohemian, and others pointedly didn't.

Bill lived with us at Sandalwood almost all the time till he was graduated from Harvard and married, to Adelaide Burr. Helen, who left us when we still lived in New York had married a young man named Dave Stewart. In 1932 we went to Hollywood because Mother was hired to write some scenarios as soon as Tony was born. When we left, Helen, married, was sick in a New York hospital. Western Union was kept busy with wires while Daddy arranged for her hospital bills and doctors, and then, since she also had tuberculosis, arranged to send her and her husband to a sanatorium at Saranac. And by Christmas of that year my mother was desperately ill in Hollywood with complications from thyroid and aftereffects of pregnancy and so on, so ill that one newspaper headlined her death.

When we returned to Cape Cod, Bill had his room on the second floor of Sandalwood-by-the-Sea, and, being so much older than I, lived in a different grownup world. I knew him to be a talented artist, a serious newspaperman, a writer of bittersweet poetry.

For a time Helen lived with us again too. After her cure at Saranac she became pregnant and came to stay at Sandalwood so she could have the care and bedrest she needed to keep her from losing this baby. Mostly she had the big guest room, but when we had to put up other people, she, being family, had to be moved to a pine-paneled cubbyhole called—I never knew why—X2, or even into a tiny writing room. It wasn't a very convenient arrangement, but we made the best of it. Eventually her baby was born well and happy.

And to complete the environment there was usually in Sandalwood Bernarr Macfadden, that much maligned wondrous old man who made the house crack with his laughter. Physical culture with BM, as everyone indelicately called him, was no mere money-making gimmick. He lived physical culture. He'd fly his plane up to the Cape and I used to love going to meet him because often he smashed up the plane but always he walked out safe. We'd put his luggage in the car and drive home while he walked the ten miles at a brisk clip. He slept on the floor. He drank buttermilk, swam in the bay even in winter, and deplored our family's uncultured physiques. Because of him we all had to wear outrageously expensive handmade healthy shoes. I had four horrid pairs in different leathers. The black dress-up ones looked as if they were borrowed from my father. I suffered agonies of soul over those shoes, but I couldn't really hate BM. He had such a good time, all the time! He fasted when he felt his body needed it. If everyone else happened to be going to a restaurant he'd wait in the car outside, humming "Ah, Sweet Mystery of Life!" Of course, he gave us a terrible reputation in the town. People, hearing that we made "that poor old man" walk, sleep on the floor, and stay outside at restaurants, thought we treated him dreadfully. Explanations were futile. Personally, I dreaded his visits because he always expected me to be thinner and healthier, but I loved him. He could forgive even me for not sharing his enthusiasms as long as I had real enthusiasms of my own.

Life in the Sandalwood three-ring circus was broken each January and February by a trip abroad. I'm most grateful to my father because he never stopped to wonder if I was old enough to appreciate travel. He took me. And Tony. And Paul. With a fantastic caravan of suitcases, numbered with green paint up to 36, he'd roam in a combination of vacation, higher education and serious journalistic work. One year we visited the Chiang Kai-Sheks in China, another we interviewed Mussolini in Rome, and later the Duke of Windsor in the Caribbean. A trip to South America began with a trek through Panama jungles to a forlorn shack, hideout of a man weary of publicity, Jafsie of the Lindbergh kidnapping case.

Crime buff and editor, my father had run many stories on the Lindbergh case, including other interviews with Jafsie conducted when he had actually stayed a while at Sandalwood. So immersed was my father in that mystery that at one time another writer publicly stated she thought Fulton Oursler had conceived and engineered the whole crime as a publicity stunt.

After that follow-up visit to Jafsie's hideout we went on to Ecuador, and to Peru, where I was bitten with the archaeological fever, and under the encouraging eye of Dr. Gieseking made my own amateur digs at Cuzco. We came home through customs that time with a genuine shrunken head concealed in mother's purse. She did not know it was there. My father thought it best not to tell her until we got home. And since no woman except Mary Poppins ever carried a more capacious pocketbook than mother, he was certain neither customs inspector nor mother herself would find it unaided. It stood leering in a dark corner of Sandalwood for the next twenty years, later posing us quite a problem when it came to disposing of our parents' personal effects after their deaths. Ultimately we gave the head a decent burial in an unmarked grave.

Through this hurly-burly of places and people I moved with solemn glasses and fascinated ears. I was aware that a few of the famous people who came to our houses were not legally married to the people they slept with. I was not shocked. I didn't snicker. Their romances lasted, and seemed most appropriate. I read my mother's books, with titles like *Twilight Cheats* and *Ex-Mistress*, and found them quite moral, as I do today. I knew my mother well, and though she had an ex-actress's racy language, and was always telling me to kite the hell down to the post office or the kitchen, I knew her shameful secret: that she was a good little girl at heart. She knew about many things, but she preserved a genuine innocence in spite of being surrounded at times by technical scandal. This innocence of my mother's was and is a mystery, and in later years my husband was to be continually baffled at finding her the most shockable of women.

I read my father's current books, including *About the Murder of the Clergyman's Mistress*, and understood his boast that he never wrote a word he was ashamed to have me read. I knew that in the past under other names he had penned such masterpieces as *Alimony Jail* and *Confessions of an Ex-Cabaret Girl*. I read *True Story*, and knew it was a very moral magazine because my father often said so. And I read a very special home-brewed magazine, now a collector's item and even then valued by antiquarian societies and unsnobbish museums, that sporadic monthly called *The Sandalwood Herald.* I read that because I had founded it, under the name of Mr. Jackson.

Most youngsters who want to write start newspapers. My first *Herald* was a methodical report of neighborhood news spiced with knock-knock jokes, typed by me in a single copy and passed by paid-up subscribers from one to the other till all names on the subscription list at the bottom of the paper were checked off. Then S. O. Shapiro, indomitable circulation manager for Macfadden, gave me a hectograph, and I mastered the messy purple art of printing a real paper. I conned advertisements from our guests. Once Victor Moore and Billy Gaxton took an ad in my *Herald* touting their new musical without any mention of co-star Ethel Merman. I got her to retaliate, and I had a good thing going there at 25¢ a column inch. Aunt Bobbie's husband, my uncle Herb Harris, who was Parfums Charbert, launched all his new scents through my media.

I had such a good thing going there that my father and mother took over the *Sandalwood Herald* and put it on a big-time basis with several thousand subscriptions, and had it printed with illustrations at the Falmouth Enterprise Press. My pseudonym remained on the masthead as the one who founded it. Mother and Daddy's names appeared as those who losted it. My book reviews were published occasionally. And the *Herald,* with articles by H. L. Mencken, Rupert Hughes, and other adult amateurs, was underway. Daddy wrote a column called "Indiscretions, by Heretic," and Mother wrote under the pen name Etaoin Shrdlu, derived from the printer's term for a worthlessly pied line of type. There were limericks, gossip, studies of the history of pornography, musings on current plays and books, politics, and all kinds of things in the *Herald.*

Recorded there in loving detail is the story of the man who was to become my Episcopalian godfather, advertising man Arthur Sherrill, who was a woodcarver by avocation, specializing in figureheads. Needing a model, he approached a maiden of Marshfield. The girl grew shy. Her mother, perceiving the ease of this novel way to earn money, volunteered her equipment. When Arthur, considering her age, demurred, the mother demonstrated the beauty of her torso, and stole the job from her daughter. The figurehead was carved, and the model's husband, a milkman, was impressed, and delighted to know that his wife's beauty would sail the seven seas. He had only one request, that since the carving was masterfully accurate the artist make a few changes in the face to make it impossible for the world's sailors to track down the model. A photo of model and artist at work, with the model's face blacked out, graced the *Herald's* front page.

There, amid sober analyses of current affairs in world politics, and other current affairs, I sampled the outhouse humor my father and his friends enjoyed in private, and first read of Steinech's hormone creams, monkey glands and test tube babies.

I remained incredibly innocent.

I can only say, looking back, that coarseness and vulgarity, like earth and loam and manure, are not the same as dirt, and do not soil the soul. Jesus Christ himself did not hesitate to refer to the privy. He said the things which enter a man by his mouth do not defile him, but pass out of him. The gospel writers did not hesitate to report this, but I can't imagine the average nice person of today, setting out to pen a tract on religion, referring to the toilet. I suspect that many people are not clear in their own minds about what is degrading to humanity and what is not. I was steeped in the facts of life, and in the kind of humor that comes from pratfalls, and because I was also steeped in poetry, laughter, music and kindness, it did me no harm.

I went each summer to a day science school in that part of Falmouth which is called Woods Hole, a center of marine biological research. This school for children gave me the chance to graduate from sea-shell collections to the dissection of cats, the serious study of how newts grow new tails, and the effect of shock treatment on unfertile eggs. One summer I became the father of thousands of sea urchins, fertilizing them myself with electric shock and highly concentrated salt water. Being an assiduous student in Woods Hole, before I was ten and went into seventh grade I knew from my scalpel and probe the anatomy of those huge laboratory earthworms, the dogfish, and small mammals, such as mice. I knew the theory and practice of reproduction from amoeba and plant life, to the insect and vertebrate world.

Yet when the kids in school started telling dirty jokes, I was embarrassed because I didn't understand why they were funny, even when they were explained. I didn't think I was a prig, so I thought I must be naïve. I went to my mother, as one is supposed to do. Mother, normally a voluble woman, grew shy and annoyed.

"Why are you pretending not to know these things?" she asked. I tried to explain that I wasn't pretending. She reminded me that, much to her disapproval, I'd been a less than reticent scientist for several years, and that I'd taught her a thing or two. She thought I was being dishonest, perhaps even prurient, in my new curiosity. Dishonesty and prurience appalled her, as they do me.

I couldn't explain then. Later I understood. True, I did know the biological facts of life, and realized that the facts didn't change much from other vertebrates to human beings. What I couldn't understand was *why*. Why should the mating process call forth on one hand the snickering shame-tainted humor of the children I knew, and on the other hand evoke the poetic fire and almost religious fervor of love poetry? If I accepted sonnets—and young as I was I knew Elizabeth Browning, Shakespeare and Edna St. Vincent Millay—if I accepted the heroic gestures of men and women in the finer romantic novels, if music had meaning, then there must be something more to human love than the joining of bodies in animal fashion.

There had to be something I did not yet know.

I knew it wouldn't be found in smut. I read the original *Arabian Nights* and the *Decameron*. On Daddy's library shelves, near the steamship models, I'd found the sex manuals, and read them unobserved. I discarded everything I found there as worthless.

Perhaps the best armor for a child's purity is complete awareness of the biology of reproduction. It sets one searching for something beyond the body.

Of course, I was pointed more in the direction of humanism than of religion. Organized religion of any sort I was hardly conditioned to take seriously.

The year my father became a bishop I was nine, and thought it great fun. My father became a bishop with degree and credentials from an ordination mill in California, a mail-order house that affably made anyone a bishop for $40. Bishop Oursler apostasized and wrote an exposé of the racket for *Liberty*. But as a memento he had lettered on the side of our station wagon the label: "The Bishop's Carriage," and occasionally deflated the pompous by parading his espiscopal dignity.

Yet, though God was seldom mentioned at Sandalwood, souls were. And not always jestingly, even in Bishop Oursler's residence. Hyacinths were for the soul. That was what one should buy rather than bread when one was down to the last coin. Our life was rich in hyacinths, no matter how confusing was our idea of a soul.

For a long time my father believed he had been reincarnated from the days of the French Revolution. He used to tell me all about Marie Antoinette. Transmigration of souls was a notion that pleased him. Numerology, psychometry, astrology, e.s.p., the mystic and eerie in any form delighted him. Hardly a month passed without some famed fortune-teller holding forth in our living room: Horace Leaf, the psychometrist, Stella Billings, the numerologist (whose analysis of my future I still check with increasing delight in its accuracy as the years go by), Barbara Collins, the astrologist, and later Litske, who brought her pet rooster everywhere. Daddy was himself skilled at reading palms, and often read mine. He always told me what he saw and, as I remember it, it's come true. But he always refused, firmly and strangely, to tell me how many children I would have. I think I know why now.

The significance of numbers thrilled him. He could deliver a half-hour analysis of the number 9, which convinced me forever that it is my lucky number. The construction of the Gizeh pyramid, into the angles and stones of which he read a whole encyclopedia of wisdom, haunted him. He had a half-avowed belief in ghosts, and the little people, the brownies, elves, fairies and banshees, poltergeists and all. To this day I have a fully avowed belief in them.

His knowledge of stage magic and sleight of hand made him adept at exposing frauds. One of his first published books, under the pen name of Samri Frikell, is called *Spirit Mediums Exposed*. He kept hoping to meet a real no-tricks magician, a witch of Endor, and he kept on for years experimenting with table-tapping and ouija boards, but he understood his search for a spirit key to another world was a lost cause.

Which is why I'm fascinated now by the people who talk to my parents. There are quite a few. For some reason, most of them are writers. Perhaps the yen for clairvoyance—or the ability—is a literary disease.

A few years ago I phoned a well-known woman writer to ask if she could remember a detail in my father's life. Quite seriously, she told me she'd ask him about it next week when she talked to him. He had then been dead seven years. I never dared call for the answer. But I know she is sane, competent and successful in her work, and truly good in heart and soul. I don't think she imagines that she talks with him. I can't explain what happens.

Another famous woman once wrote to me, timidly and with great discretion, about encountering the "presence" of my father, and wondered if I would want to hear the message he had for me. I knew, from my own observation, that even while my father lived he had psychic or telepathic encounters with this woman, so impressive that she has reason to believe he saved her life. I did want to know whatever message she had. I had never met her personally, and she had no way of determining the circumstances of my private life at the time, but the message she said my father confided to her proved to be obviously relevant to a situation then in progress. The message described the situation and the people involved, and offered advice and warning of events to come. With heroic will power I put the letter away and acted as I had intended to act anyway. The events predicted did not occur. I was however shaken for months. I believe this justly admired woman to be sane and sincere. I cannot explain her experiences, but I'm not prepared to deny them.

And this year I've learned that my mother is supposed to be talking regularly through a medium to a man writer who values her advice.

Sometimes I wonder if I should be miffed that they don't talk to me anymore. But seriously, it would have delighted the reportorial instinct and the debunking reflex in both my parents to know people think they're chatting with them now.

That reporter's instinct, I was left in no doubt, was the key to understanding and enjoying life. You had to see and smell and taste and feel and observe and question and remember, or you might as well be dead. Nightly at table my father would ask me what I did that day. The one totally unacceptable answer was that nothing new happened.

"I just went for the same old walk," I might say, before I learned better.

"It couldn't have been the same old walk! Something was different. What did you see? What color were the leaves? How high was the tide? Whom did you meet, and what do you suspect they were feeling and thinking, and why? Today is not the same as yesterday. Tell the day chronologically, tell it right, and find what it means."

Squirming, I'd tell what came to be called in our home a "chronnie," a methodical report of a day in which I must search for the unforgettable and the meaningful. An art painfully mastered, this review process has yielded me happiness ever since.

Then, having learned to give a straight chronnie, if you were Fulton Oursler's child you learned to add a dash of showmanship. You were expected to use a bit of artistic license, adding things that were understood to be "details to give verisimilitude to an otherwise bald and uninteresting narrative." All writers, Daddy and Mother agreed, were born liars: not malicious dishonest deceivers, but the kind of happy liars who knew lions roamed the tamest woods, and that the tramp drunk on the main street was probably a lost king. You were expected to know the difference between fact and fiction, and the even more important difference between fact and truth.

And, if you were Fulton Oursler's child, you never knew when your narratives would be used for startling results, so you had to be responsible for what you said. When I finally told him about what I privately called my haunted house, an old shack on the beach where I had observed strange rearrangements of furniture, odd traces of tar, and once in a pre-dawn walk heard voices—the Coast Guard swooped down on my haunted house and caught some rum-runners. When I told my father that my public school teacher proved to us that advertising is deceitful and wasteful, a hidden cost foisted on consumers, he answered me with a long series of articles in *Liberty* about Advertising and the American Way, which made me a bit pompous, probably embarrassed the teacher, and made *Liberty* the advertisers' darling.

The showman's flair for making the most of what one had was as much a part of my father as his walking stick and his laugh. As an editor he had uncanny luck playing hunches. It was the night before the biography of Mary Pickford appeared in *Liberty* that Mary fled to Sandalwood to escape the threats of kidnappers. While police surrounded our home Mary, beautiful, fragile and frightened, hid from the news services that besieged door and phone. News of the Pickford kidnapping threat was headlined across the nation. That issue of *Liberty* sold out.

Some people said he might have staged that. He said it was a surprise to him, as was Jafsie's dramatic departure just when *Liberty* hit the stands with the story "Jafsie Tells All." But at any rate, there's one little coincidence that couldn't have been staged. The week the King of England abdicated for love of an American girl, only one magazine in the United States had his picture on the cover. And again, *Liberty* broke its sales records.

Stick to the truth and play your hunches. See life. Celebrate life. And do your best to make sense of it on your own. That summed up the advice my father offered me in those dizzy years.

And when I decided to become a Christian, he didn't try to stop me.

5

Holy Land, Homeland

I first really learned about Jesus Christ in his hometown.

The first Bible I ever read I bought in Jerusalem. I still have that small New Testament, King James Version, bound with olive wood and set with all the Lord's words in red type. For all intents, I became a believing Christian in the Garden of Gethsemane, which is not what my parents had in mind.

By that time I was already an accustomed traveler, being nine years old, and a veteran of the *Roma,* and the *Conte di Savoia,* and lesser ships. I'd learned to gulp two months' schoolwork like nasty medicine early in the crossing to get it out of the way. Obediently and happily I read travel books before each stop, and kept a diary with pasted souvenirs. I understood about avoiding water, lettuce, and unwashed fruit. When necessary, I could survive on Bovril, crackers and chocolate bars, but I could eat foreign dishes without making a fuss. And I could ride for hours without needing to go, which made me a perfect traveler.

It's not true that travel is wasted on the very young. Granted, my specific knowledge of languages, world history, art and geography is still scant. The map changes so fast today that I keep reading about drastic governmental changes in countries I never heard of. And I have a thing about trying to speak out loud in a foreign tongue. But I found myself able to understand Babel's spoken languages by pretending they were codes and using a little telepathy. Children who go traveling young enough, learn to be undaunted by strangeness, to recognize sameness, and to thrill to newness. What we call culture, a sense of grandeur behind all the many kinds of men, seeps into a child, and lies there to be drawn out later, aged and distilled.

I had seen the real skeletons in the real closet at San Severo in Italy, and risen at midnight to watch Stromboli dance with draperies of fire in the Mediterranean darkness. The Casbah is mine, because as a child I walked it and smelled it. Moslems are mine because I shuffled in paper slippers through mosques in Rabat and in Istanbul, and heard the mezzuin cry the people to prayer.

I wasn't a scholarly child, really. I walked the miles of fortifications at Gibraltar on tiptoe, because someone in the ship's gym had said walking tiptoe developed the calves and produced beautiful legs. What my legs look like now is my business. But I remember Gibraltar and the warships in the harbor. About the Alps I remember most clearly the time the cap blew off our car radiator. I still have the flowers I picked and pressed while grownups fumed and feared. I remember the purple veil of twilight snow in Turkey, and the crazy way it felt to ride a camel to the pyramid at Gizeh, and the word the beggars use for alms, which is "backsheesh," and the word to send them away, which is "impshi." I remember bougainvillea and wine in Madeira, the crooked bridge in China designed to drown the devil who can chase you only in straight-line dashes, the thatched roof of the Hathaway cottage, and the sidecar ride in Dublin.

I remember Rome, where I first wished on a star from the Palazzo Albergo balcony, and I wished for a red sweater, and found one on my bed in the morning. In Rome, and almost everywhere, good tourists visit churches to see art and history. I hated visiting churches. At the end of a particular long day of trudging catacombs, gaping at paintings, and holding my nose to keep out the smell of incense and candles, they told me we were going to St. Peter's. I begged to be excused. I almost dared try a tantrum. But when I got into St. Peter's I couldn't bear to leave it. I was very young that first time, but to this day I can recall the strange, comforting stillness that riveted me to that greatest of houses of God. I didn't know much about St. Peter's, and didn't want to know. I didn't listen to the guide. I stood there without peering at altars, not liking the shiny worn foot of the statue of St. Peter, not caring about the dome, not thinking it was beautiful and impressive, but only knowing that I did not want to be anywhere else.

Of all memories the most indelible is the first visit to what was then called Palestine, and is now called Israel, but which my father always referred to as the Holy Land.

My parents took for granted that I must know something about Jesus. They'd taught me all about Minerva and Athena so I could keep Greek and Roman gods separated in my head, and the history of the French Revolution which, after all, Daddy "remembered" from his earlier incarnation, and enough English history to please my maiden great-aunt, Mary Oursler, a genealogical expert who could trace Ourslers back to the Barons of Runnymede, and to that evidently superpotent man, William the Conqueror. I knew about Thor, and Druids, Isis and Buddha.

Why shouldn't I know the story of the gospels?

The fact was that I didn't. Oh, I knew the Christmas carols about the pretty little child lying in the hay, but what happened to the child after he grew up I didn't know. And I didn't know he was seriously supposed to be God.

I had a vague idea that there was somewhere *one* God, in distinction to the many gods of mythology. The one God ran the world, and had a fascinating and much more likeable enemy, the Devil. But I wasn't good for God's sake. I was good, when I was, for goodness' sake, and out of fear of parental displeasure. One of our dinner table games was "Moral Questions," in which my father would propose a situation, ask me what I would do in such a case, and explore the results of the possible different courses of action. I enjoyed the game. And I understood that a human being, to have the dignity of being human, was honest, kind, patient, hard-working, noble, clean and quiet.

As we neared the port of Haifa I wasn't going to admit to my parents that I didn't know the story of Jesus. It wasn't that I feared to reveal ignorance. Instead, I had a definite sense that talking about Jesus meant bringing up a difficult subject, like the facts of life. Children have their own ways of knowing what subjects to avoid.

How odd a party we made as we landed in the Holy Land, I did not know then.

There was my father, who had already enthusiastically written a recommendation for a particularly blasphemous book which debunked the Bible as dirty literature. (To this day someone peddles that book, using Fulton Oursler's endorsement as if it were recent.) Champion of Margaret Sanger, more or less polite enemy of Christian piety, he had come to Palestine to write a book later called *A Skeptic in the Holy Land*. I didn't know how he felt, and he was kind enough not to tell me.

And my mother? Her last close contact with the Catholic Church and Christian faith, had been when Grandma came along to see her married. In what mood was my mother in the Holy Land? I knew only that she had a keen eye for the human failings of the priests we met at shrines, and an earnest, sophisticated air as she took home movies of famous landmarks.

Paul was with us, and what that dear tidy compact woman believed about anything I still don't know. She always was a private sort of person. Tony was only about-to-be-five, and he believed that life was wonderful and his big sister was a pain.

I stood on Mt. Carmel the first day we spent in the Holy Land, a simple, joyful discoverer. I was not being converted. I was being taken as in a fairy tale from everyday poverty and placed in an enchanted kingdom and told that this was my homeland. I was coming into an unsuspected inheritance, in the tiny country where the old and new testaments of my genealogy were lived and recorded. I believed every word I heard.

We had a dragoman, a guide, a pock-marked messy one-eyed Christian named Tumul, whose breath smelled worse than his tarboosh.

"This is Mt. Carmel. Down there," he said, pointing, "is where Elijah rode up to heaven in his chariot. And on this mountain top is where Elijah lit the fire by prayer and the 450 priests of Baal were killed. Over here is the spot where the Holy Family rested on their return from Egypt. And—"

My head reeled as I pieced the stories together.

By car we sped through the land where Bedouins camped in tents. Far to the right rose Mt. Tabor. Turning a bend in the hillside road we saw a town of white walls and red roofs, olive and fig trees.

"Nazareth!" said Tumul.

We had lunch at the Hotel Galilee, and bought blue beads said to ward off the evil eye. And we went out into the streets of Nazareth.

"It's just as it was," my father said. "Like the pictures in the Bible."

Women in long robes, children riding their shoulders, jugs balanced on their heads, wove their way to the well called Mary's. Some used gasoline cans instead of earthen jugs, but they walked barefoot, and they were beautiful. Off the narrow streets shops opened like dim stages lit by charcoal fires. Each trade had its own bazaar: woodworkers, knife-sharpeners, jewelers, coppersmiths. A Nazarene with beard and dark flowing hair made for us that day a copper tray that I still have. The bazaars of Nazareth were like hundreds of others I'd seen, but later, when I bought my Bible, I discovered that Jesus in the pictures looked just like that Jewish coppersmith. Mary and Elizabeth looked like the women I'd seen at the well. Did the people in Jesus' time play backgammon, as we saw Nazarenes doing, and drink black coffee, and smoke with narghilas in the bazaar? It seemed likely. The world had changed little here in Nazareth, so that there was no strangeness about Bible stories.

I confess the Church of the Annunciation discouraged me.
Within its labyrinth of hillside steps lay a damp cave where Joseph,
Mary and Jesus are said to have lived, and some ruins of the Crusaders' Church and St. Helena's Church, and a pillar where Gabriel
stood, and another where Mary knelt. There's a chapel called the
Workshop of St. Joseph, which was horrid with carpets and lace,
candles and silver and incense. I scurried along trying not to look at
it at all, listening for every clue in the grownup conversation that
would tell me about the people who once lived here. I knew from
Christmas carols that Mary was Jesus' mother, a virgin even though
she had a child, and the child was not Joseph's, it was God's.
Joseph was a carpenter, and so was Jesus, till he was thirty years
old. In the ornate Workshop of St. Joseph chapel, where no one
would have dared saw wood, a painting showed him teaching God's
son the trade.

The church was like a museum, and, like most museums, uncon-
vincing. I was glad to get out in the streets again where I could see
the faces of men I thought related to Jesus.

Even the church of Nazareth didn't dismay me. But Cana was
something else again. After all, I'd seen my father turn water into
wine a hundred times on our library stage, and I knew how he did
it. I remembered his telling me that the word "hocus-pocus,"
which magicians used, was intended to make fun of the Latin of the
Catholic Mass, in which priests claimed to turn wine into God's
blood. Now, as we drove the few miles from Nazareth to Cana I
heard for the first time that Jesus really did turn water into wine
for a wedding feast there. Tumul said it was his first public miracle.
I didn't quite know what to do with that information. If Jesus did
that, and he was God, it seemed blasphemous for modern prestidigi-
tators to go around blithely imitating it. But, if Jesus was God, why
did he choose such a stupid thing to do for his first miracle?

Past camel riders and donkey riders into tiny Cana we came, to
be besieged at the church door by a swarm of beggars howling and
keening, scabby-eyed, sore, hideous. They were like beggars I'd seen
in North African towns, but I hated them for being in Cana be-

cause I couldn't completely believe they were sincere. There were two churches in Cana, both claiming to be on the site of the miracle. The Greek one boasted it had the original jars that held the water, and we looked at the water jars, and hurried away before the beggars swarmed again.

As we drove out of Cana a shepherd climbed a hill, and I took his picture. Tumul said the hill was the Mount of the Sermon. Tumul and Daddy vied with each other quoting the text of that Sermon, and Tumul seemed as surprised as I to find how well my father could do. He had really studied his Bible. We went down from Cana to Tiberias on the Sea of Galilee, and Tumul, who believed in Christ, seemed to be fencing with my father, but my father smiled, dark eyes twinkling, and I decided it was only a game and that both really agreed. Storks flew, donkeys trotted along the road, and the chime of camel bells put me to sleep.

On Galilee we sailed in a fishing boat, the same kind you see in Bible pictures. And I heard from the oarsmen of the terrible sudden storms that beset those lake waters before I heard from Tumul and my father of the time Jesus ordered the wind and waves to be still. We saw Magdala, home of Mary Magdalene, and Nablus where we sat on the edge of Jacob's well, and I met real Samaritans and saw them snubbed by real Jews, and Tumul told me about the Samaritan woman to whom Jesus first announced he was the Messiah.

We slept that night in the King David Hotel in Jerusalem. From our balcony we could see the walls of the Old City, the towers and rust-gold stones of the most loved city on earth.

In a morning rain we entered the Holy City, prowling narrow cobbled stepped streets, sometimes pressing ourselves against walls to let swaying camels and robed Arabs pass. We were not tourists then, not visitors to sites of the past. We were living and breathing in the pages of the Scriptures.

As we followed Tumul down winding walled streets I heard the sound of wailing. I was afraid. We turned a corner.

"Three times holy!" cried Tumul, his bad eye oozing at the corners.

Holy? I saw a big open place in the city, with walls, and a few houses, and inside it mosques and other buildings. It looked like a badly planned museum center or exhibition ground.

"The Mosque of Omar!" cried Tumul.

Mosques are Moslem, and I was puzzled. But Tumul explained that three faiths consider this temple area sacred. Moslems believe that the big black rock in the middle of the Mosque is the place where Mohammed went up to heaven on a winged horse. Jews believe the same rock was the altar of Solomon's Temple, which Nebuchadnezzar destroyed, and on which site Herod's Temple was built. Some also believe that somewhere near that rock is buried the Ark of the Covenant.

Christians believe that it was Herod's Temple, and that in the Temple Jesus preached, drove out the moneychangers, and heard the hosannas of children. There Mary sacrificed turtle doves and presented her infant to the priests. There when he was twelve, Jesus got lost, and was found preaching to the wise old men of the place.

"Thrice holy, then," said Tumul. "And thrice dangerous. The Jews feel the others have stolen their holy place and they stay outside wailing at the wall. The Moslems hate the Jews, and they hate the Christians, and the Christians hate the Moslems. Be careful, little girl, and say nothing, and stay close in this holy place."

One lesson you learn quickly in the Holy Land is that religion makes people angry, and drives them to hate each other. My stomach tingled with fear, but I wasn't what you might call disillusioned. I was young enough, I suppose, to accept the fact that human beings were often nasty, and not to let it get in the way of finding out about Jesus.

The Mosque of Omar was dim and beautiful. Everywhere Moslems prayed to Allah, squatting on prayer rugs blessed in Mecca. Cautiously we approached the thrice-holy rock of contention. It looked like a holy rock.

Tumul whispered, "Some Jews say this rock plugs the mouth of the hole where the waters of the great Flood still roar." His breath was like old wet leather. "And here, but not out on display today, is a gold casket in which are two hairs of Mohammed's beard."

From an outside wall of the Temple area, near Solomon's Stables, Tumul showed us the view of Jerusalem's golden gate, of Mt. Olivet, and of Gehenna. Then he led us through the streets again, past the home of the whirling dervishes, to a convent. Downstairs, in what would have been a basement, he showed us the excavated remains of a city street, furrowed with chariot marks.

Over our heads was the part of the city called Old, which was not very old, being only a thousand years or so. Between that old cobbled street overhead and the paving blocks on which we stood, was the layercake of history, the debris of sieges and destructions and rebuildings. But here, in the damp dark below the convent chapel, experts had dug and found the very road on which Jesus walked.

"The Via Dolorosa," Tumul said. I didn't understand the words. I was gathering the story of that sad Way from paintings in the chapel.

I had stood on older ground, in the ruins of Rome and of Greece. History did not awe me. But something, or someone, did. I believed Jesus carried his cross on these paving stones. I heard someone say he did it to save men from their sins, because he loved them. It was in that convent I bought my New Testament.

The prayer that began in me there came to completion that afternoon in the Garden of Gethsemane. I didn't yet know what had happened in that Garden. On the way out there my father and Tumul were arguing about something, and I was eating an orange, and no one told me about the Garden.

But you cannot look at the trees that grow there, and not know that someone has suffered there.

The trees are thick-trunked and wrinkled and gray. I knew olive trees by sight. They are supple in youth, and firm but still gainly in age. These were in their trunks more like banyan trees, terrifying in their huge solidity. The green leaves on their misshapen stretched branches were normal size and color, and they seemed to me like children in a setting of desolate adult tragedy. I have photographs of those trees still, grey and shadowy in the rain. My father said there was quite a bit of doubt that these could be the same trees that grew there when Jesus wept and prayed. I didn't argue. I listened to the story of that dark night when his apostles slept, and of how Judas and the soldiers came down from Jerusalem and across that valley and up into this place where olive oil was pressed. And I wept, leaning on a tree. I have never forgotten Gethsemane.

The days were crowded with sites and tales, overlapping old and new. At Bethany I heard about Lazarus and Mary and Martha. At the Dead Sea shore I heard of Sodom and Gomorrah, and Lot's wife, and I threw sticks in the salt sea and saw them bounce. A rainbow shimmered over monstrous hills. At Jericho, Tumul picked thorn vines and fashioned us a crown. Later, as we stood on a ramshackle bridge over the Jordan, I heard about baptism, and made sense in my own mind out of the snatches of Baptist hymns Daddy had sung shaving. We had brought empty bottles, and carried them home filled with the water and silt of that swollen stream, and gave them to those who asked.

By the time we walked the Way of the Cross the next day, I'd read part of my olive-wood testament, and knew where we were going and why, and where Jesus had been going and why.

The Way led through arches and bazaars, past coffeeshops and peddlers and beggars, to a big ugly confused church. In the church were Moslem guards. Tumul said they needed guards there, and Moslem ones, to keep peace among all the different kinds of Christians who worshipped in the Holy Sepulchre. Roman Catholics, Greek Catholics, Armenians, Copts, Ethiopians, all kinds of Christians, had spaces marked out for them in the Church of the Holy Sepulchre, and timetables for their services to keep them from colliding, and they weren't polite to each other.

This state of affairs depressed us all except Tumul, who de-

clared that, after all, things were better now than back in the earliest days when a Roman emperor, wanting to erase the memory of
Christ, built a temple to Venus right over his tomb.

This church was a madhouse of ugliness and perfume, a maze
of chapels, priests, golden candelabra and darkness. You needed
tickets and a flashlight, and you had to stand in line. You climbed
down steps and around railings and stood in Christ's tomb. You
climbed up steps and around railings and saw the top of the rocky
hill of Calvary which was inside the church, and there was a hole
lined with silver to show where Jesus' cross had stood.

Years later I would know that my father, standing beside me
there, was bitter then, not only at the folderol and human nastiness
surrounding these shrines, but at the whole notion of Christ's dying
for his sins, or mine or anyone's. He was to write in his book, *A
Skeptic in the Holy Land,* his caustic opinion of the doctrines of
sacrifice, atonement and redemption.

The doctrines didn't bother me. I liked them. Ever since I'd
first read about Sidney Carton, self-sacrifice and dying for others
seemed to me the noblest thing anyone could do. I believed Christ's
death had meaning. But I did not believe in or like that church,
and I was glad to get away from it.

We went from death and resurrection to ascension, to the top
of the Mount of Olives. The Moslems ran that too. They let Christians come there only at certain times because, somehow, that site is
also sacred to Mohammed. I came to think of Mohammed as a kind
of religious squatter. But there was fresh air and green grass on the
Mount, and far off the blue of the Dead Sea, and on the other side
Jerusalem, clear and small, a miniature in a story book. And overhead was the sky into which Jesus ascended, and which no one had
ruined with candles and tickets.

When we came to Bethlehem flocks of sheep fed on the hill-
sides. The water in the Well of the Magi was star-bright. The place
looked exactly like the little town in the colored illustrations of the
carol books the Falmouth National Bank gave out, and I began to
sing "O Come All Ye Faithful," and Tony sang with me, and soon

Paul and our skeptical parents and Tumul joined us, singing as we came to the place of Christmas.

Even I had to stoop a little to enter the Church of the Nativity. The door was deliberately made very low. Inside we saw Christmas tree balls hanging from the ceiling, gaudy and wonderful. Down below, in a rock cave, was where Mary and Joseph went when there was no room at the inn. I'd seen the inns, or khans, of modern Palestine, and they smelled and were flea-ridden, and I was glad there'd been no room for the holy family in places like that. Many silver lamps hung from the ceiling. A star on the floor marked the place of the birth. A wax doll lay in a marble manger. Little Tony sang "Away in a Manger," his long lashes blinking, his voice sweet. But I still conceived an intense dislike of shrines that I've never lost.

Tumul and my parents were discussing Matthew's Gospel and the virgin birth. They didn't believe in the virgin birth and he did, and I got lost in the genealogy they were quoting. But in Bethlehem we bought a Christ-child figure and a small manger that wasn't marble and elaborate, and we used it for our crêche at home for years.

We almost didn't get to see the place of the Last Supper. Like everything else in the Holy Land, it was a place of unholy bickering. The Cenacle, the upper room where Jesus and his apostles ate, where the first holy communion was given, and the first Pentecost flamed, is of interest only to Christians. But underneath is supposed to be the tomb of King David, the ancestor of Jesus. And the tomb is of interest not only to the Jews, but also to the Moslems, who honor David too. So the Moslems controlled the whole place, and no Christian could go down to see the shepherd-king's grave, and only if Christians were polite, and the Moslems in good humor, could they go up to the Cenacle.

I remember being finally disgusted with human beings and all kinds of religion, until I forgot them listening to the marvelous things that were said to have happened in that upper room.

We were to hurry off to Egypt. A few days in the Holy Land

were enough. My parents wanted to get to the Land of Pharaohs and mummies and mystery.

I carried with me on the train to Egypt memories of the gazelles playing in the gardens of the King David Hotel, a string of colored shells from the Sea of Galilee, my bottle of Jordan water, my New Testament, and a small rough crucifix which I bought with the last of my spending money.

6

Blessed Am I?

I made another appointment to see my father. In 1936 I told him I wanted to become a Christian.

Now that I think of it, if I were in his place and one of my children made such an announcement, I'd probably hit the ceiling. He was filled with dignity and tact, even though he was at that moment writing *A Skeptic in the Holy Land,* indicting organized religion as a travesty of Christ's message, decrying theology and dogma, blasting the idea of ceremonial communion, the virgin birth and even baptism.

He was awfully nice about my decision. He asked if I knew what I was doing, and when I assured him I did, he accepted it. I'd read the whole New Testament, I'd seen the Holy Land, I'd made up my mind. Had I chosen a church? he asked. I said I wanted to become an Episcopalian.

Perhaps he was relieved that I didn't want to be a Catholic. Of all churches he considered that the least Christian. But it never occurred to me to consider the Catholic Church at all. I wasn't aware of any Catholics among people I might know.

Of course, the idea of letting a child choose a church is ridiculous. We don't let little ones choose whether or not to brush their teeth, or what school to attend, or which citizenship to adopt. But if parents don't believe in any religion, then it is surely valorous and kind to let a child be free to believe. I was allowed to choose my church, and set my own criteria. Unfortunately, my Oursler grandmother, and Daddy's hair-raising memories of immersion, automatically ruled out the Baptist church in spite of their hymns. I knew and loved the Falmouth Congregational Church building, and had won a prize from the DAR for an essay about its bell, which was cast by Paul Revere. I liked the minister's son, too. And the Methodists were also nice.

But the Episcopalian church, being not white and New Englandy but rather Old English and Oxfordy, looked literary, romantic, and somehow more sacred. The choir was beautiful. A husband and wife had the best voices in that choir, and they were both magnificent looking people, and when they sang solos across at each other it brought tears to my eyes. Their son, who was in my class at public school, carried the cross in procession. And when the Rev. Dr. Leslie Wallace prayed, it sounded to me like real prayer.

None of these reasons did I give my father. In fact he never asked me why I chose to be Episcopalian. He said seriously that if it was what I wanted he was glad for me that I had found Christ.

I was baptized a Christian in St. Barnabas' Church by Dr. Wallace, whom I came to love dearly. For the one and only time my family accompanied me to church. For godfather I chose Arthur Sherrill, the man who carved figureheads, because he was tall, blond and handsome, and because his wife Dorothy wrote and illustrated little books that I liked about Sleepy Sam and Sleepy Sally. I chose for my godmother Jean Wick Abdullah, the author's agent who was the wife of Achmed Abdullah, that self-styled seventh son of the seventh son of the Prophet.

Now I do not quite understand how Jean Wick agreed to be my godmother because, as I discovered years later, she and Achmed had both been converted to the Roman Catholic Church the year before, in Panama. Achmed was then christened Alexander, though he certainly kept that name quiet. By rite, Jean Wick had no business being my sponsor in a Protestant church. Probably she didn't know that. Anyway, she was a wonderful godmother. She began building for me a set of sterling silver from Tiffany's, and left instructions in her will that it be completed down to the last oyster fork, and it was. Arthur Sherrill carved for me a manly, forthright figure of Christ. And so I became a Christian. Nothing in my life had ever made me happier.

Of course, as the only practicing Christian in the immediate family, I was left to my own devices. Only twice did anyone intrude on me. Mother, who had said nothing about my decision, but simply coped with it as with any other social event from my joining Girl Scouts to having a birthday party, couldn't completely hide her feelings even from herself.

I was learning to recite the Apostles' Creed, studying it from a lovely purple-bound thin-leafed Book of Common Prayer.

" 'I believe in one, holy, catholic and apostolic church.' "

She wheeled on me, her huge green eyes flickering with astonishment. "What? Why are you saying that?"

I explained. In Sunday school I was taught that catholic meant universal and all-embracing. I believed in the catholic church with a little "c." Mother shrugged and went back to the piano. But I understood that she had been actually shocked to hear me recite that creed.

My parents slept late on Sundays. The household help drove me to church, and it was then that I discovered that some of these people, who were really my closest friends in the world, were Catholics. They went to Mass at St. Patrick's, and I went to the early service at St. Barnabas, and everyone was happy. Until one day Mother realized I was receiving communion at St. Barnabas, wine and wafer.

"But you have breakfast first!" she cried, appalled. "Don't you know you must fast before communion? That's disgraceful. You've been confirmed now, you should know better."

Well, I asked my pastor's wife about that one. Mrs. Wallace, shy, soft-voiced, was one of the kindest women I ever met. She told me that Catholics always fast before communion, and that while Episcopalians don't ordinarily fast, some kinds of Episcopalians do. She suggested that if it would make my mother happier, I could fast, too.

Mother apparently forgot about it. But I fasted, to please her, in the interests of Christian harmony, and in a rather smug spirit of self-sacrifice.

I made an altar in my bedroom, using Arthur Sherrill's statue and some tiny vases for flowers on a corner shelf. I read diligently through even the small print in the Book of Common Prayer, puzzled out how to use church envelopes, and the meaning of things like Trinity Sunday, and prayed. I read the New Testament again, went to Sunday school, and in years to come I taught Sunday school and sang in the choir. And I loved God according to my lights.

Though I didn't always understand the Bible, I tried valiantly to follow it. I remember trying to find out what the word "divers" meant, and finally deciding an apostrophe must have been dropped in the King James version, so when it said Jesus cured divers' diseases it meant he cured people of the bends. Presumably they got the bends in the Sea of Galilee. Later I used dictionaries when I couldn't understand.

I took my faith literally. My Bible quoted the Lord, in red type, as exhorting us to go into our closets to pray. So I did. I knelt there with my nose in the hems of my dresses, next to the sneakers, and prayed. Mine not to wonder why.

Over and over I read the Beatitudes, hoping to find a way to qualify as one of the Blessed. I did not mourn. I wasn't meek, nor persecuted, and I wasn't too sure about being pure of heart, or hungering and thirsting after righteousness. I had a good guilt complex about some snitching and pilfering that I figured had made my heart impure, and the biggest battle of my life was due to my hungering and thirsting after too many sweets.

But I wanted to be close to God, to honor and love him, and Dr. Wallace said that was what mattered. In the Book of Common

Prayer I steeped myself, composing nightly schedules of hymns and psalms to exercise my sincerity. One line from that prayerbook is still daily in my thoughts, so simple, so right: "We have left undone those things which we ought to have done, and we have done those things which we ought not to have done, and there is no health in us." I could say that to Jesus, and he would know it was true, but because he was my savior he would forgive me and make me better. I was happy believing in him, and I knew it was important to be thinking about God and loving him. At least for me it was important.

Missionary zeal wasn't part of me. When we sang of bringing the faith from Greenland's icy mountains to India's coral strand, my heart wasn't in it. It seemed to me obvious that each person must find his own way, and you shouldn't go putting clothes on savages and expecting them to be glad to leave their gods and love Christ your way. It didn't bother me at all that my folks belonged to no church. We were always a family of loners, and if they thought they should be Christians they would be, and if they thought they shouldn't then that was right for them. Loving God was, I thought, a private thing, an aptitude, like loving music or flowers. Loving God was a way of making the world lovely and coherent. There were, I guessed, many ways.

When my Catholic cousin Bonnie came to visit that summer, we prayed together at the bedroom altar in our own ways. She said Hail Mary's, and I said, "For thine is the kingdom" at the end of the Our Father, but it didn't seem very different. The only thing I can remember puzzling me about what she told me of her faith was that her school was named Mount St. Someone-or-other, and she called it the Mount, but it wasn't even on a little hill. She said lots of places were called the Mount and weren't mounts. With her I first went into a Catholic church that wasn't a tourist attraction abroad. I remember wondering why the seats had no cushions in the Falmouth St. Patrick's, and thinking the vigil candles pretty, and that was all I thought about it.

Besides, our family went off to China and Japan.

We almost weren't allowed to land in Japan. Tony blossomed out with German measles after we left Honolulu, and even though I prayed hard, the spots still showed as we neared Kobe. The whole ship would have been quarantined if Japanese immigration officials saw his condition, so with the captain's connivance Tony's face was pancaked and powdered. Paul held both his hands so he wouldn't scratch till the health officers were gone. So we saw Japan. We saw the musicals at Takaradzuka, drank tea in ceremony, and visited the Diabutsu, that magnificent giant figure of the serene Buddha. I liked Japan.

China was something else. China overwhelmed me, depressed me, infected me with desperate unease. My father said I had it all wrong, that under the rice powder and the hissing sounds that indicated politeness, the Japanese masked dangerous power and hatred. Japan would soon make trouble for the world. China would be the first to suffer, China—our friend.

China was the first country I ever visited with which I felt no bond of identity. All the Mediterranean cultures, even those of North Africa, offered some common ground. Japan, at least on the surface, was aggressively modern and cosmopolitan. But, though I'd read Chinese fairy tales, and those offensively folksy books for children about children in other lands, which tried to convince me that Chinese children were like me both now and in Mandarin days, I sensed, from the first sight and smell of China, that I was truly in alien land.

The heathen idols of China struck chords of terror in my soul. I admired, and came to cherish, the Diabutsu of Japan, but even the Chinese happiness god, with his rolls of fat belly, appalled me. China seemed a monstrous contradiction. The story and teachings of Buddha were beautiful, the legends and old prints charming, but all I saw firsthand was filth and grotesque posturing and hopelessness. I'd read of the happy festivals for children; I saw no happy children. I heard the tale of Kwan Yin, exquisite giver of mercy, a woman so good that she was to go directly to heaven. When Kwan Yin looked down from heaven's gate and saw all the suffering people who were not yet in heaven, she could not bear to enter rest and happiness, so she came back to be near us all, and help us. Who could harden a heart against Kwan Yin? I keep a carven statue of her still. But I would not find a trace of her spirit on the banks of the Yangtze or the Whangpoo.

As we walked with practiced tourist discretion and reverence through the temples of China, past prayer wheels and sellers of firecrackers into the darkness where garish gods leered, someone spat on little Tony. Not in mosque or cathedral had such an ugly unreasonable thing happened. I hated China then, and I was grateful to be a Christian.

The Whangpoo River was dirty, the ponds in the formal gardens were green with slime, the colors in the shops were too bold, the world was sad. If Japan's beauty had been artificial and hypocritical, I still preferred it. I knew that my father had, in a special sense, fallen in love with Madame Chiang Kai-shek, as he fell in love with only two other women: Hildegarde and Marlene Dietrich. Years later I was proud and grateful to be able to call her my friend, too. But then I didn't want to hear about Missimo or the Generalissimo, or anything about China.

When our visit ended it was coronation night in England, and all Shanghai, in deference to the British, was to be a fairyland of electric lights and festival. Our ship was sailing at midnight. We had met in Shanghai an "old China hand," that dauntless squat dynamo named Carl Crow, author of *A Hundred Million Customers,* a bestseller describing his adventures in Chinese commerce. Carl loved China and knew I hated it. He wanted me to see Shanghai in her gala dress, even though my parents firmly intended to board ship in the afternoon. He got permission to keep me out late, arranged for his Number One Boy to have a small launch to carry us to the liner at eleven at night, and set out to dazzle me.

Mr. and Mrs. Crow, and friends happily named Mr. and Mrs. Swann, took me to dinner in a river restaurant with fireworks exploding over the harbor, and barges of music, flowers and torches floating by.

"You have not seen China," said Mr. Crow to me, "because she offends you. If you went to visit a grand old lady when she was ill and close to death, her attempts to rally herself to entertain you might seem grotesque. If you are young and unwise you will look only at the surface, and turn away. If you are a bit wiser and more humble, you will seek to know her heart."

The night was enchanted, but Cinderella's hour came. And no Number One Boy came. We had to search ourselves for transportation to the ship, already sounding her whistle in warning. We ventured to the street. There, so it seemed, were all of Carl Crow's hundred million customers. Under the lurid light of electric crowns and electric British flags I saw what that old phrase "a mass of humanity" looks like. When now I see on television the Times Square crowds of New Year's Eve, I'm not impressed. They are not as vastly tidal and impersonal as those of the Shanghai waterfront, pressing, pushing, silent, carrying us with them relentlessly. Far off the ship's whistle blew, but I couldn't see or breathe. At the last possible moment Mr. Crow found a man and a boat, and we reached the ship. My parents made the captain lower a ladder for me.

An unforgettable night. And, in a way, it is the last night I remember as being young.

"The lights will go out," Carl Crow cried up from the sampan to my father at the ship's rail. "Here. And there. Don't be angry. Let her remember tonight, before it is all over."

He was talking of war. I didn't know much about the impending war, because I had not let myself listen to grownups talk of it. Later I was to remember Mr. Crow's words, and think that what he said could apply another way. For I personally had come to the end of the simple time. The chief lights of my life were going out. Like it or not, I was going to be forced to make a stab at growing up fast.

7

The Cocoon Falls Away

I fell sick and nearly died, making modest medical history. And at the same time I discovered trouble in my family, and home did not feel like home, the parents I loved turned out to be people like other people, and for a while I didn't dare let them know I knew.

The discovery that parents aren't perfect is made by every child sometime, and it always hurts when the cocoon falls away. As I see it, if you weren't ever made unhappy by your parents then either you or they were at least half dead.

On the way home from China I sensed something was wrong, and kept out of my folks' way on shipboard. It was an American ship, and a particularly uncomfortable one, and the fresh water supply ran out halfway back across the Pacific, and the bug supply multiplied. I supposed that was what bothered my parents.

We hadn't been home long before I fell ill with a fever no local doctor could diagnose. Because we had just come from the Orient an Oriental specialist was summoned, and he swore no such disease polluted the East. I was very sick. Suddenly my dog died. Some doctors thought he might have died of whatever disease I had, and later that turned out to be true. Finally, thanks to the unrelenting efforts of a dedicated Boston doctor, Dr. Theodore Badger, diagnosis was made. By that time I had recovered. Which was a blessing, because the disease was tularemia, and in 1937 there was no cure for it, and the mortality rate was extremely high.

I'm enshrined in the *New England Medical Journal* as the first case of tularemia in New England. As I understand it, some chamber of commerce innocently decided to import rabbits from the west, where tularemia was old stuff, and set them free on the Cape to attract hunters. Anyway, I have a scar on my right arm where a solemn delegation of doctors drew blood samples one afternoon for the greater glory of medical research. And I was sick for three strange and horrid months.

I had a nurse who had read some psychology. An illness doctors couldn't diagnose was to her necessarily and deliciously psychosomatic. As I lay isolated on the third floor of Sandalwood she plied me with questions. Had I a guilty secret? Had I acquired a carnal knowledge? Day after day she picked at me. And, of course, nothing I said ever came out right. It never does when you're talking to a quasi-psychologist. If I told her I was sick and tired of her questions, she took it as a sign of repression. If I said I was innocent, she raised her eyebrows. When I got confused and cried, she took it as a sign that I was nearly ready to unburden my psyche. It was ghastly, and it went on and on, and conditioned me to mistrust all psychology, and I couldn't tell anyone about it.

I couldn't tell anyone anything. No one could come near me except the nurse and doctors. I could have written about the inquisition in my daily notes to my mother and father, but I didn't. You see, one of those porches my father built was directly below my bedroom window. Now that I'm a parent I'm careful what I say on porches. Then I lay in bed and the windows were open and I heard the things my parents were saying, and though I didn't understand them their tone and intensity frightened me, and I felt inside as if my stomach closed up, and there were few things I could say even to myself. I didn't know then what the problem was, but I knew there was one. So I wrote long notes to them because they expected notes, and all I wrote about was how I liked sad cowboys singing on the radio, what books I was reading, and how nice orange sherbet tasted.

And fear became part of me, so I was no longer really young.

Children can have a horrid time without anyone's knowing it. I did, long after I was well. That wasn't, even then, something I felt sorry for myself about. It was just a fact and I had to learn to live with it. And another fact, though I didn't yet recognize it, was that my mother had become an alcoholic.

Looking back, I can see that Mother was almost always a little high all the time in the beginning, and only occasionally really in trouble. When she was a little high she was gay and very much herself. Her drinking had begun back in the city when she had so much entertaining to do, and when she had been given sherry and aspirin instead of a sleeping pill, or a vacation. She'd slipped imperceptibly into the habit of using alcohol to steady her nerves. For years she remained able to cope with a twenty-four hour day as a writer, hostess, wife, mother, stepmother, and companion to a man of endless energy. She used liquor as a tranquilizer, and it got hold of her physically so that her body required it, and after one drink she could not stop.

She was "ill" more and more often. At the time I thought Mother was just like Bette Davis in her more dramatic movie roles when this "illness" was on her. She didn't want me to know, but she did want me to stay with her. The demons riding her terrified me, and though I never described these vigils to anyone, I set out to avoid them. I wanted to be completely unnoticed. And I would tiptoe, or go without using the plumbing, or stay in my room inventing busyness to be absorbed in.

I never knew when my mother and father would be together and when they wouldn't. There were some peaceful, sunny islands of time. And sometimes Mother would be in the hospital and my father home, or my father away and Mother "ill" at home, and either way the house felt nasty. It was worst when they both pretended everything was fine for my sake, and grew cross with me for being lumpish, or, to use my father's word, scraggly.

Scraggly I was. Now all the years from eleven through fifteen seem muddied together like misused tablets in an old watercolor box. A few things stand out in clear tones: the way my father was afraid to tell Mother her mother had died when the wireless message reached us aboard a ship; the hurricane that desolated Cape Cod and did not harm Sandalwood; the frantic rhythm of Hitler's voice on the radio; the day Paul left us because even Tony was no longer young enough to need a governess.

One summer night when my cousin Bonnie was staying with me, she told me what was the matter with my mother. Bonnie was a beautiful girl, dark-haired and delicate-skinned, about sixteen that year, and she loved my mother as much as if not more than I did then. Mother cherished her, too, and recognized in her the gleam of true talent, taught her to write, and launched her on a career as Bonnie Gay, young columnist for a Baltimore paper. I was a bit jealous of Bonnie, but she kept assuring me I'd be sixteen too, someday, and I really loved her.

She told me about Mother with gentleness, and instantly I knew it was true, and that I could have known all along if I'd let myself.

"Does anyone else know?" I asked.

"Your father does. The help must. But no one will say anything. They all love and respect her too much. Besides, she hides it so well most of the time. She doesn't know I know. She keeps right on working harder than ten women. But it's getting worse all the time."

I thought, and the only thing I knew about drunks was that in movies they were funny and in real life they weren't. Drunks were a disgrace, they were bums, they ruined other people's lives as well as their own, and they should be ashamed of themselves. That's how little I knew. And I'd never even heard of a woman alcoholic. I couldn't have been more shocked or frightened then if I knew my mother was a murderess.

"And you want to know why she does this to you, don't you? You think she's horrible. You're the horrible one!" cried Bonnie. "She isn't doing it to you. She's the one who's miserable. It's not her fault. Don't you think it kills her to be like this? She's like a person in quicksand. You don't understand her at all."

I didn't. Such understanding would take me years. But I clung to the knowledge that Bonnie wasn't shocked. And I asked her what I should do. She said I should pray. So I did. For years.

Mother was in and out of hospitals and rest homes and sanatoriums. When she was gone I'd play the piano, choosing the most disconsolate melodies, hoping my father would hear and be pleased by my sensitivity. He'd stand it as long as he could, and finally tell me to stop this instant and go ride my bicycle, and I'd be insulted.

I was a lonesome, scared, bitter pain in the neck. And I was rushed willy-nilly into responsibilities. Tasks were thrust on me by my parents, intricate sad bits of diplomacy between them, as well as the job of being my own parent and buying my own shoes and sending myself to the dentist. That last chore I never did do. But before I was fourteen I was interviewing headmasters and visiting schools to decide where Tony was going to be sent to study. Mother was away and Daddy didn't have time to do more than decide that Tony would be better off in school, so the headmasters had to put up with me. As I hit my early teens I had sometimes to make so many decisions and handle so many problems that I felt quite nastily superior to both my parents, and hated them for pushing things on me.

And they, in turn, like most of my world, found me honestly unbearable, and occasionally seemed to feel half their troubles sprang from me. The whole thing was hell.

I remember the time I decided my father must be the one really at fault, and that he had "driven her to drink"—a conclusion I reached because of something he'd done that annoyed me—and I felt sorry for Mother. So we ate raw onion sandwiches together. But I didn't let her know I knew she was an alcoholic because I felt that would be more than she could stand.

And I remember the time I heard and saw my father cry, the most terrible sight and sound a child can endure, and knew Mother's illness was not his fault, and pitied him.

Finally he brought the subject into words between us, because he knew I knew. That helped. And he needed me to know so I could be of use when he was away in the city or on a lecture tour. It was my task to try to find any caches of liquor and pour them down the toilet, and my task to know when she was so far gone that she might hurt herself, and call the doctor. So finally she had to know that I knew, and she found that hard to take, and so did I.

Those summers I believe the only person I loved was Tony. I find in one of my spasmodic diary entries the comment: "What a fine person he really is!" double underscored with double exclamation points. He was all of seven or eight then, and was quite prepared to forgive and forget my past bullying of him. I sided with him against the whole miserable world. Though we couldn't really talk much to each other, being separated by age and gender, I read into him more or less accurately my own lonely bewilderment. He accepted the excesses of my sympathy rather graciously, contrived to raise ruckuses with his stormy best friend, and spent secret hours behind a boulder reproducing solo the dialogue and scenes of every play and movie he'd ever seen.

All I focused on was my own life away from home at boarding school. When I was twelve, entering tenth grade, it was decided I might become a lady if I went to Westover School in Connecticut. I leaped at the chance, not to become a lady, but to escape and start a new life. That summer, in preparation, Bonnie, who knew me better than I knew myself, talked me into reading *How to Win Friends and Influence People*. I read it dutifully, hope springing in my breast.

Westover didn't want to take me, because I was young and would be a problem, but, even though they didn't dream I was reading Dale Carnegie, they took a chance on me. For three years I wore a tan uniform with detachable white collar and detachable brass buttons, and big crackly patent leather belt, and became educated.

The school was right the first time. I didn't belong there. Partly because I was twelve and most New Girls were fourteen. Only a year out of pigtails, I'd never been on a date, wasn't in love. And I was still confused by the underpinnings and paraphernalia of young ladies, quite unable to keep a stocking seam straight. Besides which, I didn't know how to play bridge or hockey, owned not one lipstick, had never even thought of making a debut or doing charity work. If there was a girl lower than I on the pecking order that first year, I never saw her.

"She's just too young to leave home," one hall-mother said of me in exasperation. But home had, in a sense, left me, and I was so darn glad to get away from family tensions that I stumbled all over myself trying to fit into this new life. Rebellion, naturally, was a part of this process.

The trouble was that as a rebel I was a flop.

I knew the difference between right and wrong, ethically, as my father had taught me, morally, as the church taught. I'd done things that were wrong, like swiping change from my father's pocket-emptying place, and candy bars from stores, and telling a few lies. But always I felt guilty. And no one outside of Mark Twain had ever suggested to me that it was admirable to defy law and order. When I tried, I couldn't bring any sincerity into my efforts.

So there was this tug of war as I tried to get my bearings in this miniature world. On one side were all the good people, who for some reason were mostly tall athletic blue-eyed girls at least publicly supporting honesty, responsibility and whatsoever things are good and true. On the other side were those who seemed more sophisticated, more nubile, apparently having a wonderful time. And me in the middle. I kept trying to find out what was wrong with me.

Years later, at the only reunion I ever attended, I saw what a fine school Westover is, and secretly wished I had the fortune required to send our daughters there. Perhaps they'd fare better than I, using all the school's possibilities fully while keeping enough integrity to be about half as unhappy as I was. I would not cherish or trust any girl who completely fitted in.

At that reunion, where it seemed to me we were all the same age at last, one ex-classmate said to me, "But you were always so darn young, then!"

It wasn't only being young. Not only the heartache of the empty home I'd left. Not even an unfortunately uninfluential personality which sent me mooning and slipping on the skunk cabbages in the brook, or star-watching in the twilit courtyard between the science lab and the art studio.

I was trying to find out who I was, and why I was. That, like any other process of birth, is always painful, and naked.

8

Of Knacks, Frogs and Tears

When you're young it's much easier to believe in God than in yourself. Especially when the evidence is all against you.

There I was, a big awkward ugly child, mooning around. When I came home for vacations, my parents usually pretended to be gay and welcoming, but they didn't know what to do with me. One thing about people in the grip of alcoholism: they always fall apart at the most meaningful times, like Christmas. Only later did I learn that one hellish nuance of the suffering of alcoholism is that devastating inability to stay sober when you yourself most want to. At the time, I was sure Mother ruined things with purposeful perversity, which naturally made both of us more miserable.

Mother insisted on staying in a separate city apartment, so I shuttled between her and my father, but I was always expected to pretend everything was fine. So I'd talk about school, as if it were fascinating, and talk enough to bore even Mother, so I'd be left alone. Her emotions made me numb. Nights, I'd lie in bed sweating and pretend to be asleep. I sort of held my breath till school was open again.

Then at school I'd talk about home as if it were fascinating. I'd boast of going to Twenty-One or the theater, which is what everyone else seemed to do on vacation, but of course I never admitted that I went only with my father or his unromantic middle-aged friends such as George Jean Nathan and Julie Hayden, instead of a date of my own. Everything I said, at home and at school, was phony because I felt appearances had to be kept up. I don't think I fooled anyone. What worried me was that I began to wonder if I was personally phony all the way through.

I had then the nauseous horror of hypocrisy so often found in adolescents. I'd drive my father into snits of desperation because, on principle, I refused to say, "Pleased to meet you," or its equivalent, to people I wasn't pleased to meet. I wouldn't say I liked something simply to be polite, considered it indecent to make small talk, and shuddered with embarrassment whenever my parents went out of their way to be courtly or charming to anyone. "Truth is beauty!" I would cry. The more it hurt, the truer, and the more beautiful.

The beautiful truth which really hurt me was that apparently I could not write. I'd clung to the belief that I was a born writer as if it were my one hope of earthly salvation. But no one at Westover considered me a budding genius. Valiantly I submitted manuscripts to the school magazine, *The Lantern*. I wrote short stories with plot and without, editorials, humor. I wrote poetry: some in imitation of Browning, some in sibilant sentiment about snow, silence and stars. Almost nothing I wrote was accepted except some doggerel in imitation of Ogden Nash that, when I reread it now, makes absolutely no sense. Other girls had their work published, and were elected to the board, and taken into the tiny sanctuary of the *Lantern* room in the quad near the apple trees. But not me. Until, near the end of my last year, apparently as a consolatory award for effort, I "made" the staff. By that time I'd stopped believing I was a writer.

My marks in English were far from extraordinary. The *Liberty* magazines that were mailed to me, being less than literature, were classed as contraband and delivered to me in batches at vacation time. No one had read any of my mother or father's books, and few people admired Dickens, Dumas, Emerson, Poe or any of my old standbys. So my standards of excellence became confused, and I found it increasingly difficult to believe I had talent. I knew there were in every career, but perhaps especially in writing, many deluded hacks, muddling along fancying themselves great and unrecognized. I didn't want to make a total fool of myself.

So I got busy facing the idea that I couldn't write. I bore my disappointment with striking lack of dignity, muttering and weeping where no one could see me, and occasionally in the public privacy of the chapel.

At Westover, chapel is the beginning and end of everything. Each morning after breakfast we formed a line and marched into chapel singing over and over a many-versed hymn harmonized in four parts, held our service, and marched out to another hymn. At night at another prayer service, we sang psalms. I was fed on strong good bread of Scripture in song and word.

In group prayer I felt safe. I liked praising God. I loved him. But I wasn't sure he loved me. To be brutally honest, I didn't see how he could. No one else seemed able even to like me much, including me. And, though the Good Shepherd was devoted to rescuing lost sheep, I didn't even qualify as an outstanding sinner.

I would have liked to know how to become a better person, because Dale Carnegie hadn't worked for me at all. Of course, the blueprints of good character and holiness were always being spread out for me. But I couldn't see how I was to become good or true or beautiful, because I was really a whited sepulchre of such ordinary nastiness, and not well whitewashed at that.

For obvious reasons, I never confided this self-knowledge to anyone then. But I kept thinking provision should have been made so lukewarmly bad souls like me could be filled up with enough goodness to begin again, running the straight race and fighting the good fight. Like a new baptism every month, maybe. When we sang we seemed chiefly to be urging ourselves onward, looking forward to heaven, praising God and the new Jerusalem. I loved thinking about being holy, much as I loved to daydream about skating or dancing, but I had a hunch that when it came to actually facing God, I'd turn out to be as much of a phony as I was on skates or the dance floor. Sometimes in the evening we sang the hymn, "Dear Lord and Father of mankind, Forgive our foolish ways." I put my heart into that one.

We were always singing, even outside of chapel. We sang team songs for Wests and Overs, school songs, tree songs, garden songs, and just plain songs. Only I couldn't sing. Even in grade school teachers used to ask me just to mouth words if the singing class had an audience. My parents loved to sing, and though Daddy was ordinarily tactful, even he couldn't be polite if I chimed in on his song. The notes I sang bore no relation to melody, and I really couldn't hear the difference.

There were three of us like that in the New Girl Class. There was also at Westover a handsome grey-haired red-cheeked director of music, Mr. Congdon, who said anyone could learn to sing. He worked with me for a year. He gave me the idea that as a set of bagpipes has to be full of wind to sound musical, so must I be. He showed me it was necessary to work muscles to make music, and sent me home for the summer with orders to sit at a piano playing one note at a time and singing it. By summer's end I could really sing. Ever since, I've sung decently. That may not sound important to you. But learning to sing was a major turning point in my life.

In the first place, quite literally, singing in a well-disciplined group seems to me the nearest thing to heaven on earth. To sing you use your body, your mind, and your heart. You are committed, engaged, caught up totally. Physicians tell us too much of the deep breathing of singing produces anoxia, which can be dizzying and intoxicating. But the thrill doesn't come from lack of oxygen. When you sing in a choir, blending your own song into a wholeness with others, there's a glory and a delight which can be real re-creation.

In the second place, when Mr. Congdon taught me to sing, he unwittingly handed me the secret of success in a hundred other fields. There is, Mr. Congdon said, a knack to everything. Find the knack and you can do what seems impossible. When the knack he taught me actually got me into the Glee Club, I began searching out and collecting knacks.

I'd always been shy of reciting. I sometimes think I got a trauma from the time on an Atlantic crossing when there was a children's talent show, and everyone else said funny poems or sang cute things, and my mother for some unfathomable reasons insisted I recite: "The Lord is my shepherd."

Girls at Westover had to memorize poetry each week, and take turns reciting, sometimes voluntarily, sometimes as penance. My turn came with a section of Keats' *Endymion:*

> Spite of despondence, of the inhuman dearth
> Of noble natures, of the gloomy days,
> Of all the unhealthy and o'erdarkened ways
> Made for our searching; yea, in spite of all
> Some shape of beauty moves away the pall
> From our dark spirits.

I recited as in a vacuum, intensely yearning to sit down. My voice trembled. I was desperate. And I was a mild sensation. There was an awed silence when I finished. Miss Lowe, tweed-suited, with clipped grey hair and great coals of eyes, who was our poetry expert, congratulated me. Such repressed emotion! Such intense yearning!

Ah, so. I'd found another knack. The knack of speaking in public is to be scared and ride over the wave of fear.

I read more hungrily than ever. Westover's closets were so huge that you could read in them illicitly by flashlight all night without feeling cramped. I swallowed in gulps Saroyan and Steinbeck, Kahlil Gibran, the Brontës and Thomas Wolfe.

Since my father's most modern taste was Longfellow, I'd never read modern poetry. In a tiny dark Westover classroom facing an apple tree a thin woman with glasses read aloud:

> Jane, Jane, tall as a crane,
> The morning light creaks in again . . .

The shock of that verb "creaks" is still fresh in mind, because Miss Hibshman, who was not beautiful, shed beauty on words and on all that she taught, and so on me. I acquired the knack of enjoyment when I understood that the beautiful is not necessarily pretty.

All through my education I've been blessed with intense and idiosyncratic teachers, who knew what they knew, and cared that you should want to know. They expected you to come up to their level, and if it was necessary nagged and even insulted you till you woke up and started climbing. Those who were most important in my life were of the type that PTAs often mistrust: they were a bit inefficient by modern standards, and none had a bland personality, and they demanded a great deal and were stern. Sometimes I didn't *like* them. But they are unforgettable. I may forget the contents of their courses, but never their impact on my thinking.

It was in algebra class that I caught on to another, most precious knack: the ability to trust hunches. Miss Brown was a logical person. She chanted the rune: "Butterfat plus butterfat equals butterfat." By that she intended to make us logical persons who wouldn't mix terms. Well, I tried. I was already trying to memorize logically conjugations, French and English kings, and world exports. And I was going nuts trying to make logical notes in outline form with lots of I.'s and 1.'s and a.'s and a.1.'s, which seemed to me a fearful waste of space on notebook paper. And I'd proved conclusively that Euclid and I lived in different worlds when I nearly flunked geometry.

The more I tried to go step by step along in that sea of butterfat and xs and ys, the more confused Miss Brown and I both got. Came mid-year examination. In panic I forgot all about logic. I stared at the examination and suddenly—illogically—I had a hunch I understood algebra. Giddily I zoomed through, completing the exam in an hour and ten minutes. I checked my work, decided there was no point in sitting there, and handed the blue-books to Miss Brown. Whereupon, with logic, she reminded me that a girl with a 40 average in algebra couldn't do a perfect exam in half the allotted time. After all, no one else was finished. To please her I rechecked my work, found one thing to change, and ran. I got a 98. Two points were lost by that rechecking.

You can't make someone work the wrong way round. Right-handedness isn't inherently better than left-handedness, it's just different. Parents and educators now know the perils of changing a child's handedness. Logical-mindedness is different from intuitive-mindedness, though not better. Trying to force a child to an alien thought pattern is asking for trouble.

I was always the kind of child who, in English comp class, wrote the theme first and then made the outline from it, even though the outline had to be handed in first. To me the order and plan are part of the thing itself, and I can't make an outline of what I'm going to do until I've done it. I come up with answers and work backward to explain them. I've learned to adapt to logical minds, and to be realistic enough to make some plans and systems. But I get close to a nervous breakdown if I'm led slowly up the steps of a new thing. I want to get to the top and then look back. And I'm really miserable when anyone insists on spelling out details to me. Oddly enough, I recently discovered I was driving one of my own children nuts demanding that she be logical about schoolwork, when certainly I knew firsthand one doesn't have to be.

A singing teacher. *Endymion.* An algebra test. Those are the moments when unaware I held the coin with which I'd purchase some of my future.

But nothing consoled me for the fact that I showed no signs of being a great writer. So I decided I never wanted to be a writer in the first place. Instead, I planned to be a great scientist.

I began haunting Mrs. Prentiss' science lab. Drawing on my Woods Hole background, I launched private projects. I conceived the notion that the trouble with my mother stemmed from endocrine imbalance affecting emotions and personality and body. Mother had never been the same after that thyroid operation. Perhaps, I thought, too much was removed. So I went down among the skunk cabbages and caught frogs, and in the lab experimented, transplanting thyroid and pituitary glands from one frog to another.

It was dramatic, messy, satisfying work. At the same time I plunged into extensive study of evolution, compiling facts and theories so I knew much more about the history of Eohippus than of any Ourslers or Perkinses.

One December I was in New York on a weekend from school. I came to New York because my parents had a play opening on Broadway, a murder mystery starring Arlene Francis and Victor Francin. Sunday we sat glumly in the aftermath of scathing reviews. Once my father had written a play called *The Spider*, in which the murder occurred in the audience, who were all held for questioning till the "crime" was solved two hours later. First of the audience-participation plays, a minor tour de force of illusion and suspense, *The Spider* had tremendous success here and in Paris, and still survives in summer stock. But *The Spider* is as old as I am. None of Daddy's subsequent plays was as successful. Hope, pinned on the sleeve of the new play, *The Walking Gentleman*, was walking right off-stage.

So I sat, frightened and sad, drinking a Coke at the play's wake. Then the phone rang and someone told us the only news that was to matter to anyone that day. The date was December 7, 1941. And I had to go back to school in time for supper. It made no sense: the play's failure, the war or going back to school.

I was busy choosing colleges when the next blow fell. My father lost his job. Control of Macfadden Publications changed hands. Bernarr Macfadden was pushed out his own door. And my father was no longer editor-in-chief.

He was never much of a businessman. He had no investments. There's a faded cloth-covered memorandum book in which he entered all monies received by him year after year, his one concession to financial record-keeping. I have that book. In its cramped penned notations I can follow the history of a successful Macfadden editor, a handsome four-column weekly figure increasing comfortably. Then, from four columns under the dollar sign the next entry shrinks to two.

The only job Fulton Oursler could get was as a minor news commentator, and an answerer of listeners' questions about current events at $99 a week on New York radio station WHN. In that cash book is the handwritten record of a man almost fifty years old, forced to walk on water.

Mother was in the hospital, bills mounting. I was in an expensive boarding school, Tony in another. There was substantial alimony to pay, as there had been for so many years. And no job. Sandalwood was mortgaged and remortgaged. Insurance policies were cashed in. And he earned his ninety-nine bucks a week.

Never since have I been easy prey to panic over finances. When people ask me how we expect to meet certain probable future expenses, I remember that my father had once prudently prepared to meet all expenses, and seen his prudent plans upset when he lost everything, and that in spite of it, he pulled through.

He wrote me a brief note, telling me what had happened. He said I was not to worry, that he had always taken care of us and always would, somehow. He also said he couldn't afford to send me to college. I'd have to get there by myself, and if it meant enough to me I would.

I applied for a scholarship to Bryn Mawr College. Wise and cheerful as ever, Miss Dillingham rallied to my assistance with all the hidden resources of her role as headmistress at Westover. She had, in fairness, to warn me not to get my hopes up too high. My marks, though not bad, were not startling. Nor was I such a star at extracurricular activities that a college would feel it had to have me.

I got my scholarship, I suppose, under false pretenses. Scholarship investigators liked to arrive to meet a candidate unannounced. The New England Regional Scholarship people came to see me on a Monday, which for some obscure reason was Westover's day off from classes instead of Saturday. So I was puttering in the lab with my frogs and their glands. I smelled of formaldehyde and must have looked altogether dedicated. Explain it by providence or chance, but I'm convinced I wouldn't have gotten to college as a would-be writer, and only my temporary attachment to science pulled the trick.

I left for college, three weeks after high school graduation. It was then possible to get through college in three years by going to school in summer. If I went to school in the summer I wouldn't have to stay home, and I didn't want to stay home. Bryn Mawr had no summer session, but I could attend Swarthmore and start collecting credits. I was then a brooding tall girl of fifteen, looking twenty, feeling more like fifty, with a sullen-eyed addiction to butter pecan and chocolate ice cream, lemon Cokes, and T. S. Eliot. I had arranged to complete a premed course by the time I was eighteen, planned to go to Johns Hopkins, intern at Bellevue, then take off for some lonely laboratory by a bitter seacoast where I wouldn't have to think about people at all.

9

The Little Girl Co-ed

Does anyone ever realize that American dream of college life, of plaid skirts and moccasins scuffing in piles of drifting leaves, of learning and laughing and loving? I yearned for that dream, but my college years were woven of incoherency, smoke and exhaustion, in spite of sporadic valiant attempts to look and think like a girl in the pages of *Mademoiselle*.

As in a nightmare, I moved through college emotionally naked. I had been stripped of almost everything that mattered before I reached campus. I had lost the warmth of home and family, and the chill of that loss had made me almost viciously refuse to love and trust anyone. I had lost the security of knowing my father could pay the bills. I had relinquished the belief that I could write.

I still had my faith in God. But that garment too would be

torn from me before the first winter set in. A rent had already been made in it when I learned that Episcopalians are not all agreed on whether Christ was God or not, and that some didn't accept the virgin birth. That startled me almost as much as the time I heard a woman boast that her son was at theological school studying for the ministry and she was dying to know which kind of church he would decide to be a minister in.

The way I saw things then, belief in God meant awareness of God. Some people were blind to him as some are blind to beauty in art, or nature, or mathematics. We all have limitations. But, just as I expect all poets to agree on the most basic nature, history and laws of poetry no matter how they disagree over sonnets vs. free verse, so I expected Episcopalians to agree with Episcopalians, and Christians with Christians, if only to define themselves. If it was merely a matter of private opinion whether Christ was God (since the only alternatives were that he was crazy or a liar), then nothing mattered. Then a church was only a device for people to come together and perform certain rites as if the rites were valuable in themselves, like a hobby center where people who didn't care about art went to paint for the occupational therapy of moving a brush around on canvas.

I didn't let go of my faith all at once, but I became more private about it, and peered out at the world hunting signposts to understanding.

The United States was at war. You would hardly believe how little that meant to me. No one of my immediate family was in the armed services. My half-brother Bill, who now called himself Will, was a war correspondent and wrote splendid, fascinating reports for magazines, and was himself in danger, but I'd seldom seen him since his marrige in 1937, and he was of another generation. I knew, and rather hoped I was in love with, two young men in the Marines, but their involvement in war seemed to me only a nice detail, adding glamor to the situation. I couldn't understand the war, or follow the maps and news bulletins. Mostly my indifference to it was the result of total self-absorption, and growing general bitterness against a world that was making me miserable without seeming to care at all.

I was a-patriotic. From earliest childhood I had dismayed and annoyed my parents because flags and American history left me cold. I didn't have un-American teachers. No one tried to implant subversive philosophy in my round head. I sang "My Country 'Tis of Thee." We had patriotic assemblies, and the only flaw in my schooling as far as patriotism went is that I had only one course in American history, and found it dull. As years went on I knew far more about French, English and ancient history than our own.

Somehow, somewhere, I acquired the belief that the United States, far from being perfect, had heroes with false teeth and suspect motives. Patriotism, nationalism, was unreasonable. From whom did I learn this? It was in the air, a swaggering smart-aleck spirit spurning American heritage as corny. When I was a child it was already an unwritten tradition to debunk and ridicule love, hard work, thrift, and also love of country. Along with this was a hangover from the Snob Era that told us the rulers, generals, scientists, artists and writers of Europe were more wonderful than ours. I was told to be proud of the United States as a melting pot. But since I didn't like stews or alloys, I couldn't have been less impressed. I knew my parents took national pride seriously, and I tried not to hurt their feelings, but I felt like a hypocrite.

There's a definite tie-up between love and respect for mother and father, for fatherland, and for God the Father. Were all of us who were a-patriotic also disillusioned by our parents? Was it because we had become prey to the writing of free-love sophisticates that we lost the sense of being a nation? Or was it because we had lost sight of God? I don't know. But I believe that to honor parents takes a realism, and humility, and the ability to accept imperfections. The same is needed for patriotism. And for true religion.

The summer of 1942, war meant to me ration tickets, the food ones being given to the college, the shoe ones to Tony, because his feet kept growing and mine were grown. War meant trouble getting cigarettes, now that I'd learned to smoke them. And courses in first aid, and practicing idiotic air-raid drills, huddling in places where no one would be safe if the whole thing were real. And, acceleration.

Some unknown temporary official at Bryn Mawr had planned my course at Swarthmore, and I have now almost forgiven her. After all, it was a schedule perfectly designed for a young scientific genius, and it wasn't her fault that I wasn't one. At any rate, three weeks after I left Westover I went to college to find myself faced with German, logic, analytical geometry and physics.

The only thing I understood all summer was Logic, and I fled to it as a release and a joy because part of the time at least it dealt with English words. Even though I wasn't logical, I could understand the charm of the subject as a game. Syllogisms were amusing, and I needed all the laughs I could get. Then we progressed into Aristotelian sorites and Goclenian sorites, and I found that logicians can't wait to leave words behind and start juggling symbols. Dilemmas, which in words are fun, become horrible things that look like this:

$$(p \supset q) \cdot (r \supset s)$$
$$p \lor r$$
$$\therefore q \lor s$$

I concluded that men who constructed logic relish pompous formulae, and delight in making the obvious seem difficult. But I learned logic, and it was sane, weighty, and thereby a useful emblem to wear for safe-conduct in a crazy world dominated by men.

The rest was like a bad dream. Having nearly failed plane geometry in high school, I didn't even once understand why we were doing whatever it was we were doing in college analytical geometry. My frustration there was exceeded only by my total bafflement in physics. I was the only girl in physics, and every man there had not only had elementary courses in the subject, but seemed to have spent hours fiddling with engines and electricity. All I knew about engines and electricity was that when something didn't work my father would say: "Get a man," and no one would dare kid him by reminding him he was a man. Ourslers cultivated a convenient fear of things that worked, and lived by our private theory of the Natural Perversity of Inanimate Objects. Near us watches perversely refused to run, and drawers always got stuck. But that attitude was no help in physics class. The professor was nice about it. He even constructed a special exam for me with yes-and-no answers and a few more daring multiple-choice items, so I passed, in the very low sixties. Oddly enough, in later years, by my own illogical study, I came to understand the theories of physics rather well, and have been lately having fun studying anti-matter. But I still believe in the Perversity theory.

German, like all languages that aren't English, was not meant for me to use. Learning to read it wasn't hard. Having been raised on Sam Lloyd's puzzles and rebuses, Dick Tracy's code messages, and *The Goldbug*, I can learn to read almost anything, and—on a hunch or empathy principle—to understand them when they're spoken. But the sexual characteristics of nouns confuse me, and besides, basically, I'm lazy. To graduate from Bryn Mawr, besides passing my courses, I was going to have to be able to swim the length of the pool, which was no problem, and pass two written examinations, called orals, in two foreign languages. The exams demanded only that I be able to read the languages at sight. That is all I intended to do, but the professor at Swarthmore was hoping for a bit more.

As far as my courses went, the summer was horrid.

"How is my little girl co-ed?" Mother would write in her occasional letters to me.

Being a co-ed that summer wasn't at all like the stories I'd read. The men who were studying were either 4-F or else really seriously studying, and doing nothing else. And there weren't many of them. There was such an acute shortage of men that I was appointed to sing tenor in the Glee Club.

I was, I imagine, the only freshman arriving at Bryn Mawr that fall with a handicap of a 67 first semester average. I was late for Freshman Orientation Week, taking the train after my last mid-year exam at five in the afternoon out of Swarthmore. Around me at Bryn Mawr, tanned and healthy girls chattered happily about homes and vacations. I hadn't been to sleep in a week. I fell into bed for thirty-six hours straight, then made sure there was an English course salted in with my Biology and Chemistry.

Bryn Mawr girls, who call themselves Bryn Morons, are, by definition, intelligent. So I was intelligent. Unbearably intelligent, and I made a fresh start on academic life.

Within a year I was so intelligent that I could prove there was no God. And no truth. And no point to anything.

10

All Kinds of Long Hair

From what I read in the *Alumnae Bulletin*, I conclude that obviously it's possible to graduate from Bryn Mawr and be both intelligent and well-balanced. Lots of girls who went in as freshmen believing in God graduated still believing in God. Some even found faith at Bryn Mawr. At the time I was there that did not seem to be normal procedure.

The Quaker origins of Bryn Mawr still echoed around the campus, much as did the English madrigals and Greek hymns, which must have been meaningful and relevant to someone sometime but had become merely ornamental flourishes to small dress-up occasions. I wish more of the Quaker influence had been felt. (Near Sandalwood, in West Falmouth, stood an old meeting house with old stone stalls for horses and buggies. I had visited Quaker meetings, and the spirit of the Friends left a taste in my mind like the memory of a sunlit field.)

Dimly I recall that there were chapel services on the college campus. If they were a regular thing they certainly weren't emphasized or popular. To get to the Episcopalian church on Sundays entailed just a small hike, as I remember, but demanded an effort to go against the standard of the majority of undergraduates, happily engaged in sleeping, or lounging with newspapers. I soon stopped going to church.

Around me voices argued about the existence of God. Until then I had never heard God spoken of as something that might or might not exist, and so I found the argument a strange game. Voices argued whether there was a basis for morals, and about relative cultural values, the influence of myths, the findings of psychology and anthropology. Of all the girls I knew well, only one took God seriously, and she argued for him not in words but in unobtrusive actions. Her name is Naomi, and she lived among us in Merion Hall with a quiet loyalty to ancient Jewish law, and Naomi and her family were eventually to do more to effect my conversion than they knew. But not at the beginning, of course.

While I was there, at least, it seemed that Bryn Mawr's chief aim was to teach us that there is no absolute truth, and there are two sides to every question. It wasn't expressed in quite those terms, naturally. We were told instead to develop a questing spirit, a hunger for knowledge, and so on, which anyone would agree are great things to develop. But the chief, and announced, goal of a certain few professors explicitly included ridding us of the clutter of religion. There were deeply religious professors on campus, but they were not the type to make flamboyant impressions on students, and they didn't go in for the open-houses and coffee klatsches at which so many ideas are formed. Their voices sounded more softly, and it was easy not to hear them.

It was in psychology class that I began to go mad. I had had the amateurish notion that psychology was a handmaid to the understanding of human souls, possibly of value to both doctors and writers. And in that classroom I was taught that psychology is an exact science, revealing that there was no such thing as spirit, and that all thought and emotion rose from hereditary, constitutional and environmental factors. No soul. When we progressed to a survey of the science of psychological disorders, being unstable anyway, I proceeded to get all the symptoms of all the disorders. We took personality tests and other devices to rate us on stability, creativity, intelligence and so on. I came out as an acute manic depressive, a genius, a schizoid and also anti-social. All or nothing, that's me. Ordinarily you can't be all those things at once, but I wasn't ordinary, and I wasn't afraid.

Fear of madness didn't bother me because I ran across the concept that all geniuses are by nature mad, and are also positively devoted to evil. After all, Rimbaud and Verlaine were sick, and so were Charles Lamb and Coleridge and Wilde. Since it seemed plain that being moral and sane precluded the possibility of being a genius, I kept hoping I could turn out either mad or evil.

Yet some providence protected me from evil, kept me wrapped in innocence, so that in spite of myself I walked unharmed.

I didn't fight off sin. I rather hoped to find it. It would have flattered my adolescent spirit to plunge into a season of hell. For some reason, concerned adults often assume that the sins that most endanger youth are those of sex and drinking. Agreed, they are most common, and obviously perilous. But not to everyone. I craved the distinction of some form of ruin, more or less as a small child may wish he could die long enough to induce people to mourn him. But it could not be ruin in surrender to someone who did not love me and could not care. Naturally, drunkenness had no appeal to me, except in literary efforts. I wrote several plays, under the joint influence of Saroyan and T. S. Eliot, impossible as that sounds, and the plays were all laid in bars.

But I became fascinated by witchcraft, warlockery and devil-worship. For some reason I cannot explain, I already had more statues of the devil than of Christ, or of ballerinas, or of anything. It was as an art form that the devil first caught my fancy. The sweep of his cloak, the cunning of his hand, the intensity of his helpless battle against God, these captured me. I had one devil with a carved ivory face, another in artfully enamelled metal, a Mephistopheles ashtray with a green onyx base, a marble tempter with horns and yellow agate eyes. In the art classes for which I showed slides, I saw the strange faces of the devil through the centuries. I read of him in *Paradise Lost*, and in Dr. Sprague's Shakespeare course I learned that he had once been known to be dressed all in black, a color that seemed more apt to me than red. And I began to study what I could of the science of the devil, not believing it, yet hoping it might be true.

The night I first encountered evil was a night like a hundred others, spent in the ashy, bridge-card-littered smoking room of Merion Hall. It was late. For some reason it was impossible for me to go to bed at a decent hour. Some girls led normal, self-regulated lives. My attention was caught by those who didn't. By a little round rusty-freckled girl with sophisticated accent, who seemed to tweak at life's feathers, drink too much, and never sleep. By a big-framed stringy-haired girl with wide eyes swimming behind goldfish-bowl glasses, who affected fantastic long faded cotton skirts, and always taunted proprieties. She seemed to me a desperate, angry, aching soul, and though I didn't enjoy her, I was fascinated by her.

Desperation seemed to wear many guises. Desperation had sleek long black hair and perfect make-up and a cigarette holder, in a girl who studied archaeology and smiled at those who said out loud that they couldn't make sense of the world. Perhaps misery is good for the growth of hair? Certainly it seemed girls who burst with *weltschmerz* all had long hair, and resembled, to a degree, weeping willows. My own hair was long, but I looked more like an unmade bed.

There was then on a Philadelphia station a late-night radio program that invariably played that pure-corn record called "The Blue Bird of Happiness." *So be like I, hold your head up high, somewhere there's a blue-ue-ue bird of happiness!* It was a wonderful thing to listen to, incredibly hammed up with sighs and pauses. Yet some of us couldn't sleep till we had heard that same voice sing that same song each night.

One night, as the spirit of foolery broke through our private wasteland of unfinished long papers and stale cigarettes, I, who had been doing research on medieval witchcraft, began what was meant to be a hilarious imitation of possession and service of the devil. I began by expounding a bit of background, and went on to chant incantations to summon the evil one. I held my meager audience in the bleak set of that dingy smoking room. Self-consciousness fell from me as I threw myself into a plea for the evil spirit to come. I was enjoying myself.

Suddenly, I knew the play-acting had gone too far. I had left myself open. A force with personality was invading me. Can I describe it so that you will know the experience? I doubt it. I know only that that night, in the room where I was, I was in touch with evil. It was like a touch on my soul, a grasping, clenching, intoxicating touch, expecting surrender. Another moment of willingness and he, for it was a he, would have been no longer an outsider.

Abruptly, I stopped where I was.

"It is all nonsense," I said. "Forgive me. I'm going to bed."

My audience thought it odd, this breaking-off, and they asked what the hell was the matter with me now, but I didn't say, and I went to my room.

Never since have I denied the existence of the devil. Even when I denied God I knew better than to underestimate the spirit of evil. Never since have I trifled with him, though I was to meet him again more than once. I needed no theologian then to tell me that the devil's winning tactics are to make human beings believe he doesn't exist. Like a child who encountered electric shock, I understood the reality of this force I couldn't see.

That was about all I did understand that year.

Soon it was clear even to me that I wasn't going to be a scientist. In the old dark biology lab I kept on dissecting earthworms and dogfish as I had done for years, but I couldn't draw nice diagrams, and frankly I couldn't see anything through a microscope with or without my glasses. In the shiny new chem building at the other end of campus, I ran up breakage charges, burned myself, and nearly died of frustration trying to understand what it meant that elements had valences. I tried hard, died hard, and finally went to the dean to confess that I wasn't a girl-scientist after all.

I'd met Miss Edith Finch of the English department, one of the incredible characters of true life. Tiny, silver-haired, neat, of indeterminate age or youth, she lived with Miss Lucy Donnelly, wise and aged influencer of writers, in a house with a Welsh name. There she poured tea and served watercress sandwiches and talked of literature and greatness while puffing clouds of cigarette smoke. Some said Miss Finch had once been a bareback rider in the circus in Paris, which scandalized me for months until I realized I had by some Freudian quirk misunderstood, and that they meant the horse was bare, not Miss Finch. Then I hoped the legend was true, and that Miss Finch had contrived to have some excitement in a life that seemed to me comfortably settled in campus quiet. Still, it was difficult to imagine this dainty British-accented little lady doing anything but making clever criticisms and meaningful silences, driving her battered Austin, or sipping tea. I can't resist telling you what happened to Miss Finch in later years. She went back to England and married. She married Bertrand Russell. And I haven't gotten over my surprise yet.

Anyway, Miss Finch, God bless her, believed I could write. An austere teacher, she brooked no careless grammar, no phony tricks, no complacency, demanding craftsmanship and progress. She lifted me out of the general hodge-podge of required Freshman Comp, excused me from class, and required of me an intensive regular output of themes which we discussed in weekly conferences. She said she believed I could write, said it once, firmly, and wasn't going to go on feeding my ego after that. Often as not, I left her little office carrying her corrections with tears stinging my eyes, anger choking me, determined to show her I was a better writer than she dreamed. Which of course, was exactly what she had in mind.

And in the spring, as echoes of May Day song practice hung over Merion Green, I decided I really was stuck with being a writer. Even though I'd wasted all the beginnings of college lunging up the blind alley of pre-med, I was no further behind than most freshmen, and I could start over from where I was. I coined a word and told the dean I wanted to de-celerate. I'd take another full three years to complete college. And I'd become a philosophy major.

Most would-be writers are English majors, which I still think is a waste of time for them. Writers read as a matter of course, and too much of a critical sense is dangerous. Writers need more to know something to write about. Writers need to understand Life. Ergo, a philosophy major is what young writers should be. I remember giving my father that argument, which he accepted. I didn't explain that I also thought it would be the easiest major for me to distinguish myself in, since the field wasn't crowded, and it required little actual memorization.

Once my majors were switched I could look forward to three years of great thoughts and great words, and I was happy. I wrote my father about my glorious discovery that I was to be an author. He wrote back himself, a long letter, which was rare, as he was always miserly with his written words, reminding me with a smile that they sometimes sold for a dollar apiece. It was time, he said, I began to learn the trade. He told me that he'd made his first sale when he was fifteen, to the Sunday school magazines put out by David C. Cook Publishing Co. The same magazines were still going, and I could tackle the market that summer. He sent me *The Writer's Digest,* and my head was filled with schemes, and my cup brimmed over.

Now I looked forward to vacation. I was exhausted. Earning your way through college, in those days at least, was possible and fun. I worked in the library stacks, showed slides for art classes, helped do a huge spring cleaning for a professor's family, typed papers for other students, and even, God forgive me, did babysitting. There never was a less qualified sitter, since I despised children and knew nothing about them, but providentially no child suffered from my presence. Earning money, along with a cub reporter stint on the *College News,* and singing in the Glee Club, and being fire warden for the dormitory, was taking its toll. My dread of being home subsided, and I looked forward to getting to know my father again.

Now that I was older and wiser, I felt, we could meet on different ground, aloof to family tensions, speaking of writing and thinking and things that mattered. I'd finally grown up to his level. I thought how patient and understanding he'd been to let me follow my young impulse to Christianity, trusting me to outgrow it. I was traveling lighter now, and faster, having rejected God at last. I had learned emotionally to live without him.

And then my father informed me he was thinking of becoming a Catholic!

11

The Silent Battle

When finally my father did become a Catholic I was to ask him:

"Why did you keep it a secret? Why didn't you *really* tell me how serious you were, ahead of time?"

He replied, gently, "You weren't listening."

Of course. During those months when he inched his way into the Church, I hadn't thought him serious, and I ignored the clues he dropped. Who wouldn't think he was joking when he explained that the booklet he called "the penny catechism," kept by his bed with *The Arabian Nights*, a volume of a dictionary, and one from the *Notable Trial* series, was his "homework"? The tide was running deep under the surface, and he was fighting a silent battle to steer his course.

I knew he was at work again on the project begun after our second Holy Land trip, the life of the man called the Christ.

There had been in the thirties an unforgettable grey storm-tossed afternoon when we had sat in the library listening as he read a draft of the trial-scene from that biography of Jesus Christ. Through the picture windows I'd watched bay waters swell with whitecaps under the wind, dashing on the slick brown boulders of our beach, while his voice flung before us the strange warm midnight sights and smells of the Sanhedrin convoked to judge the Blasphemer. I'd been deeply moved. But he had set the manuscript aside in silence.

He had intended to do a job on the Christ, to show by research and reconstruction that the Master from Nazareth was not God, nor Son of God, had founded no church, was no Messiah. As a journalist, a crime reporter, my father intended to use his talents to unearth the material for exposé. He found the truth, but it was not as he expected.

Literally, he wrote himself into the Church, because he was more honest than proud. Some people, even some close to him who should understand him better, have said they thought his conversion only skin deep. They claim to find notes of hypocrisy about him. What actually happened was that a man saw that he had been wrong, and had the courage to throw away the whole past structure of his life and build it again on a new foundation. None of us, not his loved ones, his friends, his enemies, or his public, made it easy for him.

What could I have heard, had I listened to him that summer? What factors were at work on him? The man was in the middle of darkness, craved light, and would accept no devious way out. There were, he had always liked to say, three things a man needs to make him happy: The woman he loves, the place he loves and the work he loves. The woman my father loved was miserable, ill and loveless, and it seemed nothing could heal her or their marriage. The work he loved had been yanked from under him. The exigencies of war, gas rationing and fuel oil problems, plus severe financial difficulty, gave him only brief visits to Sandalwood, the place he loved.

He was doing secret work for the FBI, but of that he couldn't speak. He was working feverishly, writing, news-commentating, lecturing. And he was reaching in prayer to the unknown God in whom he dared not believe. His willingness to face truth wherever he found it left the door open for grace to lead him. The more he read of histories and ancient writers, of skeptics and Gospels, the more convincing he found the evidence against himself and for Christ. And the more, to his uneasy surprise, did he find that if he accepted Christ he must, on evidence, accept the Catholic Church.

What memories stirred in his heart that summer? He was to tell his cousin, Mary Oursler Herman, Bonnie's mother, that his boyhood love for her mother, his Aunt Minnie who was a Catholic, lay like a hidden lever in him, nudging him toward the faith. He was to remember my Grandma Perkins, Mother's mother, who had watched all her children leave the Church, and who had made that journey to Yucatán to see Grace church-wed to this divorced ex-Baptist atheist who sat now staring at the waves, hearing echoes of the fishermen of Galilee. He was to remember that his Grace had turned her back on the Church long before he met her. Though in moments of illness she wept for having lost her faith, as she wept for all her childhood days in a flight from reality, her rejection of the Church was total, and personal. Could she forgive him if he became a Catholic now? Would it not seem a repudiation of her? Or might it help her?

Certain it seemed that only God could help her. Doctors and psychiatrists had failed. Certain it seemed to my father that summer that only God could help anyone. The challenge was to find him, and no other question or consideration could interfere.

Of those thoughts, of the courage driving him unflinching to admit a truth he yearned to deny, I heard nothing. I was that summer beginning an apprenticeship in writing which drove all else from my head. I was serving as his part-time secretary, file clerk and researcher, on salary. And even the income-tax men were to agree that I earned every cent he paid me.

A taskmaster, my father asked at least half as much of me as he exacted from himself. I spent long sticky hours making scrapbooks, not the ordinary homey kind, but collated ones, filled with clippings and notes for future use, on subjects from biographies to murders. I typed up notebooks, inscribing on what he called "holey paper" details of interviews, précis of books he'd read, fact data for articles, notions for fiction. I learned to write letters for his signature, an art requiring imagination, empathy, deft English and a consideration for the feelings of others that came hard to me. I kept files of manuscripts in varied stages, outlines, drafts, revisions, and submission. The mechanics of his daily stint at the writing table appalled me. He outlined painstakingly. He rewrote each paragraph at least thirteen times, sending pages back for constant retyping, then scissoring, pasting inserts, sweating to evoke the apt phrase, cutting his own wordage with ruthless thrift.

"It's not what you thought writing was, is it?" He'd lean back in his upholstered swivel chair, light a cigarette, smile mischievously. "If I can teach you nothing else, I can at least teach you that writing is a craft, like shoemaking. It doesn't depend on the muses, or whim, or a feeling in your throat."

"But writing is a great art, not like making shoes. At least, the kind of writing I want to do."

He nodded. "But first you must learn the craft. A musician learns scales and harmony, and practices discipline. A painter learns draftsmanship, color, brush technique. A writer learns grammar, the care and use of words, learns reporting, description, polemic, and characterization, learns to be his own slavedriver. Learns to handle journeywork before he tries to soar. Technique is not greatness, but there's no greatness without technique."

"But what you're doing, and what you're talking about, is all popular stuff," I said, trying not to sound patronizing. "I want to write without worrying about popular success or money."

He bent his head, perhaps to hide a smile. "Good! But remember, no great writer in history ever did anything great except for money. Dickens, Scott, Shakespeare, all were popular. And all wrote because they needed dough. It's too terrible a task, the serving up of your soul which is writing, to be undertaken just for the fun of being a genius. And for God's sake, don't be obscure or arty. You have to communicate. I'd rather have you a communicating hack than an obscure bohemian."

That advice was thoroughly distasteful to my spirit, which craved star-shimmered solitude and the intoxication of feeling inspired. But I could see the advice made sense. And I began reading some of my father's earlier novels again: *The Great Jasper, Behold This Dreamer* and *Joshua Todd*, a long, serious, fine semi-autobiographical work. Impressive name writers of the twenties and thirties had hailed these books, and this writer, as possessing greatness. For the first time it occurred to me I'd seen him out of perspective, only as showman, editor and journeyman.

And, without any help from the muses, I began cashing checks that summer, which is the headiest feeling in any writer's life.

I was a published author. My pen name was Tony Perkins, contrived from my brother's first name and my mother's maiden name. I wrote mostly for David C. Cook Publishing Co., 250-word bits on how to make money when you're still a child, how to do simple science experiments, how to start your own newspaper. At a quarter of a cent a word I was on my way. I collected rejection slips from the big-time slicks, planned a novel, studied *The Writer's Digest*, and looked forward to my days of fame. I also wrote a three-part serial about a boy on a beach with a haunted house which turned out to be a smugglers' base, and sold that at half a cent a word. I blew the $15 on a pair of new fountain pens. Freud be hanged, I have a passion for pens and pencils.

Sandalwood was quiet. Sometimes Mother was with us. Most of the time there was only my father, Tony and me. The offices were empty, teletype and telegraph gone, no staff of help, no weekend guests, no fever of deadlines and circulation reports. I liked it. Mother's roses grew too thickly over the windows, honeysuckle swarmed over the cliff. I was tired, and when I wasn't working I let myself float on the sound of the waves and the salt smell of the breeze and the bee-hum, and I engaged in the art of not-thinking.

Not-thinking is a disreputable activity, and I used to be embarrassed about it, hiding my indulgence in it as one might conceal an act of impurity. "Whatcha thinkin' about?" someone would ask. And I'd concoct an answer because I perceived one mustn't admit she could sit without thinking. No one else did, as far as I could find out. There's a conspiracy of silence about not-thinking which should really be broken for sanity's sake. If you're drumming your fingers on the table, or twiddling your big toe, people assume you've left your body to its own devices, and are brooding, or fretting, or what-have-you, and that's acceptable. But there are times you must leave not only your body but also your mind to foolish diddling, in order to use another part of you which is called your soul. And we should start making that acceptable sometime or other.

Some, like me, have the natural knack of being able to not-think. Others learn it, as Yoga learn to stop breathing and heart-beat. The trick is to send the mind off to play, and forget about it. Minds are busy busy busy things, designed always to be conscious and chattering. Minds will chatter about trivia if there are no ponderous subjects around, and if there aren't even any nice juicy trivia like unpaid bills or what-to-have-for-dinner, the mind begins to keep itself busy with nonsense repetition. The mind may start repeating the words of a song or a commercial, counting cracks on the street, or reiterating casual phrases as if they were runes. Too much of this, some experts say, indicates you're sick or maladjusted. Oldtimers said it meant you had money in the bank or were plain batty. Perhaps. But I do that kind of thing all the time. On purpose.

A word pops into my head, for instance. And because I used to write headlines, counting letters in words in terms of the printer's measure for a specific type-face so the words fit a column, I begin idly counting out any old word. M and W $= 1\frac{1}{2}$, and i and l $= \frac{1}{2}$, and so it goes, while I try to make the word easily divisible in half. I do that the way some people bite their nails. I still do it, even though I've read that some psychologists consider it a symptom of something horrid. It's as good a bit of nonsense as any to amuse the mind and keep it quiet. And, by God, there are times when the mind should keep quiet and let the spirit be about its business.

In religion one learns about mystic states, in which the soul left free of body, mind, emotions and will, reaches out and meets God. There was no formal religion about my not-thinking. Outside formal religion, even for the unbeliever, such states exist authentically, and are of value. The spirit may not recognize where it goes, or how, may not know there is a God to encounter in the journey. The fact remains that if one is naïve enough, clever or brave enough to do what comes naturally, at times the soul gets a vacation and is allowed to do what is natural to it.

There are no immediate practical results to be gained. It's apparently a waste of time, sheer laziness. People, schooled to look not for enjoyment but for utility, resist all tendencies to not-think. They see the value of vacations, exercise, massage and sun tan for the body. They speak of resting the mind with light novels or television, or hope to develop the mind with study. They don't know there is any other part of them. For a long time I felt guilty about not-thinking, and halfway thought it was sloth or an underactive thyroid. But I kept at it, and went on sitting around like a lump, till I became rather skilled at it.

So when I wasn't writing or typing or pasting or washing dishes, I loafed and invited my soul, and grew healthy and free and new as I would never have done otherwise. Then I went back to college, plunged into philosophy and creative writing, stayed up late at night working on the *College News*, and got thrown for a loop when my father became a Catholic.

12

The First Communion Breakfast

My father's entrance into the Catholic Church came about this way, so he told me.

He studied under the Jesuits, with Father Joseph McGarry, Father Martin Scott and Father Harold Gardiner, for nearly three years. He began with the catechism and continued obediently through more complicated texts of history, apologetics and theology, until he completed St. Thomas Aquinas' *Summa*. All very high-level stuff. His mentors, magnificent souls, keen and kindly minds, hadn't gotten down to the details of conversion at all. They were, frankly, in no hurry to let him in the Church. He'd been such an articulate and loud antagonist in the past that they wanted to be quite sure he'd stay put once he got in. They knew too that he was under emotional strain. Emotions are no foundation for permanent faith, which must stand firm when excitement passes, or when problems remain.

And, too, they had to be sure of his marital status. Catholics, as the whole world knows, take marriage very seriously, because it is a sacrament. The Church considers true marriage between two baptized persons indissoluble except by death. The circumstances of my father's first marriage, to Rose Karger, had to be meticulously investigated to be sure it did not bind him before God in sacrament, and that he was indeed validly and sacramentally married to my mother. The investigations of the Catholic Church in such matters are long and incredibly thorough.

In the famous church of St. Francis of Assisi on 31st Street, in the shrine of St. Bernadette on the lower level, he had received the gift of faith. He had no doubts. He wanted to become a Catholic no matter what the cost. And he knew it would cost him, in lost friends, in bitterness and scorn from those who would not understand the turning around of his heart.

He was patient as a catechumen. But finally he went, hat in hand, to Cardinal Spellman, and asked what more he would have to do.

"I've studied nearly three years. I've read all the classics of the faith, and completed the *Summa*. But I seem to be no nearer to becoming a Catholic than I ever was. What can I do to get in?"

The Cardinal smiled. "Fulton, they're training you to be a priest, not a convert," he said. "You're ready now. Come in!"

Remarkably, there was soon after another conversion. Tony, off at boarding school in Riverdale in 1944, unknown to his father, and not knowing about his father, met a woman named Peggy Jo Reilly who led him to want more than anything else to be a Catholic. Needing parental permission for conversion at such a young age, Tony was timid of asking his father, and was stunned to find, when he did bring the matter up, that the problem was academic.

My father, whose first Baptist baptism was unquestionably valid, kept his original Christian name, Charles Fulton Oursler. Tony, who already bore his father's name, was baptized Charles Fulton Oursler, Jr. In 1946 in Confirmation they were to choose new names for a new dignity of life, invoking special patrons. They decided to take the name of Anthony. When Mother had met my father, not fancying the name Charlie, she had called him Tony, drawing tenuously on the last syllable of Fulton as a nickname base. My brother, Fulton on paper, had likewise always been Tony. Taking Anthony for Confirmation would, they felt, make sense. But a few moments before the ceremony the Bishop confronted my father:

"Aren't you Anthony Abbot?" he asked. "Isn't that the name you use to write mystery stories? There's a St. Anthony, Abbot in the month of January!"

St. Anthony comma Abbot, so listed in the calendar of saints to distinguish him from other Anthonys such as Anthony of Padua, who weren't abbots, became patron of Oursler men. My father had the fun of being actually Charles Fulton Anthony Abbot Oursler. Tony was the same, with a Junior added.

And from my point of view this togetherness was a little sickening. I didn't really mind about Tony, because he was young, and when I was young I'd gone and gotten baptized, so I could forgive him. About Daddy I minded. Even the fact that by some device unknown to me we now had a home, a New York apartment in which my father expected my mother to live, made scant impression on me.

I didn't believe the reunion would last, but I was afraid the religious conversion would.

It may sound exaggerated, but at the time the way I honestly felt was this: The most intelligent man I knew had gone haywire and joined the least intelligent, most superstitious of Christian churches, and I must fight to save him. I didn't know the reason for this aberration of his, and I loved and honored him still, but I knew I must do my best to restore him to the sane world.

I happened to be home when he made his first communion. For born Catholics that day is a special occasion when a child dresses in white and marches in ceremony and is fêted at church and at home. For converts there's no such fuss. You go to church and receive communion and hardly any one knows about it.

But Fulton Oursler's first communion was privately unforgettable. It was made, of course, under difficult circumstances. His only cohort, Tony, was at school. My parents had taken an apartment overlooking Central Park South, the same apartment, they later discovered, as was once briefly occupied by another Fulton, Bishop Sheen. But when I came home for the weekend we were all rather selfconscious in this first feeble attempt at family unity. And Mother certainly wasn't going near the Catholic Church, especially not for Fulton's first communion. Neither was I. Daddy went alone.

Then, in the kindness of my heart, I decided the least I could do would be to get up and have coffee with him when he came back, and let him tell me about it. The kindest thing anyone in our family can do for anyone else is to let him tell you about something. So I got up to welcome him home and listen.

He was in a rhapsodic mood. As Mother joined us, he told lyrically of rising in the dawn to walk through sleeping streets. He told of the pigeons, and the first hansom cabs of the day, the pink gleam of sunrise, and men coming home from night shifts under the tender veil of the new day. Even I could sense the joy of soul underlying that retelling.

"And then I went to Child's restaurant and had my favorite breakfast of pancakes and sausages," he said. "And then—I went over to St. Francis of Assisi and made my first holy communion!"

Well. Nearly three years the Jesuits had him, and they'd led him through intricacies of theology, but they'd never yet told him you had to fast before receiving communion.

It didn't seem funny at the time, what with Mother hitting the ceiling, and him feeling like a damned fool. But he was to tell the incident with relish for years after, and he'd laugh humbly at the bumbling ways of converts who think they know it all.

That weekend even I could see it wasn't time to argue with him. News of his conversion traveled fast. To some of the friends he most valued he'd written letters explaining briefly what he had done, asking them to rejoice with him. Others heard of it. The phone began ringing. No one congratulated him. I sat and listened as friends and colleagues phoned and berated him, told him to go to hell, told him he would have to go to hell, told him he had lost his senses. They considered this private alteration of his life a personal affront. They explored all kinds of strange ulterior motives he might have had. They reminded him that they knew him when he became a mail-order bishop to discredit a phony outfit, and asked if he were infiltering the Church. They asked him if he were doing this to cure Mother, if perhaps she drank because of guilt over leaving the Church to marry him, and were astonished to hear she had left the Church before she met him, would not have had to leave the Church to marry him, and wasn't feeling guilty about it at all.

When he insisted he was sincere, my father's friends and co-workers called him a traitor to free thought, freedom of the press, and the liberal American code. His dignity, his peace-making refusal to retort in anger, impressed me. His surprise and grief as letters came pouring in from still other people, broke my heart. Some took it for granted that he had been converted by Bishop Sheen, which apparently was a status-making gesture in the light of the spate of famous converts that churchman had recently made. They assumed Daddy was climbing on some kind of bandwagon.

"They will not do me the courtesy of assuming that I may truly believe this is the one true Church," he said quietly. "They wouldn't be as shocked, or as busy trying to alter me, if they'd learned I'd taken up drugs, or communism."

I felt sorry for him. But I knew how they felt. From where I stood then it was impossible for him to be both sincere and sane about becoming a convert. I thought of the Catholic Church and I thought of greed and gold and murky incense, of suffocation and rigid conformism, of torture and a love of suffering, of hypocrisy and death. How anyone with the soul of an artist and a noble inquiring mind should choose to leap back into the Dark Ages and join up with the narrow-minded censorious Catholic Church, I couldn't imagine.

Quite aside from questions of theology, I wanted to save him from the Catholic Church because I felt the Church meant a fate worse than death: imprisonment in a cultural and intellectual vacuum.

Illogical this desperate feeling of mine certainly was; many people grow totally illogical when the Church comes too close to them, encroaching on their personal milieu. I would have told you then that I *knew* the Catholic Church offered nothing in the way of art or literature, was a deadly foe of science, was a stultifying force in politics and sociology, and possessed no philosophy or logic. She was old, fat, domineering, frightening.

I knew, of course, that in the past the Catholic Church could name among her members the greatest artisitc geniuses. I knew about architects of cathedrals, about Dante, about Fra Angelico, da Vinci, Raphael, Michelangelo.

But I couldn't forget that a pope had ordered bloomers painted over the nude figures in Michelangelo's Last Judgment. And I earnestly believed that the great Catholic artists were great *in spite of* being Catholics, in spite of the accident of time and place which gave them no real choice to be something else. They lived before mankind had courage, sense and maturity to break out of the Catholic strait-jacket, or, as Nietzsche suggested, to cut the umbilical cord tying men to the idea of god. The artistic heritage of which Catholics boasted I understood to be Christian, rather than merely Catholic, and therefore part of the true heritage of Protestant Christianity, which claims as its own all that is good before the Reformation.

These geniuses I assumed had been inward rebels against the Church, paying her at most lip service. People spoke of the quickening power of Catholic faith, as if it alone were the inspiration which made artists creative. When they pointed to the grandeur of Chartres as proof of Catholic inspirational power, I simply pointed to the Taj Mahal, or the Egyptian temples.

In the field of science I knew about Galileo. In history I knew that the villains were Catholics: Spanish conquistadores, French kings, Mary Queen of Scots. The heroes were Protestants: New England settlers, French revolutionists, Elizabeth I. The monsters of current events—Hitler, Mussolini, Stalin—were once Catholics. So too were most criminals in the United States. Backward nations were mostly Catholic. Democracy, the United States itself, was the fruit of brave Protestantism.

Progress came whenever people threw off the shackles of religious totalitarianism. As far as I was aware, hardly any work of stature in human art or science had come out of the Catholic Church since the Reformation. Great men were either Protestants, or, more likely, agnostics, free men and unafraid.

Catholic philosophies certainly weren't changing the world. As a philosophy major, I sincerely believed there couldn't be such a thing as a Catholic who was a philosopher, anyway. Catholics had a nice pat creed with all the answers, didn't they? Why—and how—should they think?

Perhaps I was deaf and blind, but, though I took about all the available courses in the philosophy department, it was as though I'd never heard of Thomas Aquinas. Anselm and Augustine I knew, though not as saints, and not as *Catholics,* but only as Christians. Modern Catholic philosophers weren't taken seriously. The people who mattered were Jews, Protestants, and agnostics, phenomenologists, political philosophers. I, who was intoxicated with Bergson, and also with Kierkegaard, was looking for thought that was relevant to the modern world. *A priori,* I was sure the Catholic Church was less relevant than Buddhism.

I do not exaggerate my opposition to my father's conversion. I wanted desperately to bring him back to the joy and freedom he had seemingly surrendered in exchange for a mess of mysteries and prayers. I was convinced my horror was based on intellectual and commonsensical grounds. Only looking back can I see how unreasoning emotion moved me. I was *afraid* of the Church. But to be afraid of an outworn institution is pathetically ridiculous, so I marshalled arguments and historical data, and argued and argued and argued as time went by.

Only once more that year did I make an effort to find out if one could use one's brain and be a Catholic. It seemed I owed my father that much. Down the Main Line from Bryn Mawr was a Catholic college well-known for its football team, Villanova. It seemed the logical place to go for information. For two days I wrestled with my soul, suffering agonies of emptiness and depression that were related either to God and my need of him if there was a God, or to the flu. I hied myself to Villanova. I told the priest who had the misfortune to be the one to meet me, that I wanted to find out more about Catholic philosophy.

"I don't want to take instructions or enter the Church," I explained firmly. "You see, I'm a philosophy major, and I just want to check out a few things. My father's a convert to your faith, and he assures me the Church has some great thinkers, and I'd like a reading list or a few pointers or something like that."

Thinking back now, I can't be harsh on the poor priest, though for years I used him as a scapegoat. After all, just because I took myself seriously, there was no real reason for him to. I didn't tell him about the soul-wrestling or the flu. I just stood there in the full of the door, seventeen years old in my baggy sweater and my moccasins with no socks, a rather disdainful lump of a kid. Knowing me, I know I didn't look frightened. I seldom do. He couldn't guess what courage it had taken for me simply to approach a priest on his own territory. And in his way he tried to set me at ease.

"Tell me about yourself," he said.

I fenced with him. I wanted to keep this on purely intellectual, academic ground.

"I tell you what," he said finally. "You come here once a week and I'll give you instructions. And if you come regularly, I promise you I'll fix you up with some dates from the football team."

That did it! For years I could tell people about that conversation as proof of my sincere attempt to investigate, and of the utterly disgusting attitude of the Church. I went back to Merion Hall and surrendered to the flu. And flu it became.

13

Alas Athena

"Pallas Athena thea . . ."

Bryn Mawr girls sang a hymn to the goddess of wisdom, and its echoes clung to the Library quadrangle, and for wisdom I strived.

Against a background of war and undercurrents of Communist subversion and un-American activities on campus and off, I became, almost by default, editor of the *College News*. For the first time in my teenage life I was a big wheel. Editing the *News*, a weekly, demanded much time, late-night work, trips to the printing plant, the planning of assignments, editorial policy, and the filling of empty space. I loved working hard. I reveled in interviewing visiting celebrities like W. H. Auden, whom I couldn't grasp at all, and Marianne Moore, whom I at least thought I understood. Now, as editor, I was in on everything on campus, able to lead a few minor crusades, and sound off in editorials. Like everything else, I took it too seriously.

I was trying to decide what in the world I was going to do after graduation. Certainly I had no wish to get married. Bryn Mawr girls did wed, of course, and war-time marriages had already decimated our class of '46. But the climate of Bryn Mawr then was not conducive to ambitions for domesticity. The only people I ever heard talking much about marriage were sociology majors, who took courses in The Family, and studied matrimony as if it were an esoteric science. Everyone else, students and faculty, seemed to take for granted that if you were fortunate enough to go to Bryn Mawr you would DO SOMETHING with your life, and if you married it would be as an avocation, like tennis, or Mayan architecture. Besides, as those who roomed with me explained, I wasn't easy to get along with, and if I thought myself unfitted for wedlock I was right.

Campus life, as a lady professor, beckoned to me strongly. I was toying with the idea of becoming fully academic when, on the employment office bulletin board, I read that the Quakers, who ran a college at Assouan, Egypt, wanted young graduates to teach English lit.

When I'd been in Egypt as a child, I'd ridden in a boat rowed by chanting Nubians, and on clear golden waters had glided over the sunken temple at Assouan, a mystery preserved for most of each year in the depths of the gathered-up river, as if caught in amber. That sun-baked town, where at that time stood only a small dam, was one of many places in our travels to which I'd given my heart.

I confronted my family: I wanted to go to Assouan right after graduation. My mother, appalled, wept. My father said I could go. Said it calmly, respectfully, with a smile and genuine interest. So I didn't go.

Will I remember that when our children ask for approval for far-fetched schemes? I hadn't known that one reason the job was appealing was because I wanted to get away from what I thought would be my father's thumb, wanted to prove my independence. When he treated my decision as an adult one, I no longer needed to go. And found my own reasons for deeming it imprudent.

Besides, while I wasn't looking, home seemed to have become solid again. My father had become a senior editor of *The Reader's Digest,* a job he loved, and was again happy, busy, secure. My mother was recovering her health and joy, and at some point—I have no idea when—had returned to the Catholic Church.

And, because of my work on the *News,* my immediate future was settled for me. I became embroiled in a number of campus controversies in which the opposition was led by an ardent nonconformist. I battled her more or less well when she led an anarchist crusade to get rid of self-government, and I answered her vigorously when she attacked certain editorial policies and articles of *The Reader's Digest.* I am clever and self-advancing only by accident. The horrible truth is that being too naïve and muddled to plan ahead, I never thought of ingratiating myself with my father or Mr. and Mrs. Dewitt Wallace of the *Digest.* But the Wallaces saw my editorials defending them and their pro-American articles, and to my total astonishment sent me a telegram assuring me of a job after graduation. It was as simple as that. I abandoned thoughts of graduate work and teaching, quit my nervous little attempts to win the *Vogue* Prix de Paris, and concentrated on college.

No one person in all those garbled years stands out more clearly than my friend Naomi, who was the only girl I knew who lived a faith.

My first impression of her, back in freshman year, had been of color: the vivid orange and black of her hand-embroidered bedspread, the sharp definition of her laughing dark eyes and shining hair against always-neat brilliant sweaters and skirts. Naomi lived by rules I'd never heard of, and kept them so unobtrusively that only by diligent inquiry did I learn of them. She kept the Sabbath. And when, after many months, I learned about the Jewish Sabbath, I finally understood why she would fall asleep with the lights and the radio on Friday nights, or why she couldn't ride her bike down to the village on a Friday evening for grilled cheese and milkshakes. She couldn't light a fire, or a match, or even switch electricity on and off from Friday sundown to Saturday sundown, so it became my habit to stop in and darken and silence her room for her. She couldn't handle money even to make a pay station phone call, nor work contrivances, nor travel. She ate sparingly of the really horrid wartime college food, not because of a finicky taste, but because the meat wasn't kosher. Boxes from home, and visits with her family, kept her one notch above malnutrition. Personally, I thought the whole business rather senseless, but I loved Naomi as a person, and I admired the courage of her beliefs, and she was by far the nicest oddball of all the many around.

And, as the years passed, when I became exhausted from alarums and excursions into enthusiasms and semisophistication, I would talk with Naomi and find her sanity startling.

One night I had sat up late talking with two or three friends in my own class and one intriguingly lonesome and bewildered freshman. Let me call her Jean. There was something about Jean that bothered us all. For the past few weeks she'd carried an aura of melancholy which against my instincts drew me to her. A girl named Marjorie, who wanted to be a doctor, and I had talked about Jean several times. In our clumsy wordy way we tried to help her climb out of this mood of cynicism and sadness. We went to bed late again this night, after the Blue Bird song.

For some reason, an hour later I walked down the corridor to the bathroom, a trip which was not customary for me at three in the morning. On the way I passed the tiny room where girls could boil up tea on a little gas range, or iron a dress in a hurry. The door was closed. The light was on. Sleepily I trudged on, but the smell of gas stopped me in my tracks. I went back and opened the door. Jean was lying there, unconscious, her throat rattling and rasping. I turned off the gas. I opened the window, stepping over Jean, then came wide awake with horror because I'd stepped over her without thinking about what it all meant.

It was a shock, saving someone's life, and a terrible shock that there should be such a death to rescue someone from. The knowledge that another few minutes would have been too late woke me from sleep for nights afterward. I never saw Jean again. While she was recovering in the hospital her parents came from far away, her sweet clean parents who needed but did not want to ask me if I knew why she had tried to die. I tried to answer them. Until the night Jean attempted suicide, I could have told them all the bewilderment and loneliness that filled her, could have explained a bit pointedly where they as parents had failed her. But she had tried to die, and that put a new perspective on what I knew. I could not tell them why she wanted to *die*.

Wanting to die, really wanting to, without hyperbole or dramatics, had never occurred to me. Marjorie and I turned to each other in the weeks to come, nervously eyeing the honest-to-God reality of dying and living. Why did we want to live? We didn't know that, really, any more than we knew why Jean wanted to die, or why it happened that I was there so that she didn't die. We wondered if in our own moods and poses we skirted that chasm of reality ourselves, never knowing how we tempted final danger.

The only girl I respected who knew why she was living was Naomi. Naomi invited me to go home with her and stay for the weekend.

To this day her wonderful family, and all the branches of it, are my cherished friends. And to this day I think it surprises the good Alexanders that they were very much a part of the preparation for my own conversion to the Catholic Church.

We arrived safely before sundown. I stood quietly while they lit the candles and prayed. Graciously, cordially, they made me welcome, and there was about their home an invisible golden air of peace. I became aware of discipline and piety, of candor, of forth-right humor, and a sense of fitness in all things. I understood I could not have milk or butter with my meat, marveled at the intricate kitchen rules and the different sets of dishes for different foods, found I had a taste for kosher cooking. And I knew myself surrounded by that special God-loving concern and camaraderie that many people like to define as Christian charity. It is godly charity, belonging as much to the Father as to the Son.

Karl Stern, in *Pillar of Fire,* describes how he felt as a Jew coming for the first time into personal contact with sincere Christians. He was startled to find that they spoke the same thoughts, that there was in the religious Jewish home and the religious Christian home the same identifiable life-giving air.

For me coming to the household of Jewish friends is like returning to a family hearth. There is with them gaiety, unsoiled by sentimentality or cliché or lightheadedness, springing from a faith which stands definitely on the earth while reaching to the sky. There is with them, even in happy times, awareness of suffering, a sense of destiny in suffering. Many people spend their lives trying to pretend suffering doesn't exist. Godly Jews and Christians know it does exist, know it is related to God, and while working to alleviate it they accord it dignity and worth. In the matrix which formed both Jew and Christian is the gift of reality: the pillar of fire casts a light in which can be seen that what is unlikely may be more real than what seems probable and national.

Later it was to seem to me that in a real way, becoming a Christian means also becoming a Jew. And when you are fortunate enough to meet a family absorbed in serving the God of Abraham, you may know that you are on holy ground, even if you are a supereducated disbeliever in holiness.

Coming to the Alexanders' home was like coming to my senses after nightmare wanderings. I envied Naomi, and sensed the origin of her poise and kindness lay in religion. And, since this was an unposed, unself-conscious, hearty and human kind of religion, I determined to be as agreeable a guest as possible.

I was dying for a smoke. But I wouldn't dream of lighting a cigarette on the Sabbath in that house. They put me to sleep in the living room. When everyone else was in bed and I thought it safe, I climbed out the window in my pyjamas, slinking through the shrubbery to the line where their property ended, and lit my cigarette. If they could be technical about the Sabbath, so could I. Peacefully I huddled in the shadows and smoked. The voice of Naomi's father scared me so that I choked.

"What in the world are you doing, April?" he asked, knotting his bathrobe against the chilled wind.

At my explanation his laughter shattered the night. "For goodness sake, I'd rather have you smoke day and night in my house than be out here catching your death of cold, and running me the risk of having the police come to ask questions. You're ruining my good name, and my sleep!"

To this day, when we speak of the problems of intolerance or ecumenism, Mr. Alexander reminds me of the evening when we outdid each other in trying to make two ways of life meet. In the years since, all the Alexanders have distinguished themselves in service of their faith, and I dedicated myself to the service of mine, but we have seen no conflict. There could be none, for do we not both pray the same psalms, and rejoice in the God of Israel?

They liked me in spite of myself, and that was only one of the qualities I admired in Naomi's family. From the moment I met them I began consciously hoping to achieve in my life something similar to what they had in theirs.

But at the moment I was writing my third or fourth great American novel for Miss Finch. In a senior year with a gloriously light schedule of courses I was also trying to evolve philosophical theories of my own. When I expounded them I was told they were rooted in Plotinus, whom I'd never read. So I read Plotinus, wrote my novel, dabbled with existentialism, and finally produced an honors paper in philosophy with Miss Isabelle Stearns as guide, a small woman of incredible intensity of mind.

The thesis subject was *The Nature of the Individual*, and for me that involved sketching out a whole personal system of philosophy before I was through. Of course, students are not given credit simply for presenting their own young thoughts, and I was primarily assigned to examine the theories of genuine philosophers. I wrote on Hume, Royce, Bradley and James, and blithely drew from them all implicit evidence of the existence of a soul, of self, and of a suprarational, supernatural life, which is a feat roughly comparable to squaring the circle.

"How do I know what I think until I've said it?" someone once asked, and with me the remark isn't funny. I never suspected what I really thought about people and the cosmos until I began writing it out. Even then I didn't understand all that I had set down in that paper. I dug that thesis out of the cellar the other day and read through its fuzzy, ponderous flamboyance. From this distance I see in it a vision of truth which has become the basis for all that I know and believe today. Most fascinating to me now, rereading that paper, is the realization that the young girl who wrote it, the seeker of wisdom at Athena's shrine, somehow managed to fool herself into believing she was still an atheist.

Basically, in that paper, I began with the understanding that mind and body are actually not a dichotomy, that there is no real ultimate difference in the stuff of matter and of spirit. I went on to explain that because through evolution spirit and consciousness had developed from the same energy as had matter and bodies, so thought can affect material things, and material things affect thought and personality. And I was trying to show that each of us, while unique and set apart, is also in some degree in communion with everyone and with all creation. Life becomes an exploration of both our individualities and our oneness. To fulfill our destiny we must carry both our differences and our likeness to the final degree, and find "the aim of the world," "the world purpose" that brings us to the heights of union.

I concluded then:

"For man makes his own individuality, and when he is unaware of the universality that is the . . . cause of that individuality, he becomes confused and bewildered by his isolation from other men. Until he has come to acknowledge the gigantic workings of one common purpose behind the solitudes of men he can never be at peace with himself: he will never be able to understand or resolve the conflict of the two forces within him . . ."

I beg pardon for inflicting on you a quotation from a nineteen-year-old's homework. I offer it only as a foreshadowing of the clean-lined teaching I was later to accept: the doctrine of the Christ. There was in the world at the time I wrote that a genius named Teilhard de Chardin, whose works are now seeding the Christian world with the new understanding of the Spirit. I believe that for the average twentieth-century intellect only the insight of Teilhard can make Christianity authentically relevant. I believe that thoughts, ideas, do exercise pressure in the atmosphere of all minds, and that in some dim way, through contact in that nöosphere of which Teilhard wrote, I caught enough of the light reflected from his thought so that in years to come I could find my way a bit more easily to the faith.

At the time, of course, I carefully avoided the use of the word God anywhere in the thesis. I'd forgotten that votaries of Athena are not guaranteed wisdom, and I thought I was wise, and still pagan. I was graduated from Bryn Mawr, still an atheist, as far as I knew.

14

In Which I Really Meet My Mother

When A.A. first moved in on me, ever so courteously, I was insulted.

"I'm not the one who needs help," I said. "I'm just fine."

"All our children, all our families, need help," said the member of Alcoholics Anonymous. "It's difficult for you to accept your mother's comeback. You're going to need help from others like yourself to get used to having a happy home again."

Supercilious as all get out, I cocked an eyebrow. "A happy home? I'll be glad to get used to having one, when I'm sure it's there. If you can do something, if you can really cure Mother—"

"Only she can cure herself. We'll help her. But she'll always be an alcoholic. She told you that."

"She sure did."

"And she told you that only by remembering that she was always open to the same temptation, only by admitting the battle must be fought every day of her life, could she stay dry?"

"Yes. Sounds great. I'll believe it when I see it."

"You aren't likely to see it, if you don't get help yourself. Your attitude can make it almost impossible for her."

"My attitude didn't cause her drinking. It was the other way around. I'm not standing in her way. And don't expect me to go to any more A.A. meetings, Family ones or otherwise. Because I'm not an alcoholic, and if I do have any problems I'll take care of them myself, the way I've always had to do."

Let it be noted, as a tribute to the deepseated charity of good

A.A.'s that this one didn't rear back and take me down a peg. Instead, with genuine sweetness, he observed:

"You've had a rough time, haven't you?"

This A.A. was no stranger by now. Our apartment at times seemed to be crawling with all kinds of reformed drunks, a bookshop owner, a doorman, a widow with mink, a character actress, even a nice little old lady who looked as if she'd never had a drop in her life. I didn't know how Mother had gotten into A.A. I did know that she had been sober for what seemed to me a record number of months, and that these people were all sobered-up alcoholics who in some way helped her, mostly it seemed by talking and drinking coffee. I couldn't help liking them individually, but as a group they made me uneasy.

"Your mother feels rotten about the rough time she gave you," he continued. "One thing that scares her now is that she feels you can't forgive her. We've told her she's wrong, that she's underestimating you. We've told her that all our families have been victimized, some much more than you, but that being good souls they all rally to forgive."

"I forgive her," I shrugged.

"Well, since it's so easy for you to forgive, perhaps you'll help us out. There are a couple of kids I know whose mother's just entering A.A., and they're having trouble forgiving her. Could I bring them here and let you talk to them? You could do them good by showing them they aren't unique. Sometimes our kids think nobody else in the world ever had it so bad. But you know better. And you already know a lot about A.A. and our Twelve Steps, so you can explain it to them."

Sneaky, that A.A., God bless him.

Sure, I knew about A.A. On weekends home from college I'd heard about it. Obediently, I'd read the book that outlines Twelve Steps to recovery, a rewrite of basic Christian principles. I'd gone to A.A. meetings with Mother, and sat and listened while ex-drunks from all walks of life told with shattering frankness of their past degradation and of their adventures in rebuilding their lives. Some were, to my surprise, far worse than Mother had ever been. All agreed on one point: they were helpless before alcohol and could never again safely take one drink because they were never cured, only self-arrested cases. And all underlined the fact that they had no one to blame but themselves.

The first step in A.A. was to admit there was a power outside yourself, stronger than yourself. If you couldn't believe in God, you began by admitting in honesty that there was one power outside yourself, stronger than yourself: the bottle. Accepting the existence of God wasn't any more humiliating than accepting the domination of alcohol. And admitting the need for help was the key to health.

"Until an alcoholic hits bottom, and is scared enough to cry out for help, there's no use trying to help her," repeated A.A.

Mother had hit bottom all right. I'd seen her. It had taken a long time, and many times along the trail I thought she could go no further, but she had gone on, until at last she had no illusions left, and begged for help, and was helped.

"Live twenty-four hours at a time," said A.A. "You only have to stay sober twenty-four hours at a time. To do that you must ask help from God, and from other people, and realize you can't do it by yourself. When this twenty-four hours are over you ask for another twenty-four hours' worth of help from people and from God."

And while you ask for help in A.A. you must also give it. Perhaps most important of the Twelve Steps is the one in which you go out and help another fight temptation and stay sober, or reclaim a member who has had a slip. Or, eventually, when you go to help a drunk who's hit bottom and wants to join A.A. You're on call, and you will go where you're told to go, and stay as long as needed, and you will not count the cost in time or anguish because anyone in trouble is your brother and sister, and for God's sake you must help them.

I'd seen A.A.'s help Mother. I'd gone with Mother on some of her own Twelfth-Step work, keeping her company at midnight when she was summoned to a dark and frightening part of town. I couldn't help admiring her for doing this work. In my mind I was proud of her, grateful to her for finding the strength to fight for a comeback and win.

But, years before, I'd built a wall to shut her out of my heart. Behind the wall I stayed, watchful, superior. My attitude boiled down to this: I was glad she was finally doing what she should, but why the heck hadn't she done it before? If she loved us, why had she put us through hell? It was the kind of self-centered question that we who haven't grown up to compassion always ask.

So an A.A. arranged that I should speak to other children. Two came that afternoon, a high school boy and girl who forgot self-consciousness because they needed desperately to pour out their troubles. For two hours they told me what it had been like with their mother, and it was the same as it had been with mine.

"Some of the details are different, but the story's the same. It always is, I guess," I said. Shame is lessened when it's shared, and hurt is less terrifying when you find yourself not singled out, but only one of many others.

"And your mother has really stopped drinking?" the girl asked.

"She has."

"Well, if it's as simple as that, why didn't she do it before? That's what I want to know," flared the boy. "If she cared about us, if she cared about anyone, Mom wouldn't have done this to us. And no matter what they say, I can't believe any different. She doesn't love us. And I can't pretend nothing happened. I don't love her. Not after all she's done to us."

"She didn't do it to you. She did it to herself. She's suffered more than you have"—I began, and heard the echo of Bonnie's words to me in a Sandalwood summer so long before.

Gradually I found myself trying to tell them the truth I needed to hear. And when they left I put on my coat and went out and walked for an hour in Central Park.

For the first time in my entire life I thought of my mother as a person, apart from me and apart from what I wanted her to be for me. An unnerving experience, that, to forget yourself long enough to let another person be herself, and feel for her not self-protecting scorn but sympathy. That jolt of understanding was one of the best things that ever happened to me, but it hit hard, and nearly knocked the wind out of me for good. A good part of what I thought was me was built on reaction to her, and when it fell away it left a gaping hole.

I sat by the sailboat pond and understood that this woman who was my mother hadn't wanted to ruin her life to hurt us. She was by nature a lady, fastidious, well-mannered, high-idealed, loving. She had set high standards for herself, too high. She had wanted to be perfect, to be more than her strength would allow, partly out of pride, more out of devotion to my father.

It would be hard to do daily battle against the temptation to drink. Harder still to live with yourself humbly aware of the wreckage of your past years. To be wounded by reminders of the past when she had not been able to stand on her own feet and be herself would be a terrible burden for my mother. Far easier, I thought, to slit your throat, or stay too sotted to remember, than to try, defenselessly, to build a new life. Could I live with such humiliation? Could I have the guts to start again? To ask for help?

I'd insisted I needed no help. But in Central Park I asked for it. From whom? From whatever God there might be. I asked for help to love my mother, so that I would no longer be an obstacle to her recovery.

I came home in the dusk. Mother was in the miniature kitchenette, a bottle in her hands. In a moment I remembered that she and my father were expecting important company. She'd have to offer them drinks. It must be a difficult test for her to do this. I remembered, but not quickly enough. She had seen my face.

She wheeled on me, eyes flashing, head high in dignity, and she gave me hell. She asked me who I thought I was to be her judge.

She asked me who I thought I was to be unable to forgive her the past, and by what right I dared to not trust her. Or to look down on her.

And because she gave me hell, because she at last felt sure enough of herself to put me in my place, I could take my place. I apologized, and was glad of the chance. And I could begin to love her again, the way I should.

It wasn't easy, for either of us. Habits, patterns had to be broken. We had to get to know each other. The person who had been my mother in name for the past years wasn't the same one I met now in resurrection. They say *in vino veritas*. Maybe in a little wine there is truth. But in alcoholism is the opposite of truth. I believe that we each form ourselves by choice, rejecting by many small decisions personalities we could have become. And in alcoholism I believe that the Mr. Hyde personality in all of us is present as if by sorcery, while the true personality is chained and hidden. Drunks are not charming; they are repulsive and mean and foul. But alcoholics, sober, are the most charming people in the world, too charming, perhaps, to find it easy to live in reality. Over the years I was to come to know hundreds of A.A.'s, and, without exaggeration, I've never yet met a successful one who wasn't a better and more Christian person than the average non-drunk. Which makes sense. Because to make a comeback from the gutter, or the more polite sanatorium, you have to become a near-saint along the way.

It is, as I found out for myself, woefully simple to feel superior to other people with problems that aren't your own. We who are not prey to alcoholism sneer at those who are. Yet we may be prey to equally strong addictions which, by God's grace, happen not to be so obviously harmful. I can't stop smoking yet. And I have the devil's own time trying not to eat too much. Other people in my family eat as much and more, and stay thin. Other people complain that the things I want to eat are too rich for them and upset their systems. My system is upset going without them. The only hope for me is not in hitting a golden mean of temperance, but in swearing off certain foods forever, and this I've found downright impossible to do, so far.

Experts say that we who eat too much, or those who drink too much, or take drugs, or what-have-you, are only trying to escape reality because we're unhappy. They're partly right. But the truth is that everyone wants to escape reality because they're unhappy to some degree, but not everyone is an alcoholic or a food-aholic. Some people get to be skin and bones when they're unhappy. I think they're lucky. They don't. Others get ulcers, or spend too much money, or drive too fast, or work too hard.

The difference is that with an alcoholic there are physical factors involved that make what is a socially acceptable swallow of liquor for other people poison for them. Once he's an alcoholic, the alcoholic is no longer really responsible. He can be held to account at the beginning, perhaps, though there are individuals who were fed liquor in infancy as a harmless joke and who, because they had the constitution of an alcoholic, became out-and-out drunks before they were twenty. And there are adults who are led to drink by social custom and don't know what's happening to them before it's too late. It's pretty hard to believe that you can't get away with what everyone else gets away with. And alcoholics, like the rest of us, fool themselves a lot.

It's human nature to blame other people for our own miseries. Adam tried to excuse himself to God by blaming Eve, and we've all gone on doing the same thing. Alcoholics are notorious for blaming someone else or something else, louder than the rest of us because their miseries are more blatant. I'd heard Mother blame everyone from my father to her mother, watched her seek psychoanalysts to pinpoint guilt. But the beginning of salvation is the saying of *mea culpa*. And Mother made that beginning.

Does it sound strange to say that I believe that because of Mother's alcoholism, and her recovery, every one of us in the family became a better human being? Not the least of the lessons she taught us was the insistence that we must assume the blame for our own troubles, and, without deceit, aware of our dignity as creatures with free will, say to God, "through my fault."

I had thought once, in my bitter young days, that I'd write of the hard life I had had because Mother was a drunk. I'd thought to tell the world after she was dead of the misery she'd wrought. But I write now of my mother because I am proud of her. She came out of the depths and climbed to the heights. Till the day she died she was never free of the physical temptation to drink. Yet from the end of her first successful year in A.A. till the day she died, some thirteen years, she never gave in to that temptation again. In the last years, due to circumstance of grief and misfortune, she was to be tempted almost beyond her strength. But she did not depend on her own strength.

Who was this woman I was meeting for the first time?

She was a woman almost bewildered by love. A woman who could still hardly believe that a man she considered as truly great as my father could have chosen her. She was to write in her journal after his death:

I have lived in the age of Schweitzer, Gandhi, Carver, Merton. I have been loved by Fulton. If those men flowered in this febrile field, these years are ransomed. But my debt is clear.

She felt it obvious that she owed God more than she could pay for the simple gift of being alive and being loved. Once she found her way back to him she never ceased to keep account of herself, struggling to do better for his sake.

She was a woman of gaiety, who would clown with funny accents, a woman of music, color, style. A writer bursting to get things down on paper, stopping occasionally to play with words as if they were prism-toys, an inventor of catchy phrases. "How warm is luke?" she'd write. And, "Can anyone disappear into thick air?"

She was a woman of extravagant thoughtfulness. She'd sit up nights writing notes of encouragement to friends, draw them cartoons, send them violets or roses or newspaper clippings, take a crippled girl to see *Peter Pan,* and remember each pertinent detail about the shy hopes of even the least obtrusive people she met.

Eventually, quietly, about two years after my father's conversion, she returned to the Catholic Church, with the ministrations of Father Stephen Downey. Could it be called a return? Had she known her faith better she might not have left it. No pagan convert ever had as many mixed-up ideas and mis-remembered notions and prejudices to be overcome. And when she did finally embrace the faith she gave it her whole heart, and would have died for it.

Charmingly, she never quite grew up. She would always retain that innocence which lets a child speak knowledgeably of evil in the world without really knowing what or where it is. She would always be a creature of enthusiasm for beauty and glamor and humor and goodness of soul. She would collect silly stylish clothes and slim books of poetry, revel in the shenanigans of Jimmy Durante, and pounce on obscure news stories of self-sacrifice and gallantry. She loved best of all a good success story.

As far as I was concerned she was living one, twenty-four hours at a time.

15

In Which I Really Meet My Father

My father and I were living in a sort of armed truce. I no longer thought he'd lost his mind just because he became a Catholic. I no longer wondered if age and trouble had caused him to lose respect for learning. He was, if anything, more studious, more intellectual in the short years since his conversion. I knew how much it meant to him when I was graduated *cum laude* in philosophy. He'd always wanted to go to college and get a degree. And, quietly, delightedly, he beat me to it. He came to my graduation with a black robe and a vivid hood, mortarboard and tassel, and an honorary degree of doctor of letters awarded him the day before. In the years to come he would receive many honorary degrees, but none pleased him more than the one he brought to me that day, when he could say he went to college and got his degree before I did.

And he was earning those honorary degrees. From the time he entered the Church until the night of his death he worked overtime spending his talents to explain and dramatize the faith. He was working full time for *The Reader's Digest* from his New York apartment, executing his assignments as senior editor and contributing articles. He never stinted on the time and interest he owed to the *Digest*. But he'd rise early in the morning, getting to his desk at five while everyone else slept, and work late into the evening on other projects he assigned himself.

The book he had begun writing in 1935 to expose Christianity had become the manuscript for *The Greatest Story Ever Told*. Alarmed by the fact that so many people were ignorant of Scripture, frightened off by the fear of being bored or by a false barrier of intellectualism, he launched a private crusade to bring both Old and New Testaments into modern idiom. In the summer of 1946 he was still polishing the book about the life of Jesus. But as far back as 1943 he'd conceived the idea of a weekly radio show based on the Gospels. With the daring naïveté of a convert he suggested it to radio producer Waddill Catchings. Despite all kinds of disappointments, and the pragmatic prudence of men who knew no one would sponsor such a show, and it would be impossible to dream up scripts that would be accepted by a public made up of all faiths, my father continued to believe it could be done.

What today is called "the ecumenical spirit" was part of my father's spirit and faith from the moment of conversion, and would be of Mother's too. That was, in fact, my first good impression of the Catholic Church, that my parents, imbued with zeal and loving faith, were not *tolerant,* or *broad-minded,* which are rather conde-scending and limiting qualities, but acted instead as if they'd stum-bled on a tremendous inheritance they wanted others to share. Mother became an editor of the magazine *Guideposts,* an interfaith project launched by our great friend Dr. Norman Vincent Peale and others, featuring true stories of prayer and inspiration from all churches. My father's constant tenet was:

"I have my creed. Others have theirs. Let us ignore the area where we disagree and concentrate on the broad area of truth which we share."

Already, that summer of 1946, the radio show was close to becoming a reality. The Goodyear Tire and Rubber Company showed interest in sponsoring it. The pilot show, based on the parable of the good Samaritan, had been conceived and worked out by my father, then put into script form by a script writer named Henry Denker. By the next January *The Greatest Story Ever Told* became a weekly radio feature on the network of the American Broadcasting Company, sponsored by Goodyear at a cost of over a million dollars a year, yet presented with no commercial other than the legally necessary naming of the sponsoring company. Some of these weekly dramas were taken directly from the manuscript of the then still unpublished book. Others were original dramas, illustrat-ing and illuminating New Testament texts, born in my father's mind and heart, and entrusted by him to Mr. Denker for his tech-nical skill at preparing scripts.

"I want," said my father, "to write an elevator boy's life of Christ. To tell the story of Jesus with truth and excitement, so that it grips people today the way Christ gripped people in his day. To get out of the schoolroom and the catechism room and into the marketplace and the heart."

This was the mood and method of the book he wrote, and he carried it into the radio show. And because of his ecumenical spirit, his instinctive loving appreciation of other points of view, his sto-ries, on the air and in the book, while true to his own belief, never offended those of other faiths. It was, I think, unique in the history of relations between Catholics, Protestants and Jews, that the story of the Christ could be told by a Catholic and win the admiration and affection of the other faiths. Every script for the many years that the show ran on radio was approved by four men: Monsignor Joseph A. Nelson of St. Patrick's Cathedral's staff in New York; the Rev. Dr. Samuel Shoemaker of Calvary Protestant Episcopal Church; the Rev. Dr. Paul Wolfe of the Brick Presbyterian Church in New York; and Mr. Otto Frankfurter, brother of Justice Felix Frankfurter.

My father gave witness to his Catholic faith. But even to this day I receive letters from people who quicken to his books asking me to corroborate their hunches that he must have belonged to the same sect to which they belong. He was in his love of God a universal man.

And with love like that you cannot argue. I'd tried arguing with him and given up, because he wouldn't quarrel with me. He would not debate theology or niggle over philosophy, not because he considered them unimportant or doubted his mastery of them, but because he felt that was the surest way to lose a potential convert. With me, and with all who challenged his faith, he summoned what I can describe only as a tangible warm outgiving of love, baffling argument. It's extremely annoying to want to argue and be met with open arms.

We tacitly agreed to disagree. We met with each other in our own broad area of agreement: our genuine affection for each other, our delight in writing, literature, music, the theater, windowshopping and poker. It was an ecumenical movement of a kind, in which I still hoped to win him back from the Church, and he kept his hopes and prayers to himself.

And I found that he was now a different person. Conversion, which means a turning around or a transforming, is assumed by everyone to change a man. Skeptics and the unfriendly assume conversion turns a person into some kind of fanatic. Daddy was not a fanatic: even I had to admit that. And, being obtuse, I never thought that the change I found in him could be a result of his becoming a Catholic.

From the beginning he'd always been scrupulously honest, true to the tenets he constructed for himself. He'd had a fairly miserable childhood, but he never let himself make it grounds for self-pity. He'd always had an ideal of decency which he hewed to, even when life and the people in it played him false.

He had also been, in the days before he entered the Catholic Church, in many ways a pain in the neck. I don't say that disrespectfully. Most men of any stature and ambition are difficult to live with, precisely because their virtues are also their faults. It was always hard to get a word in edgewise with my father. He loved attention, could upstage anyone, and took himself mighty seriously. This was part of what made it fun to be his daughter, but it was also annoying, not only to his family but to others. Things had to be done his way, so much so that when I first saw *Life with Father* on stage I was startled that people found it funny. My father was the boss, the monarch, as much as Mr. Day. He was also a man who reveled in emotions and moods, who went into violent rages at inept telephone operators, who brooded, and took umbrage, who expected everyone to drop everything and come out to play with him when he was gay. And when someone did him dirt, he did not easily forgive.

Now none of those qualities is very bad, or rare. They're the kind of character traits you learn to accept in any number of successful people. I had assumed that these ruthlessly autocratic mannerisms were the necessary minor expense of Being Somebody.

But, when I came home from college I found my father a different man. The change was so gracefully unadvertised that it was a while before I noticed it. We all know people who make resolutions to do better or be nicer, and drive everyone else crazy with the showoff way they refuse drinks or keep tempers or avoid gossip. My father was working at re-shaping himself as a Christian, and was concerned with devices like the Catholic examination of conscience, but the impression he gave me was of unstudied gentleness, and love.

Now he was never too busy to see anyone. Never too important to put up with bores, or, as the Bible suggests "to suffer fools gladly." He looked at each person he met to find something to praise, and then really praised it: told the elevator girl she had beautiful hair, told his secretaries they had remarkable keenness in coping with problems. In his wake he left happiness. When exasperated by incompetence or laziness, he grew more pleasant, his voice crooning, his eyes smiling while he coaxed people into doing better jobs. For the least kindness, from a scrawled fan letter to a newspaper delivered, he gave thanks. And when he saw a chance to do good, he did it, instantly.

People he did not know would write to him, prompted by some article on faith or prayer which he'd published, and pour out to him their loneliness and despair. Writers always get letters from strangers who want to get things off their chest by writing to someone far away. The nicer writers answer such letters. But often, after the morning mail, I'd find my father on the phone conning long distance operators into locating strangers on the strength of slight clues, then talking the astonished letter-writers into believing life was worth loving.

Only after his death did we learn of the hundreds of people he'd helped with money, of the ordained priests who were able to go through the seminary only because he agreed to underwrite them, of gifts to college students, far-off missions, nearby neighbors with hospital bills or expensive hopes for a career.

He made a creative art out of forgiveness and lack of resentment. Only once before his death did I ever see him unable to rally himself to ignore a hurt, and that time it was I who hurt him. I had assured him I would do something, and found I couldn't do it without hurting someone else whom I loved, and so I simply didn't do it. I didn't know what to say to him about it, so I didn't mention it, hoping he would understand, and, in the confused way of young people, hoping desperately that perhaps the whole thing hadn't been so important to him at all. It had been important. He didn't bring it up to me, but a deep slow sadness was spreading through his days, and in my heart I knew why.

I brought it up to him sidewise. He pretended not to notice. Then I asked him point blank if he was angry because of what I had not done. He denied it, not pettishly but truthfully: he wasn't *angry*. I told him then, simply, how I'd been caught in a dilemma choosing which person to disappoint, and that I felt badly about it.

As in a puff of smoke the sadness and bad feeling vanished. A dilemma he could understand. It was my silence that had puzzled him. No more need be said.

"Then you forgive me?" I asked.

"No." He smiled. "There's nothing to forgive. There almost never is, you know. I find it increasingly hard to forgive people because I find it increasingly hard to believe they've done me real harm, or done worse than I."

Forgiveness was for him, in these days of his new life, usually replaced by an unspectacular searching for his own faults. One person who constantly broke his heart by his apparent refusal to award him courtesy, let alone affection, I shall call Dudley. Dudley and my father had not gotten on for years. As long as I can remember, Dudley had taken all my father would give him, and asked for more. As long as I can remember, Dudley had quarreled and bickered, accusing my father of standing in his way, of looking down on him. Dudley particularly resented my father's conversion, and was making it his business to tell everyone that it had been simply another clever trick to advance a career, and a concession to my mother. All ventures of friendship on my father's part were rebuffed.

Dudley made me furious. Dudley made my father puzzled.

"I've failed him in some way," he said. "Not in the ways he accuses me of, but in something about me. He hates my guts. Hatred is an illness, and when people are ill they do and say things they don't mean. He means to hurt me, all right. But if he didn't hate me, he wouldn't mean to hurt me. The things he says I did to him didn't happen as he says. But there is a wound there."

That reasoning seemed specious to me, but it led my father to search his conscience and look at himself with Dudley's eyes. He selected from within himself the qualities which most offended this enemy. Then he wrote an article, disguising the facts of the case so no one could easily identify either Dudley or himself. In the article the narrator presents the circumstances of Dudley's meanness so that any reader is quickly led to despise Dudley. Then, as the article continues, narrator and reader both become aware of the personal flaws in the narrator which had alienated Dudley in the first place: a love of the limelight, a sense of self-importance, a need to excel and flaunt, the desire to offer advice and criticism, an unconscious inability to build up Dudley's ego for fear of jeopardizing his own. The narrator accuses himself of these flaws, and works fumblingly but diligently to overcome them. And in the article Dudley forgives him, and is no longer his enemy.

He entitled the article "The Hardest Lesson." It ran originally in a Hearst magazine and was reprinted later in an anthology of my father's work called *Lights Along the Shore*. He never told anyone what lay behind that article. I read it for the first time with tears in my eyes, recognizing its origin.

"Maybe the one you call Dudley will read it and recognize himself! He'll see how he underestimated you. Serve him right!"

Ruefully he shook his head at my excitement. "If he reads it he won't recognize himself or me. I didn't write it for him. I wrote it for me, and people like me. And you still don't understand, dear. I don't want to serve him right. I'm serving someone else."

As far as I know, the real Dudley never got the point. But in reading and understanding I was beginning to see the measure of the new dimensions in my father's soul.

Suffering, of any kind, had new meaning for him. One of the things I disliked about the Catholic Church was its seeming obsession with the cross, blood and agony. My father, becoming a Catholic, never talked about "crosses to be borne," or any of the other pious clichés that repelled me. They repelled him too, not because he found them untrue, but because semantically they distorted the truth. He served the living Christ, the Christ who had lived in the Holy Land, who lived now resurrected yet gracefully present all over the world. And as his servant, late-come to the vineyard, my father felt he had not time to waste.

"I have so much to make up for," he'd say quietly, when we chided him over his long stints at his desk, his overtime hours speaking or writing to serve the Church. "I wasted nearly fifty years of my life. The eleventh hour has struck."

The last ten years of his life, in the faith, he worked with zest, taking defeat as part of growth, refusing no task asked in Christ's name. In his work at the *Digest* he was to collaborate enthusiastically with heroes of all faiths, telling dramatic tales of everyone from Schweitzer to Sheen. He'd found a new way to look at life, and yearned to share that point of view. He enjoyed finding stories from the sciences which might lead intellectuals to glimpse the intelligent design of the universe. He took erudite books such as Velikovsky's *Worlds in Collision* and Lecomte de Noüy's *Human Destiny*, condensing them so people could hear the rich overtones of godliness in an atomic world. Following up stories of juvenile delinquency, he pointed to the fact that the practice of virtue and charity could still work miracles of redemption.

And on his own time his restless pen, then held in fingers grown painful from arthritis, kept pushing to spread the good news of the gospel. His most cherished work, *The Greatest Story Ever Told*, was under contract to Winston publishers, and they wanted him to make changes in it. Their sales were mostly to small fundamentalist or literalist church groups, and they thought his approach might be offensive to them. He didn't think it was. At the time he was already undertaking a book on Father Flanagan for a quietly daring young editor named Ralph Beebe, at Doubleday, a book he was writing with Will. My father put an end to the contract with Winston, and gave the book to Ralph Beebe to read, a little hesitantly, perhaps. After all, the life of Christ had been written many times. It was old hat. And this was a most unusual way of telling that life: the book read like a novel, moved quickly, without footnotes or theological asides. Who would want to read a life of Christ not written by a clergyman-scholar?

Ralph Beebe had a wife named Rachel, small-boned with big intense eyes, and a deep faith, a woman active in the Episcopalian Church, whose quick mind complemented her husband's. Ralph read half the manuscript of *The Greatest Story Ever Told*, and looked up in a quandary.

"I don't know. It's so simple! Would people read something this simple?"

Rachel read the manuscript, and answered, "You can't make a mistake with this. Just because it is so simple. Beautifully simple."

Ralph Beebe wanted no changes. He went out on a limb, put on a major display for it at a sales meeting, and felt so strongly that no one questioned him. In February 1949 the book appeared in a resounding public silence. The history of its emergence as a runaway bestseller, eventually selling millions of copies, has been analyzed and questioned by experts. The real secret of its success was that people liked it.

Most reviewers did not. Major critics ignored it. The Catholic press ignored it especially, and those few critics who mentioned it there suggested that Father So-and-so's Life of Christ was much better, which was a habitual outlook in the Catholic press. It wasn't fun for the writer, being disparaged by his Church, nor was it pleasant when someone or other ventured that it was only because of the success of the radio show that the book sold. I've heard it claimed that he stole the material and prestige for his book from the radio scripts, which is a ridiculous backward way of putting things, because the book came first, and the radio show was his idea anyway. Claims like that annoyed and angered me then, and still do. But he would only smile, shrug, and get to work again. He was not shrewd. He had no patience with people who urged him to sue or take legal action when he was libeled or swindled. I'm still hoping to grow up myself to that point of serenity and grace that so impressed me in his new life.

"Your father was a darling, but he was a lousy business man," an old friend said to me recently. That was true. I think he took for granted that, at least for him personally, it was impossible to be a good business man and a good Christian too. Or perhaps it was only that he couldn't be bothered to spare time from more important work to tend to business. The attitude toward money in our home after my parents' conversion was, to say the least, odd, anyway. Mother kept picking out those quotes from the Bible which promise that if you love God he will take abundant care of you, and nothing is too much to ask. She tithed every dollar she earned, expected abundance, and blithely went her way. She gave lavishly to everyone. Surely God would give lavishly to her.

My father's generosity was more quiet and disciplined, and he had a hunch he wasn't meant to get rich serving the carpenter's son. He did not get rich. The money he earned from the radio show of *The Greatest Story* he never touched: it went, without publicity, into a Foundation Fund and was given to charities of all faiths. Over the years this amounted to thousands upon thousands of dollars, but he never thought of changing that policy. Nor was he motivated by tax benefits. He was neither that clever nor that wealthy. When *The Greatest Story* was a bestseller, and when in addition to his magazine salary he had other books producing royalties, he still had trouble meeting expenses: the necessary ones of his daily life, including alimony, as well as those self-imposed by his will to help others. He denied himself small luxuries, partly for economy, more to flex his willpower, as when he put himself on a newspaper diet, cutting his ration of two evening tabloids to one. He used the world's goods so sparingly that it wasn't until the year before he died that he let himself buy a car. And whenever a guest politely praised a figurine or knick-knack, Daddy would have it wrapped and delivered to him the next day.

As the years passed and he pressed on with his apostolate of the pen, he was again famous. His newspaper column, *Modern*

Parables, became a national favorite. *The Greatest Story* had been nationally syndicated, proving to boost sales of the hardcover book rather than eliminate them. In dawn hours he had written the Old Testament sequel, *The Greatest Book Ever Written,* drawing on research assigned to an old writer friend, then brooding and molding the material to the impact of current life. Words poured out as he caught up true-life dramas to illustrate his excitement about God's life: *The Precious Secret, Why I Know There Is a God,* and *The Happy Grotto,* a slim volume about Lourdes and the inspiring stories of those who were not cured there.

Yet he had become, truly, a humble man. And because I lived in his home I knew this, and marveled.

He was fond of quoting St. Paul. "Put off the old man and put on the new," he would say. "I live now, not I, but Christ in me."

I couldn't deny that this new man was amazingly pleasant to be with. Had I believed I could sincerely accept the Catholic faith and turn out like that, I'd have done so, right away.

Without exaggeration, living with my parents in those years was like living with honeymooners. They were in love. Not with the sentimental love of the very young or those in second childhood, but with a serene delightful absorption in each other, a unity binding them even while they were busy on a thousand separate interests. On a smaller scale the apartment on Central Park South was a repetition of the Sandalwood of the thirties. The editorial work, the secretaries, the phones, the visitors. *Guideposts* and *The Reader's Digest* were to usurp quantities of time and space. Books were planned and written, articles and plays hammered out, speeches written. Two personalities in separate ways lived and loved and worked for God.

And their ways were different. Mother went in for votive candles and statues and philodendron plants twining up walls and over ceilings, pink paper to type on, a bewitchingly cluttered desk. The man she loved indulged his longing for monastic simplicity in his study, following his own rule of minute schedules and orderly work.

When Mother reembraced the Church the trappings of her

faith put me off a bit. Each Catholic, I was to learn, remains an individual and chooses his own form of life with God according to the kind of person he is. Mother was a very definite kind of person, given to enthusiasms, and she enjoyed things like statues of the Infant Jesus of Prague with liturgically colored robes to be changed, and she loved novenas, especially "flying novenas" which are special prayers to be said every hour on the dot for nine hours. She usually missed up on the seventh hour and had to start all over. She liked daily quotes to live by, and her theology was as inaccurate as her checkbook subtractions. But, her prayers were answered. Small miracles fell like sparks around her. Her heart was so childlike and happy that she drew other people to her, and helped them quite genuinely. She had fun being a Catholic, and she was so quick with sympathy and thoughtfulness that she was more beautiful than ever.

This I could see, and love, but it did not draw me to the Church. And if I'd thought hers was the only Catholic way, I wouldn't be where I am now.

As far as I know, my father never made a novena in his life. He said the rosary, which at the time I thought unfortunate but probably required. The manner in which he said his rosary impressed me deeply. He kept by his bed a tiny looseleaf notebook in which he listed people and intentions for which he wished to pray, one for each of the fifty Hail Mary's involved in a rosary. He categorized these prayer intentions under Family, Business, Government, Friends, and, significantly, Enemies. I'd never known anyone who made it a practice to pray specifically for enemies before. He gave them tender, preferred position.

His other major form of prayer was the offering of his daily work to God. In both rosary and work I knew he prayed for me, that I might live enough to grow wise.

I was, I found, beginning again to have conscious belief in God. I could and did pray, though I went to no church.

But I knew I couldn't believe in things like the Mass, or transubstantiation. And I certainly couldn't believe in praying to Mary, Our Lady, as my folks called her. Anything but that.

16

The Hegira

When I was a junior in college Dewitt Wallace of the *Digest* had sent me a wire offering me a job after graduation. That summer he'd followed up with a letter:

Will you kindly compute for me the number of days and hours we must wait for your graduation?

I'm glad that you are at home this summer, able to help Fulton and Grace in their Digest work.

What fun it will be when all three of you are busily engaged in planning with us to produce a better magazine.

That's the kind of man this editor-publisher is. Incredible. But I had doubts. I wrote to him in the beginning of my senior year, to let him off the hook. His reply would disarm anyone:

But I have met you—and you are far more promising than I had dared to expect. I like the cut of your face and eyes; and we need the person behind them.

Let's have a talk during your spring vacation. How well do you know the U.S.A.? Wouldn't it be desirable to search for an assignment which would entail investigation in half a dozen states during the summer months? Suppose you cogitate on some of the possibilities which would give you helpful experience.

Meanwhile, stop worrying! We'll promise never to give Fulton or Grace preferential treatment because of our delight in having you in the organization. So there!

Oh boy! Well, I cogitated, and couldn't think of a thing. But that wonderful friend and editor, Merle Crowell, was made responsible for me. And together he and Mr. Wallace came up with an enchanting idea.

I was simply to get to know my country and its people. To take a bus trip across the northern part, avoiding large cities, soaking up small town life. There were no specific assignments for the trip, though I would do research before I went, studying states from Michigan to Oregon. I was to go and look, feel, talk. If I ran across a story the *Digest* could use, fine. If I came back with nothing they'd not count the trip wasted. I had only to tell them what I thought the United States was like.

Was ever a vaguer, more munificent command given a young-ster?

I read all the WPA books on the states, skimmed vacation and travel books, and tried to convince myself something publishable might come from me. I told Mother not to worry, that of course I'd be all right. I told my father not to worry, that of course I wouldn't disgrace him with his boss, and I'd do my best, only I wished I knew more of what I was supposed to do on this junket.

After I'd done my homework, Merle Crowell set up a lunch in the elegant private dining room in Pleasantville, where I confronted important editors who asked me important questions, such as,

"When you got into a small town and wanted to find out if there was anything interesting there, any story material, where would you go, and what would you do?"

Bravely, I said I'd thought about that, and concluded the local newspaper office was the place to go.

"Normally, yes. But we don't want you to go to newspaper offices. We have just made a widely advertised solicitation for stories from newsmen, and any newspaperman who thinks he has a story has already sent it to us."

I nodded. Boldly I suggested that I would talk to people.

"Where?" they challenged, naturally.

"Well, in small towns people gather at grocery stores, and barbershops, and . . ."

Did I seriously think I could often strike up conversations in strange grocery stores or barbershops?

Finally Mr. Crowell shifted his doughty frame in his chair and said matter-of-factly: "I think if we sent out a senior editor in these circumstances he wouldn't come back with a thing. Not one blasted story. I don't think April can bring back a story. But that's not why she's going. She's going"—he broke off for a dramatic wave of the hand—"because we're sending her."

And, as Mr. Wallace said, any editor could profit from first-hand acquaintance with all parts of the United States. I had not previously traveled extensively throughout the country, and he wanted me, for the *Digest*'s sake as well as my own, to have talked to all kinds of people, everywhere.

I went by train from New York to Detroit, scared stiff and lonesome and wondering if I should have let Mother give me her little pearl-handled pistol after all. I went by bus the rest of the way, through northern and southern Michigan, Wisconsin, Minnesota, North Dakota, Idaho, Montana, Oregon and Washington. I was gone for the three strangest months of my young life.

I learned two things, neither of which I could convey to the *Digest*.

First, I learned what an incredible nation this is. All the clichés about it are true. It is corny to remark, yet marvelous, that we can travel so simply, without visas or inspections, from one state to another. And it's food for thought that a rather naïve girl can wander around without getting into trouble, finding strangers helpful and friendly. Perhaps the most remarkable point about that is that women will almost never be helpful and friendly to strangers, even to girls, so the only people I met were men.

Unforgettably, I learned that our country is actually all the words say in patriotic songs: it is beautiful, rich, complex, and blessed. It's also ugly, dull, and troubled in places, but that ugliness is mostly in a point of view.

In Detroit I found Henry Ford's name everywhere, but the

cabs were all Chevrolets. I took a last long look at a big city, found Detroit wasn't an inspiring city, forgot it, and headed north.

In the forests of northern Michigan I walked, and went to a logging camp where men ate more for breakfast than I eat for a whole day. In Newberry, Michigan, I found a man making a good living by taking piles of slag from an extinct pig iron mine, slag which had lain an abandoned eyesore for thirty years, and selling it for insulation material. He invested $10,000. He was selling five carloads a day at $100 profit a carload, and he had enough slag for fifty years. He told me that was the secret of American success, and I believed him.

I met a man who ran a mill where veneer was made, and, visiting his family, learned not only about veneer-making but the poetry of human delight in work well done. That man loved veneer the way I love literature, and he loathed solid unveneered wooden furniture, which I personally like very much. I went through the Goodman saw mill and saw how waste-not-want-not works. Only 25% of a tree is usable as good lumber. Seventy-five per cent used to go to waste. But at the mill they salvaged all the tree. They produced lumber and veneer, then wood alcohol, acetic acid, charcoal, chips to be processed for insulation, and then they took the sawdust and shavings and used that as fuel to run the mill.

Up in Marquette, a city of iron and churches, fish hatcheries and prisons, I visited the warden and his family and became used to convicts, and learned the theories of rehabilitation. I hied off to Ishpeming, a place name I'll never forget, and found a man named George Quaal who everyone thought was crazy because he wanted to bring live professional concert artists to his dinky hometown and believed he could do it as a regular thing. He did it.

In Iron Mountain a flyboy named Mario Fontana thought I might make a story about a new kind of plane called an Ercoupe which weighed 750 pounds and was guaranteed spin-proof. He took me up in the Ercoupe and proved it was spin-proof, and I was so scared I couldn't even talk when I got back on the ground.

Through the vacation country of Michigan and Wisconsin I wandered, asking my way into dairy farms, cheese-making places and the factories that turn out maraschino cherries. I'm not sure which smelled worse, cherry places or cheese places, but the people were wonderful. Door County Peninsula in the rain with cherry-pickers in full swarm was like a scene from a foreign movie. A priest named Father Koefler, who took pity on me as I trudged with creel and raincoat, drove me around, identifying among the pickers Jamaicans, Mexicans, Chinese, Indians, Negroes and whites. And here in Wisconsin were shipyards. I stood fascinated, watching inlanders build trawlers destined for New Bedford, the old whaling port visible across the Bay from Sandalwood.

In St. Paul and Minneapolis I took a few days off to get human again. Nothing had been scarcer on my journey than bathtubs. In pampered luxury I soaked in a city hotel tub, had my hair done, and rented a typewriter. In the evening, on a whim, I followed a band of sidewalk evangelists, sang hymns with them, and eventually was asked to take up the collection. They felt I had an honest face.

Besides, who needed money? By the third week I was averaging total expenses at $6.03 a day for transportation, room, food, and incidentals. And the *Digest* sent checks to General Delivery without a murmur at such an expense account.

Up into Paul Bunyan country I went, and I jumped over the beginning of the Mississippi before my eyes grew glassy staring at the flat expanse of Dakota. There was a terrific polio scare, which made travel fascinating in a Chaucerian way, but difficult. In Minnesota I took another day off in St. Cloud, and had the idea of going to an orphans' home to see if I could cheer up a child. Actually, the one I hoped to cheer up was myself. But I couldn't do anything there because I was from out of town and might carry polio, so I tried the hospital. There I was asked to read to Mr. Murray, an old man with a clot in his head, who was, they warned me, dull but in need of comfort. Dull, heck. He turned out to be a Ph.D. fascinated by Kant, and we talked philosophy all afternoon.

I never did see potatoes in Idaho, but I saw bronc riders and bottle clubs, silver dollars and slot machines, and the people there as everywhere were hospitable, patient, politely incurious and gentle with a stranger. I stayed a bit in Moscow with parents of a young actor I knew in the East, and found that it's a blessing there are no slot machines where I live or I'd be broke all the time.

In the Beartooth Mountains of Montana I stayed with the parents of that cowgirl friend from Mother's past, the Greenoughs, whose ranch perched high near Yellowstone could serve as a set for any western movie. Ben Greenough, grizzled and silent, didn't recognize me. He'd expected a little girl in pigtails. But he was determined to show me the West. He made me buy blue jeans, put me on a horse, and expected me to follow him south into Yellowstone, not by standard trails but by his own shortcuts: sheerly vertical up and down the mountains. I nearly died of fright. When we went down my heels were at the horse's ears and my head wobbled near his tail. When we went up I bumped my nose on his neck. And Ben Greenough at seventy-seven was deaf, so he never heard the gurgles I made. Finally, somewhere in the wilderness, I saw a road. I gave Ben back his horse and flagged down a bus to ride back to the ranch, which was a mistake because buses in Montana go fifty miles an hour around hairpin turns with what some folks call breathtaking views dropping thousands of feet below the edge of the road.

Following the tumbling glory of the Columbia River, past those majestic mountains, down to the Pacific shore I fell in love irrevocably with the United States of America. Patriotism made sense. I had not words to express it then. I tried, suspecting rightly that if I could really tell of a young girl's encounter with her homeland I'd have an article the *Digest* would be proud of, but it was still too soon. Impressions swarmed in my head. The two-ring traveling circus I joined up with for one night in Minnesota, remembering as I did the mystery Daddy had written called *About the Murder of the Circus Queen*. I liked circus folk. The revival meeting in which I inadvertently got trapped by some fifty people praying and shouting for me to be washed in the blood of the Lamb. Mount Hood, so stunning it seems to have a personality.

The fog of the Washington seacoast, where I stayed with a college friend, and revived, smelling salt, for which I'd unconsciously thirsted.

Behind me lay a trail of rooms with Gideon Bibles, and small movie houses with better popcorn than movies, the jostling bus rides, and a thousand faces, sun-wrinkled, smiling, quizzical yet welcoming. At the end of September I flew home across the same country in a few air-conditioned hours. Not for years would I be able to make sense of it all.

The second thing I learned on that trip I told no one, though I had to hint at part of it to my folks. In his poem, *The Hound of Heaven,* Francis Thompson describes the uncanny intangible pursuit of a soul by God. That summer on that trip I had the unshakeable awareness of being accompanied, not by man or God, but by the person my father called Our Lady. And I didn't like it at all.

Converts, I learned later, have a saying that when Mary gets you you're lost. The story is told of a leader of the Oxford Movement in the last century, an intellectual sincerely dedicated to criticizing Catholic devotion to Mary as an error akin to idolatry. A friend who was considering becoming a Catholic came for a discussion of dogmas, and after listening to him for a while the anti-Catholic challenged him:

"You haven't been saying the Hail Mary, have you?"

"Now and then," his friend admitted.

"I suggest you desist from that practice at once," his advisor said. "It's often proven fatal."

The friend didn't desist. In a few months he became a Catholic. The anti-Mary man knew what he was talking about.

Because outsiders have jeered at Marian devotions, often with reason, because they have scorned rosaries, novenas and pious excesses, modern Catholics especially in America tend to hide this Mother when company comes. Some Catholics have more love for Mary than understanding of her. The language used to talk about Mary is often rather ridiculous in the vernacular. Understandably, non-Catholics may conclude that the whole Marian thing is either an insult to Christ and true theology, or else nonsense—and often it is.

More often, it is not nonsense, but a truth obscured by semantics and private reactions. By this time I knew that Catholics don't really put Mary above Christ, because my family was all laden down with books of answers. But the pompous schoolbook phrases about *latria* and *hyperdulia,* and other technical differentiations between the honor due to God and to Mary left me cold.

Everything about her confused me. The mere fact that there are more than a hundred different "Our Ladies"—of Lourdes, of Fatima, of Perpetual Help, of Good Counsel, of Sorrows, of the Milk, of Grace—made it sound to me as if Catholics had unwittingly built a pantheon, or Mary suffered from schizophrenia.

So I ignored her, which seemed the safest course. I ignored her until on that trip across the country she refused to leave me alone.

On what was really my first night out, away from cities and into the body of my journey, I was in "the Soo," the town of Sault Ste. Marie in northern Michigan. An elderly waitress who seemed to know everything about everyone said that the man with the most fascinating stories about Michigan, and about life in general, was a Father Bassette. I could find him at the rectory.

Since I'd try anything once, I went to the rectory. I was scared stiff, this being the first time I'd tried to pump anyone for articles. My distress showed clearly on my face. Father Bassette could see I had problems before I said anything, and interpreted those problems in his own way. He explained that though he'd be glad to talk to me, and wanted very much to be of help, he had to go over to the church this minute and conduct a novena to Our Lady of Perpetual Help.

"No, don't try and tell me anything now. There isn't time. You must come to the novena," he said. "It'll do you good, and when it's over we'll talk."

I said I'd be happier just waiting in the rectory. And besides I couldn't go to the novena because I didn't have a hat.

"I'll ask the housekeeper to lend you a veil or scarf."

But the housekeeper was already gone. Reprieve seemed certain, and I was smiling with relief when Father said,

"I'll dispense you from the rule. You don't need a hat. Just come anyway. I won't take no for an answer."

So I sat through a novena to Our Lady of Perpetual Help.

Later, when I explained to Father in the rectory what I wanted, he roared with laughter and admitted that he'd thought I had some terrible personal trouble and had been afraid to let me slip away. We became friends, and he told me many interesting stories about Michigan, but from then on I made sure not to go hunting stories from priests.

The next week, as I rode late at night in a bus through Wisconsin, the bus broke down, miles from every building in the world except one tiny Catholic church. It was storming violently. There was no hope of reaching the hotel where I'd expected to stay. No hope of fixing the bus till morning. The only thing was for all six of us passengers to spend the night in the church. The driver woke the pastor. The pastor assigned me a pew all my own to sleep on, right in front of a statue of Our Lady of Lourdes, "close up so the candles will give you enough light to keep you from being frightened."

So it went. Every three or four days by some device I'd have to confront a statue of Our Lady of Something-or-other. It got under my skin. If someone was taking me to see cheese made, or give me a glimpse of a historical site, that someone always had an urgent errand in some Catholic shrine to Mary on the way.

In a hotel dining room in the middle of Minnesota, alone with my hard rolls and smooth napkin, I reexamined what I believed about Mary. I believed there had once lived a Jewish girl named Mary who gave birth to a son named Jesus. Because I'd been in Bethlehem and Nazareth I didn't doubt the general historical accuracy of the Gospel stories. But I also knew Mary was dead, and as far as I was concerned anyone, no matter how good, who ever was dead was dead. Dead people couldn't affect current human lives directly. I'd once heard a grown woman, in drunken heartbreak, crying out to her dead "Mama!" Praying to Mary was, I thought, at the very kindest interpretation, a similar childish desperation, a yearning for Mama to make things right. And you couldn't go near a Catholic church without bumping into this dead woman, and the way to please her was to recite a string of prayers on beads, which is an old Moslem custom still not much different to my eyes from the prayer wheels of the Buddhists. Every intelligent fiber of my being was repelled by this devotion. When the number of times I stumbled over shrines and votaries of Mary on this trip flouted the laws of probability, I began to resent it curiously.

Then, somewhere in this great land of ours, a strange thing happened. I went to send a telegram home, as was my custom, to let my parents know I was alive and kicking. I stood and wrote out my message, dutifully including the name and phone number of the place where I was staying so they could reach me if necessary. Then I reread the telegram I was sending. I had written at the end:

"I am fine, don't worry, Mary is with me."

I had not intended to write that. I wasn't aware of having written it. But it was there. I stared at it, and then decided the only fair thing to do was to send it as it was.

That night my bewildered father was on the phone asking, "Who the heck is this Mary?"

All the way to Oregon the pattern repeated itself to the last day of my journey when I needed to contact a Jewish businessman in Portland and was told that he was spending the day at the Grotto of Our Lady of Sorrows, and if I wanted him I'd have to go there and find him. The Grotto's a beautiful place, but I don't know why he was there.

When I came home I decided that the trouble was that I'd been too much alone in a totally disconnected milieu, and that what had looked like a pattern had been only a summer's aberration.

Yet I carried a definite impression that this lady existed—as a real and forceful personality, with a sense of humor. Of this I did not speak to anyone. Only to myself I had to admit that the same kind of pragmatic evidence that I accepted for the reality of intuition or telepathy, love or beauty, was no more impressive than this awareness in my heart of an individual whom I couldn't see, but couldn't deny. I tried to tell myself there was no one, I tried laughing. I knew there was a serious reality behind it.

With dogmas you can quarrel. But Mary is not an abstract principle or a numbered question, and I couldn't argue about her. She is a woman, present. She was not, I understood, simply a good and holy dead woman, because by some extra dimension she had made herself felt to me as a presence not possibly to be confused with a ghost or a hallucination.

I didn't believe in Mary: I knew she existed. I couldn't understand how or why she existed. And I was afraid, because the consequences of admitting Mary as a factor in modern life went further than I cared to go. So I tried to put her completely out of my thoughts.

17

The Hard Saying

I never did find out what I was meant to be doing at the *Digest* in the months after my trip. The *Digest* seemed not to know either. I tried diligently to work, but everyone seemed vague about what I could do, me most of all. I was a third wheel in the short humor and filler department. I was treated as an adult and expected to come up with some tasks and ideas for myself. I couldn't. Finally I wrote a letter to Mr. Wallace, resigning my job. In a most gentlemanly and charming way, he answered:

We hope it isn't good-bye.
Your letter . . . strengthens still further our conviction that you have the stuff we need.

Only a magician of the heart can so transform a flop into a success. That knack is only one of many for which I admire my first full-time boss.

I had to work. By which I mean not that I was compelled by economic necessity, or by my family, but rather that I'd been brought up to believe in the value and fitness of work for human beings, and the need for everyone to do some of what my father called "drawing water and hewing wood." I needed to work, and my need sprang from my own calculation of the meaning of human dignity.

Thanks to the helping hand of my longtime friend, Mrs. Jules Joelson, I began working for Twentieth-Century Fox, reading galleys of novels, and writing résumés and evaluations of plots. That job, for which I was most grateful, had a hideous fascination for me: naturally, as low man on the totempole, I was assigned the least promising books. Daily then I was reminded by my reading that people who believed themselves to be great, or at least promising writers, had poured sweat, hope and time into books that were duds. For anyone who wants to write such a lesson is frightening, sobering. And I did want to write.

My apprenticeship with my father continued. He would now occasionally entrust to me the drafting of an article. I'd write it. Then he'd tell me what was good about what I'd done, a remarkable editorial feat in itself. Then he would take the same material from which I'd worked, and write his first draft. I would compare the two as I typed for him. Gradually the concept of form and basic structure was becoming second nature to me. I would follow his next ten drafts, typing and learning.

He'd toss a piece at me and tell me to cut five hundred words from it. Toss another, and ask for an introduction to it. As time passed I'd finally find that words or phrases, finally even whole paragraphs of mine, survived into the final version and into print.

Later, when syndication of *The Greatest Story Ever Told* was arranged, he assigned me to do the cutting for the newspapers: selecting and editing forty separate incidents of equal length and interest for the forty days of Lent. When I finished, he studied them, obviously gratified that I'd finally learned some of the things he taught, then fixed me with a challenging eye:

"Where is the story of the woman taken in adultery?"

"I left it out." I thought surely he'd understand why. "You wouldn't want that in the newspapers, would you? It doesn't seem quite proper."

"Lord save us, now you're telling God what's a proper story to tell and what isn't? He told it. Don't you know that story is the perfect one for the papers, that it'll draw people to read about Jesus who never else might read about him? Have you no sense of what life is all about?"

I blinked. "It would make a sensational headline, but it doesn't seem very—pious."

"Fah!" He nearly spat with disgust. "Religion isn't being pious or proper. It's understanding that God is realistic."

So I did a cut on the woman taken in adultery, and it was one of the most popular in the series.

We worked well together, thanks to him. It's not often relatives can make a go of any business and remain friends, or those who love each other collaborate on creative work. We never during his lifetime collaborated on anything in the sense that my name appeared with his on the finished product. Only in the handwritten inscriptions in my copies of his work did he testify to what we both were proud of, that gradually I was able to ease the burden of much of his enormous literary output. I even wrote a little book under his name, called *A History of the Protestant Missions*. This became a favorite private joke because the book, which highly praised the work of Protestant missionaries, was always listed in his publicity material. Soon I was ghosting less important stuff for him when he was asked to contribute to smaller magazines, and drafting important articles which needed now less and less changing at his hands. And the changes he made in them I could learn from. The finished piece was his, not only legally and for public consumption, but in integrity and truth. I'd been able to carry it just so far, preparing the material. He had known how to rearrange it, and twist it into living shape. Working with him was an education no money could have bought at any school.

With my half-brother Will he collaborated publicly on one book, *Father Flanagan of Boys' Town*. It was the kind of book Will handles well, with his rich background of reporting and crime writing, and his keen understanding of the craftsmanship involved in article and fact-book writing. Will already had three books of his own to his credit, and was a man with a family and a reputation.

"Dumas had a sort of factory of writing," my father said, "much like the great painters who had stables of apprentice artists to complete their work in their style. Wouldn't it be fun to have something like that? People would wonder how on earth we managed to do so much!"

Occasionally someone would suggest to me that I should resent this obscurity, being an apprentice to my father. Usually the someone was young, or thought himself young, and resented the shadow of his or her own parents' success. I was not a humble soul, understand. I still had full intentions of being a much greater writer than my father could be, which was a happy joke between us because he kept saying he was raising his own competition, with Will, and me, and Tony. I didn't resent being an unacknowledged hack in Daddy's workroom because I knew honestly how little I could yet do on my own, how much depended still on his talent and experience, and how fortunate I was to have such a comfortably built-in postgraduate course in writing.

Besides, I still didn't have anything to write about. Perhaps this is the most onerous part of being a young writer, being aware that almost nothing you have to say as yet is worth saying, yet yearning to say it.

I was learning self-discipline, the application of the seat to the chair, and the cultivation of ear and eye to catch nuances of dialogue and character.

And, sitting in the outer office, I met fascinating people. Many of them now were Catholics, many priests. There was busy tiny gentle Father John O'Brien of Notre Dame, who always called me "little girl, dear." There was dynamic Father Keller of the Christophers. And the incredible Father Peyton of the Family Rosary, incredible because he seems at first glance to be a tongue-tied gawk of a man, blushingly boyish and inept, but has a soul which leaps out at you.

They annoyed me, these priests and others, for one reason: none of them tried to convert me. None of them would give me a chance to argue with them. None even seemed to care if I became a Catholic or not. I thought then that was a heck of a way to behave, especially for such renowned convert-makers as O'Brien, crusaders as Peyton, world-changers as Keller. But they knew what they were doing. You can't get into the Church by arguing. Win an argument and lose a soul, they say. My ego would have been fed by the chance to fence with them. But their cordial insistence on ignoring my unchurched state made a longer lasting impression. They granted me the courtesy of assuming I knew what I was doing, and not interfering.

In the spring of 1947 my parents went off to Europe, leaving me to take care of my brother Tony, by then quite a self-sufficient young man, almost fifteen. I was to run the office, answer mail, pay bills, and tend the store, so to speak.

That was when Mary impinged on my life again. Tony came home from swimming at the athletic club, complained of bellyache, went out for a date with his girl, danced all night, and came home with a worse bellyache. He had also eaten an incredible concoction of things, as most young men do. I considered giving him indigestion remedies. In the predawn hours instead I called the doctor. Tony had acute appendicitis.

I tried to cable our parents but according to their itinerary they were then in Lourdes. There was at that time neither telegraph nor phone service from the outer world into Lourdes. The best I could do was cable the hotel they used as a base in Paris, but the itinerary showed they wouldn't return there for several days. I sent the cable anyway. Tony was operated on successfully, and I sent another cable to reassure my parents. Shortly the phone rang. It was my father calling long distance from Paris.

They had been at Lourdes, planning to stay. As was his custom on a visit to any church, he had gone to light a candle for each of us, naming us as he lit them: for Grace, for April, for Tony. Each time he lit Tony's candle, though there was no observable breeze, that one candle went out. Three times. He turned to my mother and told her he knew Our Lady was trying to tell him Tony was ill and in danger, and they should get to Paris as quickly as possible. He also said they must pray hard that I would be guided to do the right thing. He told me the time the candles went out. When we computed time differences we found it was the time that I had been considering giving Tony a laxative.

I filed that away with other things I didn't care to think about yet.

The summer of 1947 we spent at the Cape. I wrote a few short stories, sketched the outline for a novel, and at summer's end decided to stay on in the big house by myself and write. I wanted very much to be alone. I wanted to live on the Cape permanently and become part of a community. I might, I thought grandly, get a job, on the Falmouth *Enterprise*, perhaps, or at the Oceanographic Institute in Woods Hole. I could take care of the house, which needed warmth and tending during the winter. And I could find out once and for all if I could make myself write a whole book.

I bought myself a car. My parents believed it was wrong to buy a car for any youngster because cars aren't toys, and what you must pay for yourself you take care of, and respect. My own children know I feel the same way. The car I bought was a brand new little green tin can, called a Crosley, which everyone swore had an eggbeater for a motor. I bucketed around in it happily.

But I seemed to be unemployable. The *Enterprise* didn't need a reporter. The Oceanographic accepted my application, promising nothing. But as the fall wore on I built myself an esssentially satisfying life. I lived in an ocean of solitude, content. I wrote, potboilers for small markets as well as the novel, and I read. And I went again, quietly, to the Episcopalian Church. Wholeheartedly I faced the fact that I did still believe in Jesus Christ, and had believed in God ever since I wrote that philosophy paper. I wasn't sure I accepted Episcopalianism, but I went home to St. Barnabas on the green, sang in the choir, and let the psalms flow through me again.

I cleaned the few rooms in which I lived, played the piano, watched the change of season, made jelly from our grapes and sauce from our apples, drank in the play of wave and gull and sand and rock. I asked God to let my life stay that way always.

So, almost right away I had to go to New York. My parents had to spend Christmas in New York and insisted I join them. You can't imagine how miserable I was at having to endure holidays in the city. I had friends on the Cape, and a few dates, but I knew no young people in New York at all.

"The only man I know in New York is that guy who came around with the petition to be signed last spring." His name was Martin, and he was a personable Young Republican who had been dutifully ringing doorbells. He'd been so busy talking to my father that he forgot one of his notebooks when he left. He phoned up about it, and since I had to walk my Boxer I had brought the notebook down to him in the lobby. He had walked with me, making it plain that the whole idea of walking a dog repelled him. Once during the summer he'd written to me, and I'd written back. He had written again, some fanciful ideas for novels I might write, about banana boats or something.

At Mother's suggestion I wrote him a note saying I'd be in town for the holidays. Gallantly he rose to the occasion and made a date to take me to Radio City the night of December 26. The night of December 26, 1947, was also the occasion of an impressive blizzard. I was sure he wouldn't come, but dauntlessly he did and I had to rush to get dressed. He spent some more time talking to my parents, especially to my father, whom he admired very much as one Catholic to another. Then he took me out. Down on the sidewalk, where Central Park South had become a backdrop for a winter fashion window, he asked me the kind of question no one in his right mind would fire at you on a first date. He asked, "How come you're not a Catholic, too?"

I opened my mouth to put him in his place, but just then we turned the corner onto Sixth Avenue and the blast of wind and snow took my breath away. It was a glorious night. The city looked like a painting, and the wild air made us laugh. Radio City was nearly empty, since few people were as crazy as we were, and for us it was like having a delightful private showing. When we came out the avenue was empty. Not a bus or cab moved. Here and there a brave soul struggled, bent forward, to pierce the gale, marching right in the center of one of the busiest streets in the world. We held hands and laughed about St. Bernard dogs, and made our way on foot through the mysteriously white night.

The next day I remembered the effrontery of his question, and became very angry, not simply because he was gauche enough to ask me, but because I didn't have a nice pithy answer for him. I should be able to be more articulate about the Catholic Church. Goodness knows, I felt strongly enough against it. But I needed more information. Any writer knows that to be concise you have to know more than you do to be wordy.

I couldn't ask my parents for information because after all, having lived with them for quite a few years I had, one would think, absorbed all anyone needed to know about the Church. I had to do some research to crystallize what I knew. I decided to go to an inquiry course down at St. Francis of Assisi Church, where no one knew me.

I kept attendance at those classes a secret, taking the bus as if I were going to the library. To my surprise I found that whatever I heard there drew from me a nod of recognition, not as if I had heard it before. but on a deeper level of identification. It was a bit like walking into a foreign language class and discovering that the professor was teaching English.

The nearest analogy I can think of for conversion to faith is falling in love. In both cases you can be deceived. Both may be passing fancies, or passing fanatic desires. Both are to a degree irrational, or superrational, and yet to endure must eventually be absorbed and ratified by the mind. Is there a person who can love another on purely logical grounds? Appraise, admit the value of, and decide to love another human being? I doubt it. The impetus to any form of love, from desire through friendship to love of God, doesn't come from the mind. But neither friendship, affair, marriage or religious service can continue long mindlessly.

My reason for going to those inquiry courses was subversive, specifically to draw the evidence to refute the Catholic claim to truth. But my reason for continuing to go was a fair certainty that what I heard there was truth. With all due respect to the nice Franciscans who ran the course, it was not any personal spellbinding talent of theirs as teachers, or any particularly subtle or magnificent presentation of the Catholic message which kept me there. The classes were ordinary, even boring. The people who attended them kept their anonymity. No one did more than speak a welcome and a good-bye to me. No one asked my name, address, or intentions, though I knew that those who wished to stay and speak personally with the priests could do so. I wasn't being confused by anyone's fervor, nor attracted by a feeling of goodfellowship, not emotionally excited, not intellectually challenged. I'd have been suspicious of theatrics, or of anything which could be interpreted as an effort to catch me in a net. I had the feeling these classes went on forever, like the subway trains, utilitarian, available to take you as far as you needed to go.

Somewhere along the line Father Bertin remarked that if you hoped to come close to God and get the most out of these classes, you should be praying. That seemed, like everything else he said, so obvious that I wondered why I hadn't thought of it. On the rack in the vestibule was a pamphlet of prayers commonly used by Catholics. The Our Father I knew, of course. I knew the Hail Mary not only because my parents said it, but because I'd sung those words to some fifteen different settings in Latin and in English, in choirs and glee clubs. I decided to learn the prayer called the Hail Holy Queen, and I set aside the bus ride down and back in which to memorize it, punctuating it with those lurching yanks of the arm as the bus screeched to a stop and I tried to keep my balance. I didn't like that prayer because it asks Mary to listen to our sighs as we weep and mourn in this valley of tears, and I didn't feel that I was in a valley of tears, but I memorized it as a sort of token of my goodwill.

Nights passed, and as the catechism unfolded before me I understood quite clearly that most of this I already knew. The Episcopalian Church, as I understood it, was so close to this Catholic Church that I was startled that no one had pointed out the similarity to me before. I slipped a question into the box for the Fathers to answer, grateful for the ability to remain anonymous. The answer they gave reminded me that the Episcopalian Church was rooted in the Catholic Church, and that indeed some Episcopalians called themselves Catholics, Anglo-Catholics. The Episcopalian Church was a Protest against the Catholic, which stemmed from the time when Henry VIII was unable to accept the Pope's stand on his marriage.

Now I knew all that, yet, in a way, did not know it. I mean, I'd never stopped to think that the original reason there was an Episcopalian Church was because of Henry VIII and his philandering. I'd never admired Henry. It angered me to think that the Church I loved was the outgrowth of his gluttony and lust, and angered me more to think the Catholics believed that.

But Catholics didn't believe that, and the priest-lecturer was still talking. He said that all Protestantism was a criticism of the Catholic Church, and that some of the criticism had been justified. He added that, in his opinion, if you had just criticisms to make of your family or your country or your church your best bet was to stay in it and try to change it from within. And he explained that ever since God became man, and Jesus Christ was born, the Church, all churches, had been stuck with the fact that faith is both human and divine, and human beings keep getting in the way of their fellows looking for God. Since we are all less than perfect, he said, if you look only at human beings you'll be disgusted with any faith.

Briefly then he outlined the differences in belief and practice between most Episcopalians and the Catholic Church. I had expected a list a mile long. Instead it came down to this:

1. Belief that the Pope was St. Peter's successor, and the representative of Christ on earth, chosen with the direction of God the Holy Spirit, and that the Pope, no matter how stupid or sinful he might be personally, was infallible when, as Pope, he spoke about faith and morals.

2. Belief that all the saints, and especially Mary, were grappled to us with the life of grace, able to hear us, willing and able to pray to God for us, helping us reach heaven.

3. Belief that Mary, who was the closest human being to God, who was holier than any other because God wanted her to be and she willed to be what he wanted, loved us all as if she were our mother, and for love of God was doing all she could to bring us to him.

4. Belief that in the Mass the bread and wine of communion actually became, at the priest's words, the whole presence of Christ.

Four propositions then separated me from the Catholic Church. All the other problems, the stand on marriage and divorce, on birth control, the statues, candles, Latin, incense, novenas, the garrulous grotesque trappings of the Church, either followed from these four or were, so the teacher said, incidentals which you could choose to ignore. If there were only four, it was easier to think about them. These hurdles had fancy names: papal infallibility, transubstantiation, communion of saints, and mariology, which included the immaculate conception of Mary, the virgin birth, her role as Mother of God in distinction to being merely mother of Jesus, and her role as intercessor of all graces.

Oh, Catholics, and the words they've been burdened with! The appalling jargon of the Church in this country has as much to do with making people like me despise the Church as any amount of faults or dogmas. Catholics get so used to their words that they don't even think how they sound to others. Take the word "passion." Catholics are always talking about the Passion of Christ.

Now, being a normal American girl, I knew darn well what passion meant, and it had nothing to do with Gethsemane or Calvary. I knew what immaculate meant, and conception, and the way it looked to me as an outsider Catholics were talking of Mary as if she were a test-tube baby. Indulgence to most Americans goes with either permissiveness, or gluttony and drunkenness. To speak of gaining indulgences for saying certain prayers or performing certain good works sets up a semantic reaction in the American mind long before you get as far as the doctrine at question.

But what I caught from the friars at that inquiry class was this attitude: that you must realize the wonderful and difficult truth that the Church, which is Christ's, is on earth in a human form. You can't judge her by her current dress or language, her present hobbies or foibles, or by her servants, because all these change, and the Church does not. Cut through to the fundamentals, and let the rest take care of itself later.

So I put aside the fancy words and posed myself the four questions which alone seemed to keep me from being a Catholic. Here was the material for my answer to Martin. I must make of it what I could.

That olive-bound New Testament was still with me. I believed the Bible was the word of God. I understood Catholics weren't supposed to read my Bible, which was King James version, but I'd read their Douay version and I didn't like that. Being in the household of two such workers as my parents, both engaged in interfaith popularization of Scripture, I knew precisely where the King James and the Douay differed in content, and why. All by myself I read Gospels, Acts, Epistles and Revelation, searching Scripture to know what God had said about my four points.

So I read through once to see what was said about Popes, or Peter. And I read, in red type in St. Matthew:

And I say also unto thee, That thou art Peter and upon this rock I will build my church; and the gates of hell shall not prevail against it.

And I will give unto thee the keys of the kingdom of

heaven: and whatsoever thou shalt bind on earth shall be bound in heaven; and whatsoever thou shalt loose on earth shall be loosed in heaven.

That seemed clear to me. I knew it hadn't convinced many Protestants. But when I read it I thought it would be a frightful waste if Jesus gave to Peter all that power and then that power all disappeared from earth when Peter died. And I thought that Peter had many obvious and shameful faults, and Jesus knew those faults long before the cock crowed, and still gave Peter that power, so it wasn't impossible for God to entrust the same power to later Popes who were more flamboyant sinners.

I read on. In St. John I found the repeated promise that God the Father would send in Christ's name the Holy Ghost, to stay with the apostles and teach them all things, and bring all things to their remembrance. So God had said that there would be this Spirit of Truth which would guard them forever from error.

To me it seemed then not only possible, but almost necessary for God's dignity, that having gone to the trouble to come to earth and redeem men and set up the Church to teach and to continue applying the work of redemption to others, provision would be made to insure that that teaching and means of salvation didn't get all fouled up.

Then for the first time it occurred to me that there really had to be only one true Church. If I believed, as I did, that Christ was the Son of God, and that he built an organization called Christianity or the Church, in order to teach all nations and feed all sheep, then it should still be around, unchanged. There is only one Church now that has been around since the beginning of churches. You couldn't logically say that any of the reformation versions was the one true Church, because each had dropped some of the truths which had endured from the beginning.

About infallibility of the Pope, the Catholic Church didn't even get around to defining it until a few years ago, and, with all reverence, that isn't the most important aspect of the truth. There has to be a visible head of the Church, and the name given him is

Pope, and the Church is guided and preserved from error by the Holy Spirit, so obviously God is not going to let the Pope lead the rest of the Church into error. And if you have trouble detecting in the Acts of the Apostles an absolute dictatorship or autocracy by Peter, but find him rather as the head of the apostles taking advice from, consulting with, and sometimes influenced and guided by those apostles or bishops, that is true. Popes still take council with bishops. If Vatican Council I had ever been finished, probably the other half of the truth would also have been defined, about the impact and wisdom and co-importance of all the bishops, who are successors to the apostles today. When the Church proclaimed as dogma that the Popes never make mistakes when they teach publicly, as Popes, on questions of faith or morals, the Church was simply saying again in a different way that Christ promised us the Spirit to keep the record straight.

My problem, I'd thought, was whether I believed the Pope to be some kind of superman. My problem was instead, I found, whether I believed Christ founded a Church and somehow still kept it intact, custodian of truth and life. This I did believe.

But all over the world there were Christian denominations that sprang from the one root of Rome, all claiming they had corrected Rome's errors and returned to the solid truth, and were therefore each the one true Church. And if I were searching in Scripture alone I might get confused. After all, the red type in my Bible seemed to promise that the mark of a true Christian would be ability to handle snakes safely and speak in tongues. There was at least one sect in the mountains which handled snakes and talked gibberish and claimed to be the one true Church, and I couldn't accept them. How could you figure out whether a reform had really kept essential truths intact when reformed churches disagreed on so many points?

And I read in the Gospel of St. John:

Verily, verily, I say unto you, Except ye eat of the flesh of the Son of man, and drink his blood, ye have no life in you.

Whoso eateth my flesh and drinketh my blood hath eternal life; and I will raise him up at the last day.

For my flesh is meat indeed, and my blood is drink indeed.

He that eateth my flesh and drinketh my blood, dwelleth in me and I in him.

No one outside the Catholic Church that I knew of believed those words were meant literally. Nowhere in Protestantism had I heard anyone take the bread and wine of communion as more than a sign, a memorial, a symbol.

Could Christ have meant those words literally? It is hard to take them that way. The people to whom Jesus addressed those words "murmured" and "strove among themselves" and called it a "hard saying." Jesus knew this, knew that even his disciples were offended by such talk.

Could anyone be more scandalized at the notion of drinking blood than a good Jew? Jesus was a born Jew. His disciples ate kosher food, kept Passover, and had a holy horror of consuming blood, which was the symbol of life, set apart by the Law, and used only in sacrifice and worship of the true God. The Christ would not speak idly or carelessly, or in unexplained metaphor, when he spoke of his own blood. He could have watered down what he said. He could have said he spoke in a parable, that he didn't really mean people were to eat him. But he wouldn't do that. He watched hundreds of hitherto ardent followers turn their backs on him and go away rather than believe what sounded like repulsive nonsense. He let them go. Because what he said was true, and couldn't be explained away to accommodate those who were scandalized.

When I got that into my head, I couldn't sleep. In the darkness, while the steam heat of the apartment radiator died away and the night sounds of the city came in through a sooty window, I lay pondering the fact that only in one Church and its Orthodox sister was there still being offered the real flesh and blood of the Christ.

18

Decision

"What ever made you leave the Church?" I asked my mother.

"The people in it. I got mad at the people in it, and one priest in particular. So I flounced out. That's the kind of silly sad thing at the bottom of most people's falling away."

"What was the hardest thing about coming back?"

"Being willing to say I was wrong when I walked out as a kid, thinking I knew more than everybody at the age of sixteen. And saying I'm sorry."

I went to my father. "What was the hardest thing for you to accept about the Catholic Church?"

"What they call transubstantiation." He lit a cigarette. "I believed God could change bread and wine into himself. I could even believe he would and did delegate that power to priests. But you know, I had a dreadful squeamish feeling everytime I thought of receiving communion."

He leaned back in his chair, his eyes rueful. "You know, the Romans, confronted with the first Christians, sometimes referred to them as cannibals. They didn't conceal the fact that they truly believed that when bread and wine were consecrated at Mass they became in sacrament the real body and blood of Jesus, to be consumed, eaten by the faithful. That belief affronted some Romans. To the more philosophical, cultured Roman minds it had hideous overtones of human sacrifice and blood-drinking from pagan days. But Christianity has always had overtones of every mistake and excess in history, because it alone is true, and everything which is not Christianity either approximates it or garbles it."

"But what bothered you was the idea of yourself eating . . ."

My voice trailed off because it seemed a strange thing to say, that someone could eat the body of God.

"It bothered me very much. Whenever I told Father McGarry that he'd patiently remind me that I was human, and human beings in general are nourished in rather repulsive ways, on dead animal carcasses, and on milk. He reminded me that as a baby I nursed at my mother's breast, and so, in a way, consumed her body after I was born as well as when I was in the womb, and so it shouldn't shock me to consume the body of God. Then I had to tell him what kind of fellow I was, because now that I was grown up the idea of suckling babes was repellent to me, and no help in getting used to the idea of Communion. I was frank about it. Most people have these thoughts and don't say them out loud for fear of not sounding proper. But Father McGarry, God love him, explained that before I could hope to share God's life, I had to share human life, and get over any squeamishness I might have about being a physical, living creature. Christ chose to be formed in a woman's womb, whether I liked it or not. And he chose that in the womb of the world I and the rest of men should be fed on his sacramentally living body and blood."

He put out his cigarette. "Why do you ask?"

"I just wondered."

"I see." He nodded with mock solemnity. "Idle curiosity, I presume. Well, did I answer your question?"

"You did. Funny though, the idea of feeding on God doesn't seem disgusting to me. But you sure took it seriously, didn't you? You believed they were really doing what they said they were doing with all that hocus-pocus on the altar?"

"Yes, honey. I took it seriously. I still do."

So again that evening I went "out to the library," and said the Hail Holy Queen on the Sixth Avenue bus, and ended up in St. Francis of Assisi Church. Only this time, because I was early, I went into the church itself, instead of the classroom, and walked up the aisle toward the altar.

Catholics genuflect, which is a clumsy word for bending a knee, before they enter a pew. Though I'd been to Mass once a year on Christmas Eve with my folks since their conversion, I'd never genuflected because I didn't believe in empty show. Now I hesitated before the pew, looked at the altar, and saw that little container called the tabernacle on it, and understood that the bread that had been, so Catholics believed, turned into the sacramental presence of Christ, was there. If you believed Christ was there, the least you could do was make a sign of respect or homage. I bent my knee awkwardly, and sat down.

I sat, not-thinking, in the old true way of my childhood.

When I got up I was late for class. But quietly, almost matter-of-factly, I perceived that now I had no more arguments, no more hurdles. I had only ignorance, and willingness to learn. I looked at my watch, started to hurry, then turned back and genuflected, dropping my purse, and wondering if the strangers scattered in silent prayer throughout the church knew I was a non-Catholic who didn't know how to do anything right.

By now I had a different quandary. I had to decide whether to go back to the Cape and finish that novel, or stay in New York and do who-knows-what. I'd already stayed way past Christmas holidays, and if I weren't going to settle down again in Sandalwood I needed to return there quickly and close the house down properly, so pipes didn't freeze and so on.

For two reasons I wanted to stay in New York. One was to find out more about the Catholic Church, but I could do that somewhere else, perhaps with Father Kelly in Falmouth. The other reason was Martin, with whom I was having a wonderful time, and with whom, perhaps, I was falling in love. I say perhaps because then I still clung to the belief that I was never meant to get married, and I was afraid of falling in love, and besides I hadn't known Martin very long.

Meanwhile, I had acquired a literary agent. That magnificent Boston newspaperman, Harry Gray, longtime friend of the family, had out of the kindness of his heart suggested that he'd take on guidance of my career in the hope of someday being able to sell something I wrote. I had no illusions about his getting rich quick on me, nor did he. I dumped in his lap all my rejected short stories, and the first half of the novel about Valkyrie. Early in January he sent for me to come to his place in the Hotel Lexington.

On the way over I stopped in St. Patrick's Cathedral and walked furtively back to the Lady Chapel, and sat down to try talking to Mary in my own words, without that Hail Holy Queen bit. I just sort of sat and let her look at me. Then I knelt and asked her, if she could hear me, to please let me know whether to stay in New York or return forever to the Cape, because I didn't want to make a mistake or waste time just because it was fun going out with Martin.

Then I went over to the Lexington and Harry Gray met me with his bluff smile and giant red nose, saying:

"I'm not sure yet what I think about your novel, or what I think you must do in the future, but this I can tell you for sure— you're not to go back to bury yourself in Cape Cod. You must stay here in New York. Why are you laughing, for God's sake? I'm serious!"

I was serious, too. So I ran back to close up Sandalwood and returned to New York to see what would happen. I learned that the novel wasn't very good, in fact was very bad, which broke my heart naturally, but when I took a good second look even I had to admit it should be quickly forgotten.

"You're just not meant to have an ivory tower, kid," said Harry. "You got to have the guts to be human like the rest of us."

I didn't really understand that, then. But I was back to living by ear, following the nudges of circumstance, letting myself be surprised by patterns. I went back to work for my father. I wrote a few articles of my own, and met that charmingly adroit editor, Geraldine Rhoads, then editor of *Today's Woman*. Secretly I still attended inquiry class. And openly I still saw Martin.

With him I saw New York as I'd never seen it before. Tacitly we agreed we'd rather spend time than money. Ours was the enchanted city on a shoestring, the route of free entertainments like a theater on the lower East Side, long before off-Broadway shows attained status, where the play was free and a hat was passed. We window-shopped, and walked in Carl Schurz Park, staring out at the East River boats, and had coffee in the Automat where we could sit and talk for hours. And up in the east eighties was the 9th A.D. Republican Club, which encompassed both Martin's home and mine. At the Republican club there were lectures, study groups, and even dancing lessons. From the Republican club came tickets to balls, real long-dress and tuxedo balls, made to order for us. Martin was an active worker, precinct captain, poll-watcher and what-have-you, and clerk to the president justice of the municipal court, Keyes Winter. Under the amused and friendly eyes of the older guard we studied the politics of the future on a personal level.

When I finally confessed to myself that I was in love with Martin, I had a dreadful problem. For at the same time, and on a separate track, I'd been falling in love with the Catholic Church, and I'd already discovered that I wanted to become a Catholic.

But I absolutely did not want to become a Catholic just because of Martin. We'd never talked about marriage for us, and had never again after that first night talked about the Church, either. But I was pretty sure that he, being Catholic, wouldn't consider marrying a girl who wasn't. Would he think I was becoming a Catholic because I wanted to hook him? Did I think so? Was that my subconscious motive? Catholics have a horrid informal phrase for people who become Catholics. They say they "turned"—which always sounds to me like cream gone sour. Sometimes you hear them talk approvingly of people who "turned" accommodatingly to get married. I had no intention of turning for such a motive. And, being the introspective type, I kept probing around inside me to see what reasons might lurk there.

Oh, I got so confused. I kept going every single day to St. Pat's to kneel at Our Lady's altar, or just sit in a pew, asking her to help me out of my muddle.

Finally I told my parents of my furtive study of the Church.

"The trouble is, I don't know whether I really believe it or just want to believe it. After all, I didn't believe it when any of you entered the Church. I didn't even think of converting then. How can I know if I'm sincere?"

They were awfully sweet about it. They showed no great surprise that I was considering becoming a Catholic, I suppose because they had been praying for me. Mother did remind me that I had deemed myself in love with another Catholic man two years before, and had never let the thought of conversion enter my head then.

"You'll have to decide for yourself," my father said. "It's between you and God, and you two are the only ones who have to believe in the validity of what you do. What other people think is of no importance. People may think you became a Catholic to catch a husband, if you happen to marry this Martin, who as far as I know hasn't asked you yet! If you know you didn't that's all that matters." He smoothed the now-greying but still unruly cowlick at the back of his head. "Remember, April, I've told you so often that I took a motto from Sir Walter Scott. When someone told him the things that were being whispered about him, he said, 'They say, do they? Let them!'"

"But I'm not worried about any they! And you're no help in helping me know what I want to do."

Oh, how I wanted someone to tell me what to do. No one would. I wanted someone to urge me into the Church. No one would. This is a step to be taken by each lonely soul, alone, and it's a frightening one. More frightening even than marriage. Marriages last for life. Joining the Church lasts forever, way past death.

Living as a Catholic, if you believe it, gives you a new dimension of life, and a special relationship with God, and in a way practically gives you a million bucks head start on getting through this world and making it in the next. But along with all the benefits comes a terrible responsibility, because you're given a pretty clear guide to what's right and what's wrong, what's good and better and best, and you must live up to those standards or pay the price.

Like many outsiders, I'd been accustomed to think that Catholics had an easy way out. They could do horrible things and go to confession and be forgiven, and the past was wiped out after a few prayers were said. Outsiders like me, seeing a gangster get a fine Church funeral on the strength of a deathbed or deathrow repentance, thought you could get away with murder in the Catholic Church.

It didn't seem fair, that deathbed repentance bit. But when I read the Gospels I found that God didn't play fair at all in the usual human sense. Take the parable of the eleventh hour, for instance. Jesus tells of the man who hired workers for the vineyard early in the morning for a set fee, then hired more later for a shorter day at the same fee, then at the eleventh hour of a twelve hour day went and hired more for the same fee, so all got paid unequally. When the workers who had toiled through the heat of the whole day complained, he told them it was none of their business because he'd kept his bargain with them, and played fair with them, and kept another bargain with the eleventh hour workers. What he was teaching there had nothing to do with social justice, or unions, but with the justice of eternal reward in heaven.

Christ said there was more rejoicing in heaven over the repentance of one sinner than over ninety-nine just men who stayed just. Rather than worrying about being fair, he would remind us that we're supposed to love everyone as we love ourselves, and lovingly want everyone to get the very best, even at the last minute. If we don't love enough for that, we'll lose our own place. It's tricky reasoning for human minds, when love counts more than what looks like justice. But God's ways are not natural to men.

I'd heard people who resented what had been done to them in the past by men who became Catholics mutter bitterly that now everything was supposed to be forgotten and wasn't it an easy sneaky way to shake off guilt, just going to confession. Now that I was learning what would be expected of me if I were to become a Catholic, I saw the other side. I'd be bound in love and conscience to make amends for every evil I'd ever done, directly and indirectly. To the degree that I understood and loved, to that degree I was responsible.

I'd long ago been disabused of the wrong idea that Catholics think only Catholics go to heaven. I knew you didn't have to be a Catholic, and in fact can't be one unless, in the mysterious workings of providence you're convinced that this Church is truly the one, holy, Catholic and apostolic church. But, if you're pretty sure it is, and that the way for you to please God is to be a Catholic, and you ignore the conviction, you might as well be dead.

Well, I remembered, too, that without an actual grace from God you can't believe in him, or in Christ, or in the Church. "You have to have the gift of faith," a priest had said.

So I kept waiting for the gift. It was a nervous time, because I didn't know what I was waiting for, or how to know it when it came. I didn't really expect angels or visions or to be thrown like Saul to the ground. But surely there'd be something special?

At last I spoke to Martin about it as we sat drinking coffee and eating sticky buns after a movie. A little shyly, I brought him up to date on my spiritual search, and my quandary.

"Everything they teach me sounds right. So right I almost take it for granted. But—I don't believe it."

He was puzzled. "How can you think it's right and not believe it?"

"I don't feel anything. I feel so cold and casual about it."

"Feeling has nothing to do with it."

"I know. They teach that. But—? But, I don't believe it, inside me. I don't have the gift of faith."

I licked my sticky fingers and we laughed, and how long can you go on being serious on a date?

But a few days later Martin brought me a sliver of a clipping from a Catholic newspaper, a quote from Tanqueray which read: "You have to will to believe."

"That means you must decide to believe?" I asked.

"That's what it means. You have to make up your mind to believe. You need the assent of the will. You do have free will, remember? Put the clipping away and think about it. But not now, for goodness' sake."

Often the missing piece of truth is so obvious you can't see it by yourself. Alone I went to St. Pat's, knelt down, and made the first decision, which was to stay there till I made up my mind whether or not I willed to believe.

I was frightened. I had the impression of the Church, the whole world-wide human and divine Church, standing like an invisible person, breathing, mysterious, still a stranger, beside me. I knew I couldn't be aware of all I'd be getting into. I believed that my decision here and now would be forever.

I thought of Peter walking on water, and how the minute his common sense told him this was impossible he fell in. I thought of all the people from Peter's time on who had willed to die for this faith rather than deny it. I thought of the little Jewish girl who'd been asked to risk everything so God could become a man. I thought of Daniel and Isaiah, David, Solomon, Moses, Abraham, and saw the pattern that held Old and New together.

There, before a statue designed to make people think of the woman who understood it all, I willed to believe.

I walked sedately out of the cathedral into March slush. But inside I laughed and skipped and made a perfect fool of myself. I hurried home through Fifth Avenue crowds, and heard myself beginning to sing out loud, and people stared, and I laughed and sang some more.

19

The Bishop, and St. Anne

I asked the young man of the blizzard if he would be my godfather, since he had been indirectly the cause of my conversion. But Martin refused to be my godfather, and he would not give any reason. So I went home and bawled.

When I told my mother and father that he refused to be my godfather, they laughed and laughed.

They knew what I did not know, and what Martin had not cared to tell me, that in the Catholic Church godfathers contract a spiritual relationship with godchildren so that they are not permitted to marry their godchildren. Of course, I didn't know he was planning to marry me. But that July he did.

And that was how the year 1948 became for me the year I received five of the seven sacraments of the Church—all that were available, since the other two are Holy Orders and the Last Anointing, and I had no wish to receive them. In a very real way I was born again.

On March 22, 1948, in the church of St. Francis of Assisi, I was received into the church in a nice quiet ceremony. I was conditionally baptized, which is a way the Church has of being quite sure its Christian converts have received the basic sacrament. My godmother was my mother's sister Bobbie, in Mexico, represented by proxy by her good friend, Mrs. Billy Gaxton. I took the Christian name of Mary.

Immediately came the second sacrament. I made my first confession. Had I been a non-Christian, unbaptized all my life, and just become a Catholic, I wouldn't have had to make a confession right away, because I couldn't have lost any grace or offended Christ before baptism. But it seemed likely that I'd been living in Christ ever since I was eleven, and was responsible for all my sins since that baptism, so I had to cover ten years. Appalling prospect! Father Bertin suggested it would be easiest to sit down and make ourselves comfortable. So I made my first confession sitting at a round table in a parlor with him, and I was sure I'd be embarrassed and miserable, but it was very simple. With so much time and territory to cover he asked me questions, beginning: "Did you ever?" And to most of them I could say "No," because he picked out the most ghastly sins in the book to ask me about first. By the time we got down to the level of my sins they didn't seem too bad. We were through in ten minutes, and I was absolved of guilt, and started all over, a bit wobbly under the stunning impact of grace. I could see that that vehicle of a new start, for which I had longed back in schooldays, would be forever at hand in the sacrament of penance.

I'd become what they call a child of God. And it was like a new childhood. I never felt more uncomplicated in my life.

It was as if I'd worked awfully hard, and waited a long time to get born, and now all my soul and mind had to do was rest and enjoy themselves. Becoming a Catholic when you're grown up is like becoming a citizen of a new country, or perhaps like one of those children's tales about a pauper child suddenly being adopted into the household of a queen. It's everything you ever dreamed, and you're happy, and you're always making blunders, and you don't know all the customs of your new country, or all the private little jokes of your new family, and your accent and language strike others as a bit ridiculous.

I kept on going to classes at night because I hadn't quite finished the course. And there were so many things to learn! It took ages for me to find my way around the Mass, let alone the missal. There were prayers to learn, and grace before meals, and every Catholic I met had some pet devotions and habits and I tried to learn them all.

But I was content to be a child. I made my first communion on Holy Thursday, anonymous in a crowd at St. Francis. I'd been warned by my father and by Martin that I wouldn't feel any great emotion, and I didn't. I understood that the host was the food of my soul, and knew my soul needed food, and I kept going to Mass and being fed, and doing the best I could to grow up all over again.

And I was in love. Truly in love. Which, as everyone knows who has been truly in love, is a miracle all its own. It makes you without warning start caring more about making someone else happy than making yourself happy. And there comes a moment when all the romantic poetry you've read suddenly comes true.

Martin and I were to be married in St. Pat's. Only six months before, that statment would have seemed to me impossible. Now the hermit of the Cape was picking out towels and a wedding gown, and praying daily to Our Lady that this marriage would be all a marriage should be, and that if it were the wrong decision for either of us she would make sure it never happened.

Then one night in those weeks after Easter the friars announced at class that the next Sunday, Pentecost, there would be the sacrament of confirmation administered up at St. Paul's Church. Any of us who had been baptized and not confirmed should go up there.

My parents were away on a business trip. Martin was the only Catholic in town I knew well enough to invite. I'd studied the seven sacraments, of course, but I was still a bit vague about confirmation. It was the special coming of the Holy Spirit, I knew, and it was appropriately scheduled for Pentecost, anniversary of the coming of the Spirit to the apostles.

"Who's going to confirm you?" Martin asked.

"I don't know. I don't think they said. A bishop?"

"It has to be a bishop," he said patiently.

"Yes. Well, all I know is they said Clare Boothe Luce is going to be official sponsor for all the women!"

I was nervous going over to St. Paul's, and I hoped I was well disposed to receive the sacrament, so when the Spirit came he'd find me ready. But to tell the truth to myself, a habit I was cultivating, I had to admit I was more interested in seeing Clare Boothe Luce than I was in the Holy Spirit. Which was, I thought, scarcely the way for a good Catholic to be thinking, putting Mrs. Luce ahead of the Paraclete. So I told myself that, as penance, I wouldn't even look at Mrs. Luce when I got to church.

Adults from all over town were at St. Paul's that evening, sent from their own parishes and inquiry courses for confirmation. Bewildered, and feeling very much alone, I padded around following directions and reading my missal, hoping I wouldn't lose the card with the name I'd chosen written on it. Only at the last minute had I realized you were given another new name at confirmation.

The time came to go up the aisle, men in one line, women in another. Way up in front of the altar was what looked like a golden throne, a bishop in full regalia seated thereon. Before you reached the bishop, flanked by important looking priests, you reached the sponsors. Out of the corner of an eye I could see Mrs. Luce prettily presenting female candidates for the sacrament. But I wasn't going to look at her.

So I didn't. And when I got next to her she put her hand on me in that sort of combination gesture of helping me up the steps and sponsoring me, and I was so busy not looking that when she helped me, I tripped.

I lunged forward, my arms out, and my hands landed plunk against the bishop's knees. The throne rocked. The bishop teetered. I screamed, and it wasn't the gift of tongues but horror which gave me voice. The bishop caught his balance, his mitre only a little askew. The throne settled down. Someone asked for my name, which was on a white card I was supposed to hand over. I whispered that my name was April. An attending priest, who looked a bit familiar, shook his head. "Anne?" I asked, trying to remember back to the time when I knew what I was doing and why. Someone disengaged my hands from the bishop's knees, took the card from my hand, and read it. Anne.

I have it on expert testimony that I was indeed duly confirmed and named Anne, but I don't remember any of it. I was shown the way back down from that throne, pointed in the general direction of my pew, and I didn't breathe again for at least an hour.

As June softened the city, the time drew near for my fifth sacrament, the sacrament of matrimony.

"Who do you want to have marry you?" my father asked. "You must be married in your parish church, which is St. Patrick's Cathedral. If there's no priest you or Martin have in mind, there's one I'd like to ask. Bishop Thomas J. McDonnell, who is head of the Society for the Propagation of the Faith. He's nice. You'll like him."

So one warm night Mother and I went to his residence on East 38th Street so I could meet Bishop McDonnell. We were ushered into his study, and I carefully remembered to genuflect, and kiss his ring as a sign of respect for the Church and his office as bishop. He did seem, as my father had said, kindly, gracious. But for a reason I couldn't name I was terrified in his presence.

Then he got down to business, asking the questions the Church must ask of prospective brides and also of grooms. First he had to record officially my status in the Church.

"When were you baptized?" I told him.

"Who baptized you?" I told him.

"Who confirmed you?"

"A bishop," I said, apologetically. "I don't know his name."

"You don't know his name?"

"I could find out. It was on Pentecost Sunday over at St. Paul's. Someone must have a record of who the bishop was."

"On Pentecost Sunday at St. Paul's. I see. How is it that you don't know the name of the bishop?"

"I don't think anyone ever told me," I faltered. "Clare Boothe Luce was sponsor for the women, though."

"And you don't remember who confirmed you," he repeated.

I looked into those twinkling eyes, and knew why I had been terrified by this gentle man.

"It was you."

"It was," said he. "And though you may not remember me, I shall never forget you. It was, shall we say, an unsettling experience."

So Bishop McDonnell agreed to witness my marriage to Martin as long as I promised not to knock him over, and thereby began a friendship which lasted till his death.

But in the meantime, there were the rest of the marriage questions to deal with. The Bishop had to speak with me alone, with Martin alone, and then with both of us together, to be certain we knew what we were doing before we embarked on this sacrament.

Naturally, since I was a convert, the question of birth control was one that must be made quite clear. Carefully the bishop made sure I understood the Church's teaching about limiting births and planning families. The law of God, he reminded me, did not require me to have as many children as I could. The law of God did require me to use the gift of sex with full awareness of all it entailed, so that if I enjoyed the rights of marriage I must be willing to accept the responsibilities that went with that joy. I was to use only self-control and abstinence by mutual consent to prevent the conception of children in the rhythm system, when and if it became prudent to limit the number of children.

I understood. "I'm willing to accept as many children as God may send me," I said. "You see, I know God is all-wise. And because he's all wise he knows I couldn't stand to have more than one or two children. He knows I'd be no good as a mother of a large family. It's as simple as that."

We were married most beautifully in the Lady Chapel on the hottest day of July. My father, veteran of public appearances and all, became at the last moment so unnerved by emotion that he could hardly make it down the aisle, and I supported him instead of the other way around. Martin's brother and sister were in the bridal party, and my brother Tony was an altar boy, and my friend Naomi, whose marriage under the traditional arbor I'd witnessed that past winter, was one of the bridesmaids, and I didn't knock over the bishop.

He had obtained for us the papal blessing, and the reception was held in magnificent style at the Waldorf, and we left for our honeymoon in Mexico. In such a happy blur, of the whole ceremony I remembered only one detail.

"Until I heard it out loud," I said to my husband as we headed off into the future, "I never really thought about that funny little prayer the bishop said about how the Church hoped our children would spring up like little olive trees around the table. It's an odd simile. But I never thought of praying for children before. St.

Anne's day is just a week from our wedding day. She's my patron, from confirmation. And someone told me they pray to her for a husband, saying, 'Good St. Anne, get me a man.' But also for kids. Maybe we should pray to St. Anne for a baby?"

We did.

20

Ink in My Blood

I don't know what exquisitely chosen bits of advice other girls' fathers give them the night before their wedding. Mine took me sombrely into his study and said:

"Whatever else you do, don't let anything get you away from your typewriter."

Well, really.

"Don't look so shocked," he continued. "You have to be yourself. And you've got ink in your blood."

At the time I decided he couldn't help being himself, but that his advice was totally irrelevant. I knew all about marriage. Until I was really married, that is.

Marriage was a matter of love, and self-sacrifice. And I knew that the vocation as wife and mother took precedence over all other vocations. What I didn't know was that my father, as almost always, was right, and that you can't do a good job at anything unless you keep on being true to yourself.

Martin was surely the perfect husband. Tall, handsome, intelligent, earnest, a lawyer with ideals and a sense of fun, he took real joy in my writing. He was born in Savannah, Georgia, but bears no trace of Southern accent because when he was a boy his family moved to New York City. His father was a skilled telegrapher, his life bound up in the excitement of news wire services and deadlines.

His mother, a beauty in her youth, has still the most luxurious white hair I've ever seen, the kind I hope to have someday, and a Franciscan heart, so that animals and birds are as much a part of her family as blood relatives. Martin's younger brother Henry, a masterful man with marine machinery, was to live in exotic ports with his Australian bride, passing inspection on ships built in Singapore or Kobe. His sister Mary is a cytologist, unrivaled expert at the detection of cancer, head of the laboratory in Roosevelt Hospital. His family is fascinating and pleasant, which is a help to any marriage. But after all, I wasn't married to them. I was married to him. I thought I saw our life clearly. I'd go on writing for a while, and when and if a baby came I'd quit. That was what love meant for me, I thought.

Loving is living in a torrent of clichés leaping to life. It is also a practical business of finding out what they really mean. That business usually begins on the honeymoon.

My aunt Bobbie and her Mexican husband, my new uncle Henry, were perfect honeymoon hosts. Their children, little Henry and Susie, Maru and Rosita, played like dream figures around the patio fountain while we learned to drink tequila and tried out our Spanish. I was determined our honeymoon would be perfect, if it killed me. And the strain of not being myself, of not wanting my image as a bride to be marred by showing any unhappy emotion, nearly did kill me.

We went to see bullfights, which I loathed, and I was cheerful about it in a horrid noble spirit of self-sacrifice. In July it rains every afternoon for an hour in Mexico City, regular as clockwork, so we wore raincoats to the Plaza de Toros. Mine was trousseau new. Under it I wore an equally new navy blue dress. The rains came. The new raincoat was no good; it was as waterproof as a paper towel. When the sun came out again not only was my dress wet, but running. My body was dyed a startling radiant blue in perfect imprint of the dress. My aunt and three maids scrubbed at me for hours, but I stayed blue. It was horrible, but I pretended not to care, and made myself be blithe and laugh.

Then Martin got a bad sunburn on his back and couldn't stand to be touched. Staunchly, I smiled.

Then we went for a boat ride in the floating gardens of Xochimilco, amid orchids and gardenias, gondoliers, and labyrinths of gardened canals to be lost in. But this was our honeymoon comedy of errors, so I suddenly came down with tourists' complaint, which involved several bilingual emergency debarkations from our gondola of love.

Then a few nights later we were nearly arrested because Martin unwittingly photographed a policeman in the act of taking a bribe, or *mordida,* as it's called, from a cabdriver.

Through it all I kept being sweet and serene, so phony I nearly burst. At last, in a deserted square at night I blew my stack over nothing. We had a glorious spat. When it was over my husband gently pointed out that I had been unbearable trying to be nice, and if I'd please just be myself from now on everything would be fine. That lesson learned, I relaxed, and loved him more than ever, and complained when I felt like it.

Honeymoons, like youth, are wasted on the young, but we had fun. We climbed pyramids and fell in love with the town of Taxco, and swam in Lake Tequesquitengo, the mud of which is said to remove warts, and did remove a three-year-old plantar wart of mine. We came home with a charro suit, rebozos, serapes, silver, and happy memories.

And I was a different person. My twenty-first birthday, which seemed absolutely ages before, had been spent at Sandalwood, an interlude in my chosen solitary literary life. My twenty-second found me being that young Mrs. Armstrong, still learning how to market and cope with laundromats. We were living in Knickerbocker Village, which was the granddaddy of the apartment house projects on the lower East Side of New York.

Martin was then law secretary to Judge Keyes Winter. A compact, energetic, smiling white-haired man, Judge Winter had the unique distinction of being able to prove that he had been the genuine model for Penrod. Booth Tarkington had been captivated by him as a boy, and I was captivated by him now. Under the solemnity of the robes of justice lurked the laughing Penrod still. Judge Winter remained our close friend, even after Martin left his court to become an assistant district attorney under Frank Hogan, another fabulous man whom we were blessed to have influence our lives.

It was a short walk from our apartment through Chinatown to the D.A.'s office, and I found that stroll precariously romantic because Martin would point to front stoop or back alley and tell me about the corpses which had recently bled there. I went to Mass on this twenty-second birthday, so far from Sandalwood, in our parish church, San Giuseppe, an ornate place of candlelight peopled with old women in black who made their confessions so loudly in Italian that I was glad not to know the language. That morning a letter came from the Oceanographic Institute in Woods Hole notifying me that a position there was now open if I wanted it, and I had to stop and think before I could remember ever wanting it.

The only thing that was the same about me was that I was still writing. Out of self-defense. Nothing had prepared me to run a home.

I had a junior high school course in cooking in Falmouth, and one in sewing, which I flunked. Westover had made me sew for charity in the Junior Dorcas Society, where we made little clothes for Dr. Grenfell's missions, and Westover had tried to teach me neatness. I had learned to make a bed. But I knew nothing about how to keep things really clean, about detergents, scouring powders, polishes, mops, vacuums. I had to learn it all alone, so I bleached navy blue socks and ruined them, and ironed rayon clothes on a cotton setting and ruined them.

Gradually I learned competence. I also resolved that any child of mine, girl or boy, would master the intricacies of kitchen, market, laundry and checkbook from the beginning. I've broken many resolves, but not that one.

And whenever I could I turned naturally, happily, to my typewriter. There at least I knew what I was doing, and liked it.

I was exploring the Church too, not only in research but in life. Bishop McDonnell was the first priest I came to know well, and he set my whole orientation toward the hierarchy. Back in the first weeks after our honeymoon we had decided it was proper to invite him as our first dinner guest. Then, having invited him, I got a rabid case of stage-fright. After all, what do you do with a bishop in your apartment after you've kissed his ring? Do you call him Your Excellency all the time? What do you talk about? Surely you don't tell jokes, or serve cocktails?

We had been given the usual wedding presents of silver and crystal, and had stowed them in our tiny closets against some remote future day of elegance. I got them all down and polished up each piece, including the little silver bell to ring for a maid, and the five pairs of silver candlesticks. We had a dining table borrowed from Sandalwood, and I unfolded all its leaves in front of the one livingroom window in that first tiny apartment, laid out the cloth I had brought from Madeira years before, and three complete settings of that sterling service from my godmother. By the time I was through the table looked like a display at Tiffany's on sale day. There was barely room for food, but at least a guest would hardly have time to notice that the floor had no rug, or that we owned only three chairs and a hand-me-down daybed.

The bishop came. Martin kissed his ring and took his hat. I kissed his ring and stood appalled. Awkwardly we got ourselves to table. We had debated whether it was proper to offer wine, and decided that would be all right, so the poor bishop had to go without the cocktail he would have enjoyed. I squeezed past the table into the kitchenette and produced the meal. He offered grace. Silence. We had exhausted our store of politeness.

Suddenly the bishop fixed me with a solemn eye, cleared his throat, and intoned:

"Boy, you sure put on the dog tonight!"

I blinked.

"I never saw so much silver on one uncomplaining table in my life," he said laughing. We all laughed, and from then on we were friends. He had the fullness of the priesthood, but he hadn't lost the fullness of human realism that stemmed from a childhood in New York's west forties. Politeness, formality, elegant speech, ritual, were necessary parts of his job, and he handled them expertly. As head of the Society for the Propagation of the Faith he had immediate knowledge of the problems of the poor and sick of all nations and faiths, pressing concern for the men and women working in the missions. In his own office he labored long hours, choosing to use a stand-up desk long out of fashion, unobtrusively imposing on himself unstinting rigors. But in his off-hours he needed a chance to return to himself and relax. To our delight he took on with us the role of a privileged and difficult uncle, making a hobby of being insulting. He would, when not hampered by other guests, suggest that I go out to the kitchen and wring out the mop again when he wanted another cup of tea.

His two sisters, Miss May McDonnell and Miss Anna McDonnell, lived in the family house until at last, driven by neighborhood changes and the encroaching bus terminal, the bishop almost forcibly transferred them to an uptown apartment where, as he predicted, they soon became happily acclimatized. They were his hostesses, in the old style of grandeur, entertaining among gilt chairs, fine linens and crystal, the spectrum of his friends from those of childhood days and outstanding current laymen to the romantic assortment of clergy and nuns from six continents. Unpretentious, endearingly jolly, the bishop's sisters spent their strength in church and charity work, in the debilitating labor of card parties and ticket-selling and bazaar-running, and in hospital work and service to the sick poor. The bishop teased them unmercifully, and expected them to rally without notice to guests or trips. They teased him, and irked him with their congenital inability to be on time. A more admirable and enjoyable trio would be hard to find.

Through them we came to know the Church on many levels. From the bishop we might hear a true tale of mission valor, an anecdote about the human side of a famous clergyman, an analysis of world politics and little-known conditions in foreign countries, thoughts on modern moral problems, or a vignette of early Irish-American New York when a monsignor had been a monSIGner, and the Church had been the Choich. We could and did turn to him with spiritual problems. He took intense interest in our careers, in Martin's political activities and law, my writing, and the lecture dates which more than once he arranged, and especially in our understanding of the lay apostolate.

Our first married year began happily and quietly. Then the day came when Martin brought home a gift from Judge Winter, and proudly unwrapped it on our kitchen counter. There lay a big fat shiny fresh-caught fish, with a big fat shiny fresh black eye staring at me. I went into hysterics, crying and shaking.

Poor Martin, who knew of my triumphs in Woods Hole, couldn't understand it. Neither could I. But soon enough the doctor explained it. Pregnancy does odd things to women. And we celebrated our first wedding anniversary in the hospital a few days after the birth of our first baby.

Martin Francis Armstrong III was delivered by Dr. Virgil Damon, the same obstetrician who, seventeen years before, had delivered my brother Tony up at Sandalwood. Only in the labor room did I learn that Mother's health, precarious after the thyroid operation, had been threatened to the point of death by that pregnancy. She had refused medical termination of it. And that was how she'd met Dr. Damon, for he'd come by her hospital room to offer his help. Now, dear friend of the family, he was with me, and having a baby wasn't frightening.

When I held little Marty in my arms, and laid him in the fairytale tester-bed crib my father gave him, I decided I must stop writing. All kinds of experts, in slick magazines and in the Catholic press agreed that motherhood should be a full-time vocation. I covered up the typewriter and turned to the bathinette, which wasn't much of a turn because in our two-and-a-half-room apartment furniture was packed so tight it couldn't be moved.

I quit being a writer and my abandonment of that career lasted six days. The seventh afternoon I was back at my desk. By the time

Marty was six weeks old I'd written and sold an article called "Is Your Baby Running Your Life?"

Giving birth to a child and tending it is a privilege not at all diminished by the commonness of it. I understood that parents cooperate with God, are indeed indispensable to him for the fulfillment of Christ. Martin and I through our love had given God the occasion to create an immortal soul. When we brought little Marty to San Giuseppe, where Bishop McDonnell's coming to baptize him caused a glorious stir, the God-life was born in him and a new son of God was in the world. Our care of this child, menial, economic, affectionate, spiritual, was care given to the most precious thing in creation: an individual destined for divine union. I knew and believed that Catholic view.

And Marty was a good baby.

But the mechanics of baby-care, as far as I'm concerned, are an exhausting, naturally distasteful routine requiring a disproportionate amount of work, a clutter of equipment, a messy cleaning-up process. And it's no sooner done for a baby than it has to be done for him all over again. Of course, like logistics, pediatrics is absolutely necessary. I do not like burping small mouths, tending small bottoms, or having my sleep at the mercy of small cries that sound enormous in the night. Neither do I like marketing, cooking, scraping garbage or washing dishes. Both jobs are irretrievably mine. Both have done me immeasurable good, furnished material for meditation, taught me discipline, thwarted tendencies to laziness, cultivated self-abnegation. But I've done them only because I had to, and frankly, I've disliked every minute.

I love eating, and having my loved ones well-fed. And I love having children. Therefore, I'm willing to do what is necessary. And once I had the courage to admit I didn't revel in the mystique of either Dr. Spock or the Good Housekeeping cookbook, everything was fine.

Self-sacrifice is sublime, if you sacrifice yourself properly. It's suicide if you don't know the rules. I was going crazy trying to be and appear something I was not. I thought I was meant to abandon writing and spend all my time domestically. The instinct for self-preservation rescued me, and the family's sanity with me.

To deny your inborn personality is to mock God, which is the sure way to insanity, despair and degradation. Some women are totally fulfilled by babies and ovens. They are to be admired. For them to berate themselves because they don't take an interest in politics or read The Great Books or have a Career is dangerous nonsense. But for me to fret over my inability to run up a dress or drapes on the sewing machine is equally wrong.

I didn't reason all that out then, any more than a man being suffocated reasons out why he needs the pillow taken off his face.

But I found that without pen or typewriter I'm a cripple, less than myself, and it shows. I'm nicer, more efficient, and have more to give those I love when, for whatever moments I can contrive, I am also writing.

In the years since I've more than once stopped writing again, either because some expert needled and meddled me into reconsidering, or because I was exhausted after giving my all to meet a deadline. Then I take a vacation, clean cupboards, go on extra excursions with children, and start elaborate unnecessary projects with paper and sticks, glue and sequins. Then I begin fussing over little things like the color of shoelaces, and I magnify small problems like water pistols. After two weeks, long before I'm ready to admit I'm restless or bored, the family begins hinting.

My problem, I began to learn as soon as Marty was born, was not whether or not to work, but how to juggle all the parts of my life so I could be the person my husband married. If I had ink in my blood as well as a baby in my arms, that's how he liked me.

21

"See! Motorcycle!"

I would love to be able to start a chapter by telling you how I became a great writer. But unfortunately I can't, because I'm not.

And I know it. The only time I think I'm a great writer is when I'm actually writing, and that helps me keep going in spite of obvious flaws in the work at hand. You have to think you're great when you're doing anything important to you, whether it's baton-twirling or complaining. It's a special kind of conviction that is produced by absorption, effort, hope and pleasure.

I had vowed my first book would be the Great American Novel. Instead it was a little volume called *When Sorrow Comes*, designed to be read by the recently bereaved. I have no idea where the original impetus for the book came from, but somehow Mother latched onto it, and asked me to co-author it, and I did. It was a book dealing with all aspects of death, and containing true stories of how many different people of many faiths found peace of mind and purpose after the loss of a loved one. I took it seriously, gave it the best I had to give, and concealed my reluctance for the subject. It was a proud moment when Miss Finch, my college writing teacher, dropped in to find me on the floor correcting galleys of my first work, with a nice little baby boy in the playpen. She was awfully polite when she discovered what the book was.

Writing that book did two things for me. It taught me first to take whatever job comes to hand and do the most you can with it, because chances are that if work comes to you asking to be done some unforeseen advantage will come of it. No matter how unlikely or distasteful it seems, I believe it prudent to take what providence sends your way. *When Sorrow Comes* let me learn the mechanics of having a book published, introduced me to the men and women of Doubleday and Company, to galleys, and to publicity.

Through that publicity came the second bonus of the book. After publication, publishers strive to get authors interviewed on radio shows to arouse public interest. Naturally, I wanted no part of speaking in public or on the radio. Mother was scheduled to appear on the Martha Deane program. But Mother came down with one of her bronchial coughs and couldn't go, so at the last moment I had to go, encouraged by Miss Deane's charming assistant, Marion Johnson. My father went along for moral support, and also so Martha Deane could be sure that someone would fill the blank air time if I fainted, as I was sure I would.

Only I didn't faint. The buried streak of ham in me came out. I found I liked talking. That good old nervous twinge which had made a hit with that one bit of poetry back at Westover came into my voice, and I sounded not bad. The next thing you know, Mary Margaret McBride, that fabled empress of women's radio shows, called and asked me to come on her show, solo. The day after that my father called me up chuckling with mischief.

"My lecture agent, Colston Leigh, just phoned to inquire if I knew anyone by the name of April who was said to be related to me. I allowed I did. Some ladies in New Jersey heard you on Mary Margaret's show, and want you to come lecture there. They were sure Colston Leigh would know who you were and get you. So he pretended to know you, and now he wants to put you under contract. I told him you wouldn't be interested, because you hate standing up in public."

So I took up lecturing to patient women's clubs, making dreadful faux pas such as not wearing a hat or gloves, and more serious mistakes such as sounding pompous and reading from a manuscript. Then, before one of those jaunts, Daddy got hold of my briefcase, and substituted blank paper for my speech. After a moment of panic on stage I found I could talk better without a manuscript, and a new side career was born. Characteristically, he explained the dirty trick he'd played by saying,

"No daughter of mine is going to go around disgracing us by reading a speech."

My first really big paid engagement was an address to the convention of the American Cemetery Association. Because of *When Sorrow Comes* they thought I was appropriate. Graciously they extended an invitation for Martin and me to be their guests for a long weekend at Atlantic City. We leaped at the chance for a vacation with spending money.

They are dear, wonderful people, the members of that Association, and I remember them with affection. They rallied swiftly from the initial shock of meeting me in person. Poor dears, from the book they'd somehow expected a nice white-haired lady. They hid their disappointment, took pleasure in watching Martin and me swim and dance as if we were honeymooners, and kept inviting us to share all sorts of diversions, including the outdoor display of automatic grave-digging equipment in action.

Specifically they'd requested me to discuss the public relations aspects of their business. Not their personal problems, though these were acute because, as several couples explained to us at that convention, once you've buried someone in a family the family is usually slow to have you visit them socially, and so after a while your circle of dinner invitations gets limited in any town. What the convention was officially concerned with was communicating more effectively with the public—dignified, religious public relations.

I'll never forget the introduction given to my speech. The man said:

"For the first time in the history of the American Cemetery Association, we have gone outside our own field to dig up a speaker."

I giggled. No one else moved a dimple.

"Speaking on a subject of grave interest to us," he continued. I giggled again. Alone. But at least I had a place to start with a public relations campaign: with the use of words. We got along famously, the morticians and funeral directors and graveyard keepers and I, and for years after some would write to me, calling me the Darling of the American Cemetery Association, and that's a title not everyone enjoys.

Martin and I had moved from the tiny lower East Side apartment to an echoing barn which was the bottom half of a duplex on West 57th Street. The livingroom fireplace mantel was over my head. The livingroom windows were thirty feet high, draped in miles of old velvet which obviously no one had ever afforded to take down and have cleaned, and which we left severely alone. Our 9 x 12 rug made a nice scatter rug by the hearth. In the livingroom a glorious staircase led to a locked door. Behind the door, taking up the second floor of the apartment with a separate entrance, was a dentist's office. The dentist owned the place and sublet the bottom to us. We had happy parties in that room. When Bishop McDonnell came to our gatherings he would insist on posing at the top of the stairs as if just coming down, impishly hoping to give arriving guests an impressive illusion of our wealth. The trouble was we never had anyone over who could be impressed.

Even had we wanted to impress people it's difficult to give an illusion when you're swamped with diapers and baby food. When little Marty was fifteen months old his brother was born, a serious-looking professorial-nosed infant, who was also irresistibly loveable and beautiful. The bishop baptized him Michael Anthony in the font of what was again my parish church, St. Pat's. So we had our two babies, and friends and strangers told us how lucky we were to have had our family while we were so young. They implied it was clever of me to have done my duty and endured my two pregnancies so early in life. By now I wasn't so positive God agreed with my notion that two children were the maximum I could handle. When I countered congratulations with casual remarks that there might someday be more children to come, everyone laughed merrily.

We were learning the business of parenthood fast. I had used up three paperback copies of Spock, read some Gesell and Ames, and Martin and I together evolved all kinds of high-sounding theories of our own about child-raising. Marty, toddling, and Mike, crying with a colic no doctor could find, kept bringing us back down to practicality again. We pushed them to Central Park, and up and down city streets, loaded them into the little green Crosley for excursions into the wilds of Westchester. To us the sight of green from the Parkways, the weeping willows and country roads, were exotic refuges from the soot and concrete of the city. One of our babies, placed without warning in an unmowed field by a stream, screamed at the tall twisting green monsters which he didn't recognize as grass. Just so might a country baby panic at sight and sound of the subways which ours loved.

Our pattern of life as a young family was shaped on one hand by my writing, on the other by the exigencies of Martin's career as an assistant district attorney. In the homicide bureau he saw the miseries and horrors of city life, babies hidden to die in bureau drawers, knifings, shootings, welfare cases where the husband by not working was receiving more than Martin got by working, death in the playgrounds, death in the streets, death in the park where we took our little ones for sun. It made us appreciate the treasure we had, the fact that we loved each other, and lived plain and simple lives.

We were near enough to visit Martin's family and mine, bringing to each the first grandchildren. My brother Tony, busy with school and a young man's fancy, having his first poems published at Georgetown University, would drop in to discuss literature or French songs or his girl friends, or tease us by trying to teach Marty the wrong words for things. "Apple!" this handsome young uncle would say, diabolically holding an orange for Marty to see. Martin's sister Mary, slim, dark, and stunning, trailed sophistication through our nursery. Martin's brother Henry came home on far-voyaging ships, bringing the babies boomerangs and stuffed koala bears from Australia, or shimmering blue butterflies from the Amazon.

One room of the apartment we made into a study, and when the babies napped I wrote, and at night when Martin was out investigating murders I wrote, grateful that I'd finally outgrown the notion that one needed muses and atmosphere to write. I worked when and as I could, training myself to concentrate and be interrupted and concentrate again. From Adela Rogers St. John, who had written in the hubbub of family all her life, I learned another trade secret. The best way to pare extra wordage is to set yourself to typing a final draft of a manuscript late at night when you're so exhausted you'll dispense with any poetic phrase or pet irrelevancy just to get finished.

I was turning out short stories, which seldom sold, and articles, a few of which made top markets, and writing a weekly syndicated column with Mother called *Genius for Living,* retailing true stories about inspirational achievements of otherwise ordinary Americans. And I was working on a fearfully ambitious project, contracted for by Doubleday but now long-since abandoned, which was to tell in one huge Work the lives of all the Catholic saints in dramatic terms with historical backdrops.

The idea for that book grew out of the feeling Daddy and I shared of revulsion for unrealistic quasi-pious books and pamphlets about saints. Nothing could be better calculated to misrepresent the Church than the average "life" of a saint. Nothing could more discourage the Christian who sincerely hoped to live the life of faith in a modern world. Most biographies of saints made them sound as if they'd never had contact with human problems or history, and as if they didn't like life or people at all. Much work had been done then, and is still being done, to free individual saints from insulting plaster haloes. Some fine honest biographies exist. But no one had tried to make a synthesis of the saints, to show where they fitted in the great overall scheme of history and the biography of the Church itself as an incarnation. The vast army of thousands upon thousands of holy souls were lost in the calendar as vague martyrs, virgins, confessors, or bishops, known chiefly as patrons invoked against lightning, toothache or boils.

Working on research and writing, I saw the saints in a different light, as human beings with faults who by grace came close to Christ in the context of their times. You cannot separate the history of the Church and of nations and of literature, thought and human consciousness. Each era, each stage of human awareness and forward movement, produces its own kind of holy people, and no two are the same.

I saw that if you believe each person is a potential saint, that we are expected by God to fulfill ourselves uniquely through him, then it must be that we become more individualized as we become saints. Evil is the great leveler. Sinners are conformists with deadly similarity. The dynamic of grace produces non-conformists, remarkable first editions of humanity. Yet, in print, it usually appears just the other way round. Saints are presented as boring and predictable, and we find sinners intriguing, and in tune with the times. I was never able to finish that work on the saints, but I still hope someone more capable will set things straight so that these heroes and heroines of God are recognizable again.

As file cases and chapters piled up, I found saints quarreling with each other, saints who liked to sit up on pillars, saints who ran shops, saints who were explorers or writers, actors or clowns, saints with happy marriages and saints who abhorred marriage, scholars and beggars and neurotics and rich men, politicians, kings, whores, children and ugly old ladies. Their infinite variety, the intricate interrelationships of them from one age and country to another, the fact that the Spirit evokes from the mass of the faithful first one type of genius then another, the fact that even at death most saints still have besetting faults lingering like splinters in their flesh, this knowledge fascinated me.

Struggling to express the truth about them, I found myself immersed in Church history and then in world history. From the early days in Rome to the settlement of North America I worked, and in some forty countries, trying to tie in the impact of art, science, politics and business, seeing the weakness of human beings inside the Church as well as out. It is a cliché to say that the finest proof of the divine strength of the Catholic Church is to look at the evil human beings in spite of whom it has survived. But it's true. The Church has had wicked Popes, not-so-good Popes, and great Popes, has been persecuted and has persecuted, has inspired and discouraged, has been maligned and has maligned, and it's still alive. One advantage converts have over cradle Catholics is that they're not easily shocked by the human truth about the Church. I already knew all the bad things about Catholics now and in the past before I joined up.

Eventually the dentist decided he needed the rest of his duplex, and we had to move. We ended up on Park Avenue, in an apartment which, being on the second floor in the back and rather dark, was much cheaper to rent. So we had a glamorous address, we were next door to St. Ignatius Loyola Church, a few blocks from the Mc-Donnells, in easy reach still of both sets of our parents, and if we were conspicuous as the only parents of small children in the building it didn't bother us. We had settled into a happy rut.

I didn't realize how much of a rut until the day I went to lunch with Ralph Beebe, Doubleday editor, to discuss contracts for two books. It was midwinter. For what seemed endless weeks I'd been in the apartment with Marty and Mike, mumps and flu. When we did emerge I'd push the carriage with Mike inside and Marty riding a sort of jumpseat, and we'd go to the grocery store, the fire station, and Third Avenue to see the el train. On these rare outings I'd dutifully point out every crane and street-cleaning truck, every garbage truck chewing up refuse, and every horsie. It was a heyday of conversation, as you can see.

Ralph wanted me to do children's versions of *The Greatest Story Ever Told* and *The Greatest Book Ever Written*, with my father. All dressed up, eager to make an impression on this editor, of whom, though he was a friend, I was in awe, I stood waiting with him at a traffic light on our way to a French restaurant. Suddenly I grabbed his arm, and without thinking pointed out into the street:

"Look! See! Motorcycle!"

Years later another mother-writer confessed to me that once in a lull at a dinner party she'd heard herself turn to the gentleman on her right and say that she bet she could finish her soup before he could make his all gone.

At lunch Ralph helped me scheme to avoid this hazard which

besets writers who are also women. We agreed that I was in danger of stagnating, and I wouldn't be any good to anyone including my children unless I kept wits sharp enough to sustain adult conversation when necessary.

"Very true," observed Bishop McDonnell later when I talked with him about it. "On the other hand, remember that being a wife and mother not only comes first, but also should prove not a handicap but a help to your career as a writer. Because you have a family you've been compelled to be more fully alive, to give of yourself, to love, to be drawn out of yourself. You're more a person now than you were when I first met you. If you're getting in a rut, it's not the children's fault but yours. The Lord placed you in a position where thanks to your daily tasks you can grow so that someday you may write with immediacy and understanding of a very real world. That same position demands that you use every ounce of strength and curiosity and talent he gave you to fight against decay, which may make you ill and poison you."

"But what shall I do to keep out of a rut?"

"Whatever you see to do. God's done a good job of planning your life for you this far. Don't try and take over. When you need more to do, it'll come to you to be done. Your problem is to recognize what is at hand, and accept it."

At the moment I was determined only that never again would I catch myself talking to an editor as if he were a child.

22

Nothing in Life Stays

Most books by or about converts end up when they enter the Church, much as fairy tales end with the princess marrying, and living happily ever after.

Everyone knows marriage is only the beginning, and that things don't go smoothly ever after. The same is true about the new wedded life of a soul with God in the adventure of grace. Only I didn't know that. I somehow thought once I became a Catholic I had it made. That was that, and while I'd of course go on praying and keeping commandments and all, at least I wouldn't have to spend much time bothering about problems.

Nothing in life stays done, except mistakes. One day I suddenly realized I didn't know very much about the Church at all, which rather threw me. I had that "Where am I? How did I get here?" feeling. It wasn't that I had doubts, then. You don't get tormented with doubts until you really know what there is to doubt. It was rather that a part of my brain had apparently fallen asleep after I climbed my way into the faith three years before. Now my mind came prowling out of hibernation, hungry and cross.

Unconsciously, I had assumed that faith was a static inanimate possession, or accomplishment. But of course faith is a life, and no life stands still. I'd been an enthusiastic, busy, noisy child of the Church for these few years, but God, as soon as you're ready for it, demands your whole consciousness. I'd thought I'd given it to him, until there came, without obvious cause, this panicky awareness of confusion and discomfort over what I'd gotten myself into. This feeling is rather common with converts, and it is unnerving.

Converts are a peculiar breed, and a lot of generalizations are made about us in the Catholic Church. We're said to talk too much, and that may be true. We're said to make much better Catholics than those born to the faith, but that's not noticeably true. We're said to take ourselves and things too seriously, and to run about making foolish nuisances of ourselves, and often some of us do. We're also said to know more and care more than those brought up in the Church. Usually that's absolutely and naturally true. The adult convert worth his baptismal salt can't take for granted the truth he found.

There are, thank God, thousands of born Catholics who feel the same way. But unfortunately, all too often, converts meet many who don't. And often we meet, in our formative years, what can seem a muddling group of holy souls who appear to live what would be for us an unforgiveably pallid religious life, and who don't want anyone rocking the bark of Peter. We hear, sometimes, an expression of religious viewpoint diametrically opposed to the one we thought was *the* Catholic way. We hear the lukewarm voices, the don't-try-to-be-too-holy, be-polite-and-blend-in voices. Or the stay-in-a-ghetto mentality. Converts are taught that theology is something they should know at least as much about as politics, outer space or television programs. But many Catholics are shy of theology, which is the one science designed for all men and women to master to some degree. Many still think that "layman" really means "amateur."

There's such a gap between the modern, return-to-the-original form of Catholic truth, and the slightly irrelevant conservative brand, which is a hangover from the last century, that the convert can be totally at sea when he's in the community on his own. But not for long. A special providence watches over him, and eventually he sees that in the Church are many ways of serving and loving God, 99 per cent of which won't fit him.

Born Catholics have their own special problems. They learned about Christ as children, and children don't always get everything straight. Besides, as children they were exposed to teachers who may well have had everything straight for themselves, but who used words and stories which confused and distorted truth. At least converts never had the chance to be mixed up as youngsters. We were forced to think for ourselves to get into the Church, and so we expect to go on thinking, and don't feel presumptuous or scared. But many of our fellows, raised in the Church, were taught that "the faithful," the laity, shouldn't think. They are frankly having a confusing time now in the Church because the Catholic Church is so full of new currents of grace that it makes them understandably nervous. It's the same Church, but it neither looks nor feels nor sounds the same, thank God.

Not knowing about this problem, converts may naïvely expect

to share an enthusiasm that simply isn't there to be shared in every rosary altar meeting or every pulpit. We have to get over this, but it takes compassion, insight and knowledge to understand why the very things that attracted us to the Church as she re-expresses herself today either seem to mean nothing to many cradle Catholics, or else to appall them.

By the end of my first few years I was a baffled wreck.

"I need a graduate course, or something," I explained to Martin. "What I got out of the convert course wasn't enough."

"Now," he said, "the old philosophy major comes back to life."

The problem was where, how, when I could learn more. Reading alone isn't enough until you're well oriented in a field. Reading the wrong books can be perilous, and there are a lot of wrong books for converts to read. Dogmatically free from error, these tomes may also be free from truth, anachronistic, geared to monastic life, which is, happily, different from modern married life, or to combatting intellectual moods and dangers that have nothing to do with our day.

Questions swirled in my head. Just how does one as a Christian reconcile the fact of free will and the fact that God knows all things? Does the Church have an esthetic? Is there behind the commandments and lists of the degrees and kinds of sins and virtues any system of ethics to compare with Aristotle or Kant? What, actually, is grace? Is it, as I was first introduced to it, a life, a living power, God-in-you? What about evolution? And curious little problems bubbled to the surface, including one about time. Time, I understood, was only in this world, and was by nature related to change. After death we entered eternity, which I was told was by nature changeless. But if purgatory was a state of change and improvement to prepare souls for God, was it in time or in eternity? Either way, how could you explain the answer?

To anyone who would listen I found myself saying that there should be follow-up graduate courses for converts. People agreed more or less politely. Mostly they said that if I felt that way about it then when our children were grown up I could go to Fordham or someplace and take some courses.

Martin knows an immense amount about religion, but he was already teaching for the Confraternity of Christian Doctrine to public high school youngsters in our parish. Besides, being married to me, he didn't want to also have to teach me, because I'm prone to argument. My parents agreed that I should learn some more, but they were preparing for a long-awaited trip to Africa. My father's advice was to write my own course in religion.

"You'll learn more from your own book than anyone's else," he said. He always quoted the writer who said that he wrote books because he wanted to read them.

Only I wasn't about to write myself a book. Mr. and Mrs. Robert Hoguet, whose charming city mansion was a gathering-place of lay and clerical literary men and thought-leaders, graciously gave a party to honor my father. In her salon, where one felt in the air the electricity of such minds as Martin d'Arcy, Maritain, Verner Moore, I said to a fellow guest, almost by habit:

"I keep thinking someone should offer converts a graduate course. I need one."

"If you're serious, I'll give you one," said he. Father Wilfred Thibodeau, S.S.S., a Blessed Sacrament priest, measured me with piercing eyes.

Week after week he taught me. I'd go to the church called St. Jean's, more formally St. Jean Baptiste, and he'd give me private lectures on philosophy and theology, assigning me homework, designing his course so that my reach would always exceed my grasp. On we went through causality, essence, and existence, through ethics and esthetics and mariology. He taught me Scholastic philosophy, the approach originated by St. Thomas Aquinas, who based his system on Aristotelian thinking quickened by Christian impact. Aristotle and I had never gotten on well, but while I mastered rudiments of Scholasticism, Father Thibodeau pointed out other approaches within the Church. There were, I learned to my surprise, several schools of Catholic philosophy and theology, often in sharp disagreement on everything except the defined points of dogma. And these defined points of dogma, to my greater surprise, are really few. These absolute revealed truths are the truths around which any attempt to explain all truth must center. In addition to dogmas there are certain absolutely rejected errors. But, avoiding these errors, one can explain and connect the fixed stars of the truth in many ways.

Somehow it had been taken for granted that the only way was Thomas Aquinas' way, and Scholasticism is taught in most Church schools as if there could be no other. Yet there are in the Church neo-Scholastics, who have radically updated Thomas, and other groups who follow the lead of St. Augustine, and others following Duns Scotus, and mavericks who can't be classified under the aegis of dead saints, including some Catholic existentialists.

Under Father Thibodeau's challenging guidance, I discovered that you could think and argue with a startling degree of freedom inside the Church, and that one mustn't be dismayed by the fact that most folks, in Roman collars or out, didn't approve. The only requirement was that you learn the rules of the game, clearly understanding the officially defined truths first.

By the time I understood all this, my parents had returned with a lion rug and tales of Africa, and I'd forgotten I was ever in a rut. I was still serving as the wife of an assistant district attorney, though now Martin was in Special Sessions Bureau, and no longer washing blood off his hands when he came home after midnight. I was still trying to figure out how to be a good mother, and Marty and Mike were mischievous teachers. Once, while I made the mistake of lying down when they were supposed to be napping, they turned their bedroom into a reasonable facsimile of Jones Beach. They were proud of themselves, and they'd used much imagination, lugging toy wheelbarrows full of water from the tub, sopping pillows to make sand. And, snatching hours when they were actually asleep, I was still writing.

But because I was again immersed in the one totally satisfying subject in the world or out, I was finding ours a full wonderful life. As far as I was concerned, it could go on forever, just as it was.

Then, one midnight in May, 1952, Mother phoned to say my father had been taken ill. She had summoned the doctor. My father was almost never ill. Just the week before he'd been through a thorough physical examination, and been pronounced in fine health. He'd never been busier or happier. For the first time in ten years it seemed he would soon enjoy a measure of financial security. His books were doing amazingly well. He had been up till eleven this night discussing the possibility of movie or television sale of *The Greatest Story Ever Told*. His guest left. Then, without warning, my father had a heart attack.

I went down to their apartment. He was resting in bed. The doctor assured me he could not believe this attack would prove fatal. I asked Mother if she'd called anyone else, particularly Tony, then at Georgetown, in Washington, D.C. The doctor said that would be unnecessary: everything would be all right if my father had a couple of weeks of rest. I asked if I could see him.

He smiled from his bed. I asked how he felt. He answered me with a look which said there was no time for such trivial conversation. I reported the doctor's happy prognosis. He nodded impatiently. Then, as if explaining his impatience, he said:

"April, you will have to finish the manuscript of *The Greatest Faith* for me. Will you promise to do that?"

He was speaking of the third in his trilogy, a book dealing with the Acts and Epistles of the New Testament, the lives of the apostles, the start of the Christian Church.

"You'll be able to finish it yourself," I said.

"No," he answered simply. "I won't. I am asking you. I would like you to promise me you will."

"I promise."

"I've done the best I can. I would like to go on a little more, but at least I know I've done my best. And I know I have left your mother well provided for, and she'll have no worries." He closed his eyes. After a moment he said, "You had better go home now. Who's staying with the babies?"

"Martin's there. And I don't want to go home."

"I'll be all right for a while," he said. "I told them to send for the priest. You go home. If you stay it will worry your mother."

He knew he was going to die. He lay there calmly and spoke as he might if he were about to fly out to Chicago for a day. I kissed him, and told him I loved him, and my voice cracked.

Using a pet name, he asked, "Did I ever think you didn't?" and told me again to go home.

In the livingroom I told Mother and the doctor that he'd asked me to finish his book. I said he expected to die. I insisted we phone Tony and make arrangements so he could begin the journey home. A priest arrived. He gave Daddy the sacrament of the sick, and said he would return in the morning with Holy Viaticum. He explained later that he was sure that Daddy was in no danger of dying. The doctor and Mother told me to go home to sleep.

Before I slept I called Will, in spite of the doctor.

In the morning Martin went to seven o'clock Mass next door at St. Ignatius to pray for my father. While he was gone the phone rang. The doctor said to come quickly. I was dressed, but the little boys weren't. I phoned around desperately, and could find no one at that hour to come and sit with Marty and Mike. Who can you make understand you at that hour? I dressed the boys haphazardly, phoned Will again, and ran with the carriage to the church steps. It's a big church, and many people attend daily Mass there. I couldn't get up the steps with the carriage, couldn't find anyone to find Martin. When at last he came out I left the children with him and sped in a cab to my parents' apartment.

Will was pacing nervously on the sidewalk. Together we went up in the elevator. The elevator girl with the beautiful hair was weeping. Daddy lay unconscious in the bed, an incongruously amiable look on his face, with none of the ugliness I'd come to expect of death. At ten minutes after eight he was gone. It was the day the Church honors Mary as the Help of Christians. The morning was the kind of pink city spring day he loved. Knowing full well it sounds invented, I report that in spite of hours of physical distress and illness following his heart attack, the room at his death smelled of flowers. I was afraid to remark it out loud until others said it first.

It's always hard to believe someone you love is now dead. Yet, as you stay beside the body, it seems you can almost mark the moment the soul is gone. If this was death, it was, I thought, gentle. I couldn't weep for my father's sake, for he knew he was going, knew to whom he went, and why. He had not seemed fearful or disappointed or resigned. Only ready and waiting. People said he worked himself to death, as if that were wrong. It was what he wanted: to spend himself in the use of his talent for God. He could not have done less.

23

Lesson of Love

There's a similarity between the fuss of a funeral and the fuss of a wedding, some of which makes sense only to a mind conditioned to think of death as the triumphant passage to new life. Bereaved, you are plunged into making arrangements, notifying family, friends and strangers, keeping a record of who sent what favors, flowers and condolences, so acknowledgments can be made. The hours of reception at the funeral parlor are bewildering, awkward, yet humanly wonderful.

To my father's wake came groups of strangers who, though they'd never met him, felt they knew him because his writing had affected their lives. They considered him a friend, mourned him. Bishop Sheen stopped in to say the rosary. Arthur Gans, Daddy's still close ex-magician friend from Baltimore, quietly came. And Cousin Mary Herman came, his only living blood relative aside from his children. And the men and women of all the different worlds of his life: from early days at Macfadden, from the publishers of his first novels, from the *Digest*, from Broadway, FBI men, police, crime experts, members of the Society of American Magicians, of the Dutch Treat Club, of that esoteric group of Sherlock Holmes devotees called the Baker Street Irregulars, of the Players' Club, of the Catholic Press Association. Actors, directors, playwrights, doctors, psychiatrists, lawyers, doormen, clerks, atheists, Protestants, Jews, Catholics, priests, ministers, they made a montage of biography.

In *When Sorrow Comes,* Mother and I had written that the hustle and bustle of funeral arrangements serve to baffle the demon of grief, divert and quiet the heart. I was grateful that Martin and Tony were able to handle so many necessary details. And while I abhorred having to buy a black hat and dress, and arrange for babysitters, still the busyness was a help for a time. I didn't suspect what a hurly-burly of busyness would start for me after that funeral.

Grief is a private thing, unpredictable in its eruption, a physical reaction to shock that doesn't respond to logic or faith. You can only keep it to yourself and wait for it to pass. Or, if you are of different nature, wait for it to erupt. I become quiet in the time of most strain. Perhaps for some a cocoon of tranquilizers and sedation is needed and good. I can't believe it wise for most of us to medicate ourselves at the meeting of the mysteries of life and death.

The Mass offered for my father at the main altar of St. Patrick's was the first funeral Mass I ever attended. The dignity and realistic concession to grief in that service pulled me forth from numbness. I expected to weep. Instead, I found myself smiling with irrepressible joy, because Jesus Christ had come to be with us in that hour.

At every Mass, of course, Christ comes sacramentally to the altar. At this Mass, as the priest in regular ritual raised the host for all to witness, I understood that what was daily ritual became in this instant an act of tender courtesy from our God, who came to Mary and Martha when Lazarus was dead. He came to us when my father died.

We buried my father in Gate of Heaven cemetery. Always he had particularly liked hawthorne trees which, as Longfellow said, "ope in the month of May," and somehow we got permission to plant one by his grave. The gravestone is in the shape of an open book, inscribed with the quotation, "Behold this dreamer . . ." It's a quotation from the Bible story of Joseph, son of Israel, the one with the coat of many colors. It's the opening phrase of the words addressed to Joseph in scorn by the elder brothers who resented his uniquely favored position in their father's house. One day, they said, they'd see what came of his dreams. They did.

My father had used *Behold This Dreamer* as the title of his first novel, the tale of an artist burdened and misunderstood by a whining, prosaic first wife, then committed to an insane asylum for his dreams of beauty. All of his life, brotherless, except in his role among all men who are brothers, my father had hewed true to his own dreams, and followed where God led. Like Joseph in Egypt he had gathered up the bread of truth and dispensed it.

A funeral, a burial, a reading of the will: that is the pattern. We gathered in Mother's apartment. Will read the document aloud. In it my father left everything to my mother if she survived him.

I learned soon enough that writers stand in a peculiar position in the matter of wills and estates. Maybe some writers have lots of cash, but I never knew one who did. Some few have investments, stocks, bonds. My father didn't. It had taken him years to climb out of the slough of debt after 1942, and he'd used what extra money he had for charity for close relatives and friends, as well as the army of unnamed. He left almost nothing negotiable. His estate was reported as being substantial, but it consisted of copyrights, the ownership of books, manuscripts and other literary properties, which might earn money in the future. The government, assessing estates for inheritance tax, puts a value on copyrights by guessing their probable earnings for years to come. On *The Greatest Story Ever Told,* for instance, they put a tremendous monetary value because it might someday become a movie. The estimates were all flattering and made fancy headlines, but they posed a problem when the estate had to pay the tax on values which weren't current. The money wasn't in sight, and the government had no intention of waiting. Raising money to pay the estate tax was an urgent and difficult feat for Mother. She was reputed to be a rich heiress, and she was close to being broke, and it was extremely confusing. But we didn't worry. Her co-executor, eminent, genial, and astute business expert Al Cole of the *Digest,* and her lawyers, were superb.

My father's death catapulted me into a new urgent challenge of work. Ralph Beebe and Joe Marks, then vice-president at Doubleday, spoke with me. They didn't want to rush me. They wanted to be of as much help as they could. But I had three contracts to fulfill. There was *The Greatest Faith Ever Known.* After that, the young people's versions of the first two books of the trilogy. Doubleday was willing to take a chance on me, wanted to get at it right away. Why should I be afraid?

But I was. At twenty-five I had fewer illusions about my writing ability than I'd had in my teens, and a more accurate appreciation of the ability of the man whose work I was to finish. I went into his study and stood by the massive solid wood table which served as his desk. On the floor under ceiling-high bookcases lay two green metal lock-boxes containing all his work on *The Greatest Faith,* the book that, more than any other, he'd longed to finish. He could have asked other, more experienced writers, in our family or out, to finish this. He asked me. I opened the boxes. The work ended in midsentence in his own handwriting in the middle of Chapter 86.

Mother had told me, and the publishers, that he had almost completed the book, and that the manuscript was in nearly final draft. She described it as needing only a few additional chapters, and minor cosmetic work at the beginning. She thought that was true. But this was no final draft. There were in the boxes 1027 handwritten pages and a typed version of the same, and altogether it was only a first shadowing of a book.

I'd worked with my father long enough to recognize that these were only introductory indications and false starts. No more than a few sentences here and there would stand unchanged. Disconnected, not yet proportioned, these were the pedestrian paragraphs typical of his first handling of the clay from which he would evoke a living figure.

To finish this book I'd have to write it all, beginning to end. Stunned, I turned to my mother. It seemed to her best not to let people know this. She felt the book might be better received, and therefore more to his credit, if the public thought Fulton Oursler wrote most of it. I felt it would be better to tell the truth, so that if the book didn't turn out well I could take full blame. I consulted the publishers. It was too late. The publicity release had already gone out stating that the manuscript was almost entirely done by my father. The decision wasn't mine. The unintentional untruth was already in print, and it would look odd to go around printing retractions.

So I tackled writing the whole book and never contradicted anyone for years. I was to be amused later when reviewers remarked that I'd captured with amazing fidelity my father's technique, and that they couldn't mark any difference in style between the first part of the book and the last. It would have been remarkable if there had been a difference. In case anyone feels he was cheated, I apologize, but you can see how it was. To this day I keep his manuscript pages to remind me of the truth about that book.

I had those pages, and ten tall looseleaf notebooks of research, and I was to get to work right away, and I was terrified. Without the encouragement and concrete help of Mother, and of my father's secretaries, Charles Cross and Thomas Fleming, who was soon to begin his own bright career as editor and author, I'd have gone to pieces in those first months. I had two immediate tasks: to organize my life so that while remaining a full-time wife and mother I could also be a full-time writer; and to steep myself in research.

Until then I'd written in snatches. Now I had to learn to write and study through the din, cultivating selective hearing. The knack is not really difficult: even a child can master it, and most do, screening out adult voices unless the word "candy" is mentioned. The trick is to hear only what is vitally important, like a cry that means your child is hurt, or the excitement that comes when he needs congratulation for a really good block tower. We all know we can do two things at once. We can iron and think about what so-and-so said, and what we could have said to her. Or we can iron and plan out a chapter.

I ironed and planned out chapters. I became an expert at house-keeping shortcuts and eliminating nonessentials. And all the time I was soaking up the life and background of Peter and Paul. That July I was going around sort of expecting drachmas and denarii in change at the supermarket, and mumbling about tabularia, loggia, Roman emperors and their mistresses. Martin and the children over the years have come to accept the way I got lost in other worlds, and often inquire tentatively before beginning a conversation, "What century are you in?"

By then Tony was courting a tall, wise and lovely girl named Anne N. Nevill, whom he'd known since 1951 at Georgetown. She was taking a five-year combination course there, had her R.N., and was still working for her B.S. Tony called her by her middle name, Noel, and Mother remarked once how charmingly calendarish it would be if she should have two daughters named April and Noel.

That was also the summer we learned first hand the rather incredible torture it can be to be thought rich.

We weren't rich, and we knew it. So did everyone else with a grain of common sense. Mother was having trouble converting things into cash to meet bills. I was an expert at conning the grocer and butcher into helping me cut corners and saving for me the special bargains. Woolworth's and Lamston's were my interior decorators.

Then came startling news. Walter Winchell announced on the

radio that Mother had sold *The Greatest Story* to the movies for 2 million dollars.

Usually we followed Winchell with special interest. Daddy had given him his first job as a columnist, and Winchell, unlike so many others who got their start from him, had remained always a loyal friend. But this night we missed the flash. Our friends heard it. Some called Mother. And Mother called us, breathless, confused, laughing.

"Well, did you? Where's the 2 million, doll?" I asked her, as we enjoyed the joke.

"It's the first I've heard of it," she said, wonderingly. "Maybe someone stuck Winchell with a false lead. Or else it's going to happen and they've just neglected to tell me."

Tentative negotiations for the possible sale of the book to the movies had been going on before Daddy's death. Since then Mother had heard once in a while that sometime a sale might be made. But she hadn't had an offer, hadn't signed a contract, and no money had been offered or paid that night when public announcement was made.

People believe what they hear, what they read, and what they want to believe. The next day there was a report of the sale, and the two million dollars, in the papers. Those closest to us, naturally thought us perverse not to have mentioned this wonderful news. We tried to explain, but honestly, who would believe our story? We tried to laugh off the misunderstanding, but people thought we were making a poormouth, and were very unfriendly. Thus far it was a problem of private and personal relations, difficult enough.

Then it really hit us, on the first of the month. We always opened bills with sinking hearts. This time we howled. A man who had performed a small service usually running about $25 sent a bill for $100. A doctor doubled his fee because his nurse-secretary read and believed the newspapers. A magazine that had offered me the chance to do a little article for $50, money which I was by now counting on, politely suggested I was undoubtedly too busy and gave the assignment to someone they thought really needed the money. The grocer and butcher suddenly had nothing to offer but the best. Collectors for charities, who had been awfully nice when we could scrape up a dollar or five, now apparently intended to throw such pittances back in our *nouveau riche* faces. A real estate agent who had been desultorily trying to find us a $25,000 house suddenly offered me a monstrous estate on an island with a private bridge and a gate house. A swell buy for only $75,000. He didn't give up on that dream sale for five weeks. We were able to set the doctor straight. But things were never the same again.

Our friends went through their own private contortions. Some who were, in the natural course of things, about to write us or invite us, put off doing so lest they seem overanxious. Others, close enough to us not to worry about that, when we tried to share the nonsensical story of our nightmare listened earnestly, lovingly and decided we only had one million instead of two. And some, close friends, distant relatives, and strangers, kept hoping we'd help them with mortgages or college educations, and were disappointed. And we were busy fending off new would-be friends, and invitations to be on committees for this and that.

Eventually, of course, the powers that be in Hollywood did get around to talking to Mother, and did make a contract. Twentieth-Century Fox was highly excited, announced they'd film the movie immediately, or at least in the next year, and paid an advance against future earnings. The advance was a goodly sum, which at any other time would have impressed us. But it wasn't the tiniest fraction of 2 million dollars. And when it was split with some men who were involved before my father's death with another project for the book, there was about enough left to pay Mother's rent and taxes.

The contract gave Mother a percentage of the money made from the film after the expenses of making the film were paid.

"Someday maybe you'll be really rich, after the movie's made, and anyway it'll be fun to see the movie," I said.

"I should live so long," laughed Mother, who knew Hollywood from way back. As it turned out she didn't live that long. Sometimes I've wondered if I would. Mother kept saying it comforted her to know that Daddy died thinking he had arranged to take good care of her and spare her financial worries. And she kept on writing herself, and continued her magnificent work on *Guideposts,* and coped with the muddle of his estate.

Everything presented problems. For instance, absolutely no one wanted to buy Sandalwood. It was, after all, idiosyncratic, an ungainly chambered nautilus that fit my father, but that was not sensible or grandiose enough to attract people who had money to spend on large homes. More than anything, I'd have liked to live there, but none of us could hope to earn a living on the Cape. We were torn between wishing the house would sell for Mother's sake, and wishing no one would buy it because we couldn't stand the thought of anyone else living there. Eventually it sold for less money than most modern three bedroom ranches. It was sold to the Franciscans, and is now a priests' retreat, rechristened Quam Bonum—How Good!, the first words of a psalm about brothers dwelling together in love. Franciscans are the only people I can picture there without pangs of jealousy. It pleases me to know that where once moved skeptics and magicians, the holy sacrifice is offered on many altars day after day. I always said Sandalwood had a personality that matched our family. In the end it too joined the Church.

But estate problems multiplied. Only the astute direction of Al Cole and the lawyers kept things on even keel. My father's first wife, to whom he'd paid alimony for more than twenty-five years, brought suit. She seemed to feel alimony should continue after his death until hers. Because of the terms of the original divorce agreements, the dispute was handled by an arbitrator. He awarded her a settlement, and Mother had to borrow from the bank to pay it. A larger loan had to be taken out to pay taxes.

Mother kept looking for ways to cut corners, but like many other women left alone in their older years in the city, she found corners hard to spot. She thought it should be wise to move to a smaller apartment, but smaller apartments are, oddly, rather expensive. The one she had provided some hotel service, which meant she used their sheets and towels. She'd have to buy a small trousseau to set up housekeeping. It all seemed very complicated. Mother was forever making out budgets, trying to see how sometime she might have money to do things close to her heart, including helping Helen and Will and Tony and me, and in particular helping Helen and Will's children to get to college. As long as she could she continued music lessons for one of Helen's daughters, which Daddy had been paying for. It was a pleasant pastime, a sort of solitaire, shuffling the income which might be hers if ever a movie were made, or the copyrights began living up to government expectations, or if some of her own projects paid off. But at the moment it was impossible to get the cash for an urgently needed redecorating job on her apartment.

Still, there was always enough to get by. And Mother and Tony and Martin and I used to giggle over our reputation. We decided the best we could hope for was that people might think us eccentrics who simply liked bargain basements and subways, and affected outdated clothes. I've heard it said you have to be very rich to dare to look shabby. So in a way we kept up the myth of being rich without much effort.

And I was too busy being in a panic about *The Greatest Faith* to worry over other problems. The publishers' news releases had filtered into the hinterland of religious periodicals. While it certainly wasn't headline material, the story about all the work I was going to do kept appearing, and people sent clippings. The attention gave me stage-fright.

I resolved to begin each day's writing with prayer. When I did, the work went well and quickly. When I did not, hours of work would earn me only a full wastebasket.

Working over anyone's manuscript involves intricate questions of style and intent, interpretation, even diplomacy. The trademark of my father's books on Scripture was their enthusiastic acceptance by leaders of all faiths. With the Gospel story this had been difficult to achieve, with the Old Testament less so. But with the early days of Christianity, which involved questions of sacraments, and the Pope, and relations with the Jews, and other prickly points, it would be even more difficult.

I was acutely aware of how little I knew about Catholic lore, Scripture, Theology. I'd been a Catholic only four years.

Our pastor at St. Ignatius then was that deceptive gentle genius, Father Robert Gannon, S.J. One rainy night I confided to him my feeling of inadequacy.

"I feel foolish," I began.

"That's a good sign," he said, eyes twinkling.

I explained that I was frightened because my task required an expert, and I wasn't one.

"You know how little you know," he said, "but no one else really does, except God, so be grateful. Nobody knows all about Theology. We just do the best we can with what we have. Any dead tramp knows more than a live Doctor of Divinity. So that's that. The only time we can get into trouble is when we start taking ourselves too seriously."

He smiled.

"You're a very unlikely expert. I agree. Which is as it should be. Do what he seems to send you to do, in the livery he gives you to wear. But if you're too self-conscious to be a fool for him, he won't give you anything more to do. And for that you'll pay later. Relax. Don't take yourself seriously. And pray."

Added to these technical problems were those of combining writing and mothering. Marty and Mike that fall went to St. David's, a superb private Catholic school, founded by Mrs. Hoguet. They were possibly the only children in the world to have scholarships to nursery school and kindergarten, a kindness done us by Mrs. Hoguet. I wrote while they were in school, wrote while a babysitter watched them in the park on certain afternoons. As pressure mounted, Mrs. Hoguet gave me the use of the library in her home, a haven of silence. Still, when I came home there was the housework, laundry, marketing, and all the rest.

And that fall I discovered we were expecting another child.

The baby was due about the same time that the publishers expected the book.

Yet, with prayer, I worked my way through, surrounded by what seemed to me increasing evidence of God's help and loving concern. The human heart is froward, contrary. I believed God was helping me with a special personal love—yet I couldn't understand why or how such a thing could be. I was still afraid that the reality of God was too good to be true. In a self-made agony I began wondering if I weren't being presumptuous, thinking the Lord, wonderous and loving as he is, would bother about me. It is so desperately hard for human beings to understand about God's love.

I'd come across a book on the technique of mental prayer. Timidly but sincerely, I followed the directions for the first of the formal exercises in that book. The meditation was on God's love of individuals. The special emphasis for the exercise was concentration on the truth: "God loves me."

When I put aside the book with its planned steps for thought, affection, and prayer, and dwelt on that truth, the experience was almost more than I could take. It was inundating.

Giving love to God is only half of the business of religion. The more difficult part comes in being honestly trusting with him. I had been still, like most of us, I suspect, attempting to put up a front to God. I was unconsciously terrified that he might discover that underneath I was a totally helpless, insufficient, profitless servant. Of course, he knew that all the time. I was the one who had to discover the truth about myself and him.

To let yourself be loved by God demands more than natural strength. To be able to accept the incredible intervening personal love of God for you is what religion is about. I imagine that when you completely accept his love, and surrender to it, you have reached the point that puts an end to life on earth.

24

Of Priests, People and Coping

At last *The Greatest Faith Ever Known* was finished.

"God help you when this manuscript gets to the censor," said a worried-looking fellow at the publishers.

"Oh," said I stupidly.

One thing all converts must do, and most born Catholics should do, is learn to cope with priests and hierarchy. They in turn have to learn to cope with the plain people of God, and that's not easy either. Centuries of formidable history, pomp and stereotypes of behavior make a barrier over which it is hard for the people and the mediators to see each other. Some priests have good reasons for mistrusting the laity, having been trained by a generation of other priests who were made nervous by heretics and schismatics, mistakes and aggressiveness. Some priests are taught to be wary of lay groups with opinions, and of children of God who try to do anything more than give money, or attend Holy Name and Rosary Altar meetings. They're sincerely frightened of the laity. And some lay folks are scared stiff of priests. They're annoyingly awed by monsignors, bishops, archbishops and cardinals, and want as little to do with them as possible. Converts usually get caught in the middle. But because we're naïve, enthusiastic, and in the hands of providence, we usually get to meet enough men in Roman collars to form our own opinions, and there we're lucky.

When I was a young girl I read Emily Post cover to cover, memorizing which forks go where, when one removes gloves, and how to introduce an ambassador to a senator over cocktails. With the same gallant impracticality when I became a Catholic I read about Church etiquette so I'd know what to do if I stumbled over a member of the Curia. I was impressed, but confused.

One night I was seated at a banquet beside Monsignor Aloysius Dineen, flamboyant pastor of the Grand Central Station commuters' church, St. Agnes. Msgr. Dineen, a friend of my father's, had recently been made a prothonotary apostolic, which I could hardly pronounce, let alone understand.

Never one to mince words, Msgr. Dineen explained: "A prothonotary apostolic is a mule bishop."

"Ah," I said, in what I hoped was properly reverent tone.

"He can do anything a bishop can do except reproduce his own kind!" Msgr. Dineen returned to his dinner, eyes twinkling. He meant that as a prothonotary apostolic he could perform many functions of a bishop, but he could not ordain priests. He also meant it was time I stopped expecting the hierarchy to be solemn.

Thanks to our cherished friendship with Bishop McDonnell, I'd already come to know first heart essential truths about the priesthood. All men, even atheists, I fancy, accord honor and respect to officials of religion, to rabbis, ministers, priests. But in the Catholic Church a priest is more than an official, he is truly a person who can never again be the same as he was before ordination. In the sacrament of holy orders he receives an irremovable gift from God, the power of acting for Jesus Christ in his role of go-between for human beings and the three-in-one God. Men who became priests are carefully chosen and trained, and once they've been ordained they are priests forever. Whether they are intelligent and gracefilled or bumbling, boring and ungraceful, they are, by virtue of this God-given priesthood, set apart. With this largesse and burden they must live.

God, in ordaining priests through his bishops, does not change their personalities, opinions or mannerisms, because God has, in a real sense, left himself at the mercy of human beings. Unfortunately, many lay people in the past, and many converts today, become confused and wretched because they haven't learned that, while they honor the priesthood and the man who bears it, they must also respond realistically to the human nature of particular priests. And, of course, for outsiders it can be disillusioning and difficult to come up against priests' human ramifications.

The man at the publisher's was quite humanly appalled at the prospect of coping with the ecclesiastical censor, who happened then to be Msgr. John Fearns, now Bishop Fearns. The man at the publisher's had worked chiefly with Protestant books, and Protestants don't have censors or monsignors. Because he was appalled, I decided I should be nervous.

The word "censor" immediately sets up a nasty semantic reaction in any writer and in most readers. But though my writing had never required a censor's eye before, I knew from my father's experience what censorship in the ecclesiastical sense was all about. If a Catholic wants to publish a novel, or a book about cats, politics or history, the Church isn't officially interested. But if a Catholic writes a book involving the explanation of faith and morals, a nonfiction work about the truths entrusted to the Church, the rule is that he must have it read by an appointed representative of a bishop, known as the *censor librorum*. The censor's sole concern is that the writer isn't, knowingly or unknowingly, misrepresenting Catholic truth. The system is, actually, a comforting safeguard for writers, who ordinarily have no wish to teach heresy, but who know that slipshod phrasing or an exuberant literary device may give others a different impression from the one intended. The censor is not a literary expert, isn't the least interested in a writer's style, or even, officially, in his accuracy on any non-theological topic.

My father's books on Scripture had always come out in two editions, one labeled Catholic, the other Protestant. The two editions were precisely identical, word for word. The only difference was that the Catholic one had the *imprimatur* printed in it at the beginning, and the Protestant one didn't. Catholics will not buy a book about Christ or the Bible unless it has the *imprimatur*. Protestants will not buy one if it does. Protestant editions of my father's books, naturally, always sold out first, because Catholics are notorious for not buying books anyway.

The Greatest Faith Ever Known was also to appear in two editions. Some of the Protestant clergymen who read it before publication were distressed by parts that they found offensive and divisive. They reminded me and the publisher that my father had the genius of being ecumenical, and of staying within the area of agreement. Obviously, I lacked the gift. Yet what could I do, to remain faithful to myself and to truth? I couldn't honestly see what so irked these readers, for they seemed disturbed not simply by well-known divergences of point of view, such as the question of whether Peter was the head of the apostles and the Church—but rather by an overall feeling in the manuscript.

To our family friend, Dr. Norman Vincent Peale, I turned for advice. This brilliant Protestant leader had often worked closely with my father, and as founder of *Guideposts* he was Mother's good companion and co-worker. He is also one of the downright pleasantest men I know. I was sure he could show me how to achieve the apparently impossible task of telling the story of Peter and Paul without alienating thousands of good Christians.

In his charming family livingroom in a Fifth Avenue apartment he gave me of his time and wisdom. So often, he explained, dissension rises from a mere matter of words, from conscious or unconscious semantics.

"You knew that, before you entered the Catholic Church," he said, smiling. "But you've forgotten. You've lived among these sounds so long now that you don't remember how they hit ears outside. If you once understand that certain phrases strike up angry overtones in other hearts, your charity will enable you to find other ways of saying the same thing more courteously."

"Show me?"

"In this manuscript, for instance, you have a habit of referring to Mary as the 'Mother of God,'" he said.

"Why not?"

"Let's say that each time you call her that you're reminding other Christians of old wounds. Let me ask you: would you feel you'd seriously compromised your own beliefs if instead here you called her simply the 'Mother of Jesus'?"

Under his expert and tactful guidance, I gradually understood. As a Catholic, I believe that Mary is Jesus' mother, and Jesus is God incarnate, so she is also the chosen mother of God. But some people separate Christ's humanity and divinity. Others consider him to be only human and not divine. They can't understand how any woman could be God's mother, even by God's decree. But we all agree that Mary is the mother of Jesus. It's a lesser phrase, but on it we can meet, and keep within ourselves the understanding we attach to it. In this book I wasn't trying to teach catechism or argue dogma; I was trying to tell the story of the days after the resurrection, to move people to new awareness, to lead them to read Scripture for themselves. Surely it was a small concession to choose words which would let others listen to a story about the Christ whose love we all share. Yet it took insight and patience for Dr. Peale to get this through my thick head.

"When you come to something you feel you must insist on," he advised, "dig in your heels, and stick to the words you must use. But in Christ's name, save the fight for something immediately worth while."

I edited out the trouble-making phrases I didn't deem worth fighting for in this particular project, stood firm on those I did deem important, and the manuscript went to the censor, a minor experiment in ecumenism.

The editor I'd been working with then was, I think, developing ulcers. A Protestant, he was afraid the censor would think I'd watered down the manuscript too much, or that the censor would find lots of mistakes and insist on a whole rewrite. I suggested it might be best if I went and talked to the censor myself, explaining the problems of this book and how I handled them. The editor told me no writer was allowed to talk to a censor, reminded me of the need for ceremony and protocol in the Catholic Church, and scared me out of my wits with gossip about what happened to laymen who dared inquire about the prospects for an *imprimatur*. The book had been incommunicado for what seemed a very long time. I assumed that was because the seminary at which the censor resided was involved in all the extra work of graduation and end-of-term. But the publisher's deadline was approaching.

And so, of course, was the advent of our third child.

That really threw the editor, who figured no woman could juggle a new baby and censor's changes at the same time. I'd practically forgotten about pregnancy while I'd worked, and that had lulled the editor into serenity he now judged false. In the faint hope of spurring the censor on, with little faith in the sympathy of the hierarchy, he informed the censor that I was about to become a mother.

On a hot July afternoon in 1953 our first little girl, Catherine Grace, was born. I had nightmares under anesthesia of an inquisitional demon in modern clerical garb, a censor chasing me down the corridors of Columbia-Presbyterian Medical Center. But holding a beautiful little girl in my arms filled me with joy.

Two days later a priest entered the hospital room, the monster in person. Monsignor John Fearns, gentle, charming scholarly priest as well as censor, had come to talk about the manuscript. We had a glorious laugh together about the notions of him that had been conjured up in my mind and went over the galleys. Actually, as he pointed out later, we found the unofficial censors of the publishing house much more severe and rigid than the ecclesiastical censors, both on the matters they'd expected the Church to disapprove, and on what they themselves disapproved.

Msgr. Fearns had taken the trouble to go far beyond his own official concern to point out to me historical and geographical anachronisms that had escaped the copy editor, and which would have been embarrassing. Complimenting my work, he said jokingly that I should be entitled to a licentiate in theology—a phrase I love because semantically it sounds positively lurid.

"This is a milestone in my career," he explained. "Never before have I worked with an author in the maternity ward. The world is changing."

A few years later, after his name had appeared with the *imprimatur* on several more of my books, I was to have the privilege of witnessing his consecration as a bishop. Meanwhile, I'd found through him one more proof that the official Church, the Church in panoply, dignity and authority, is still made up of fine, often misrepresented, men.

We brought little Cathy home to Marty and Mike, celebrating the final delivery of both baby and book. Miss May McDonnell, sister of Bishop McDonnell, was Cathy's godmother, and Martin's brother Henry her godfather, and our pastor, Father Gannon, who was assisting the bishop, disappeared during the baptism service. We found him telling stories to our little boys on the church steps, the most renowned and loveable babysitter they ever had.

The next thing we knew we were on our way to Portugal.

I'd started leisurely on the children's version of *The Greatest Story*, and we left town for a little vacation, when suddenly we got a phone call offering us one of those wonderful but rare rewards of lucky writers. Ralph Beebe wanted a book done on the shrine of Fatima. If Martin and I would do the book together we could have a trip to Europe almost free. Mother was delighted to have a cute snub-nosed baby girl to fuss over at her place, and a trusted sitter would hold the fort for us, moving in with Marty and Mike at our apartment.

We were to go to Fatima in time for the major anniversary of the appearances of Our Lady there, October 13, the date on which occurred the "miracle of the sun," witnessed and recorded by thousands of believers and agnostics. We knew the more popular facts and legends about Fatima.

Back in 1917, before World War I ended, Mary the Mother of Jesus appeared to three shepherd children in the mountains of Portugal. She confided to them a plea for the world to pray and to turn from sin. In what have since been called the Secrets of Fatima, Mary also entrusted to the children certain messages not then to be made public. One included a vision of hell, emphasizing the reality and damaging effect of sin, the need for prayer and penance. One was a prophecy of the rise of Russia's power, the coming of World War II, and an understanding that war and human suffering were the result of individual personal sins, the refusal of grace. This message, popularly known as The Second Secret, had been revealed by the surviving seer long before the world at large considered Communist Russia a menace. There remained one more message from Our Lady of Fatima, not yet made public. Two of the shepherd children, Jacinta and Francisco, had died while still very young. The third, Lucy, still lived. After many years as an obscure teaching nun, she was now where she'd always wanted to be, in a Carmelite cloister in Coimbra.

In 1953 the song "April in Portugal" was being sung, and with that melody lilting in our ears we dug into hard preliminary research in the month before our departure. We turned for help to Father James Keller of the Christophers. He promised to put us in touch with the most informed expert on Fatima. And thanks to him into our life walked a small tender-voiced Italian-born priest, Father John de Marchi, I.M.C., then superior of the Consolata Society for Foreign Missions in this country. He was to become an integral part of our lives, an unofficially adopted member of the family. But during those formal meetings in which he briefed us on Portugal, Fatima, and the personalities and facts involved, we were aware only of his keen mind, and his immediate knowledge of human and divine nature.

The story of our adventures at the shrine, our personal interview with Lucy, and the gradual penetration of our spirits with the message of peace, Martin and I told in our book *Fatima: Pilgrimage to Peace.* But one of these adventures bears repeating here, for it marked a small milestone in my encounter with the clergy.

At the time of our trip, as later, there was among American Catholics acute curiosity about the so-called Third Secret of Fatima. Lucy was known to have written it down, sealed it, and given it to the Bishop of Leiria, in whose diocese lay Fatima. It was public knowledge that decision had been made to open and read the Secret in 1960, or at Lucy's death, whichever date came first.

Of course, the age of revelation, as far as the Church is concerned, is passed, by which the Church means that heaven's not going to add any new articles to the creed. Or confide to anyone, saint or not, something startling about God, faith, or morals. For this reason and others, no Catholic has to believe in any visions since the death of the evangelist St. John, unless he wants to. It's considered rash, imprudent or impolite, to say you don't believe the appearance of Mary at Lourdes, Beauraing, Pontmain, Fatima or a score of other spots. But ignoring those visions doesn't make you a heretic. Even when the Church has agreed after much investigation that the visionary, such as Bernadette, was a saint; even when the Church officially approves a devotion, such as devotion to Our Lady of Knock, or Our Lady of the Miraculous Medal, and says it's safe to believe in these because they're not opposed to faith or morals, and there's reasonable evidence that the apparitions genuinely occurred, still the Church properly leaves these devotions as sidelines that may or may not appeal to you. You don't absolutely need to say the rosary, though Mary requested it at Lourdes and Fatima, or make the nine first Fridays, to be a good Catholic, let alone get to heaven.

The Church is also aware that people who are saints, or who are, while perhaps not saints, at least judged to have received authentic visions, may have visions which contradict each other in details. St. Paul said it was impossible to put in words his vision of heaven. Human beings report even earthly events in their own ways, because they see and remember and describe things differently. Even saints make mistakes, or, trying to pour the magnificence of spiritual insight into the skimpy vessels of words, adapt truth to terms natural to them and their milieu. One fascinating book takes the visions four very holy people had about Mary's life and tries to combine them into a sort of autobiography. The spirit of the visions is the same. But the anecdotes don't agree.

The Church has been around a long time, and so it is cautiously insistent that the contents of private visions be not taken as gospel truth. The Church officially, and by her nature, doesn't get excited over prophecies, messages or secrets. But people do.

The Fatima story was known in Europe long before it filtered to this country, but by the 1950s interest here in the Third Secret was almost unbearable. One of our tasks as reporters would be to find out whatever we could about it.

In Fatima itself every person, no matter how devout, seemed nearly disinterested in the Third Secret. The solitary, contemplative mood of that shrine and of the hamlets around it conspire to turn the soul from tabloid curiosity toward the unchanging strength and love of God. But our curiosity wasn't totally dimmed.

The Bishop of Leiria granted us an interview. If we had expected the man in charge of this world-famed shrine to live in suitable pomp, we were quickly set straight. He lived in endearing poverty. The ground floor of what was euphemistically called his episcopal palace was given over to other people's shops. His home was a walkup, and we walked up. The door at the top was opened by a young Portuguese maid, barefoot. She ushered us into the one formal parlor, obviously seldom used, then into the Bishop's study.

At first we could hardly find him. The study was a magnificent clutter of books and papers, and the bishop, maneuvering in a wheelchair, was lost to sight. In the Portuguese revolution, when for a time atheistic socialism held the country, he'd been made to stand in a barrel of ice water for days. He'd lost the use of his legs.

We made an odd company, coming to call. Martin and I weren't totally fluent in Portuguese, so to ensure accuracy we brought interpreters from the Consolata seminary founded by Father de Marchi. There was a young seminarian with a thick Scottish accent. He translated our English through his dialect and into Italian. An Italian Consolata priest stationed in Fatima translated again into Portuguese for the bishop. Also with us was Father Ado Trabold, O.S.B., a German home from African missions, who asked his own questions directly in Latin. Our queries traveled the chain from English to Scottish to Italian to Portuguese, the answers coming back along the same route.

Eventually, we got to the Third Secret. Yes, we were told, Lucy had written it down, and it was in the bishop's keeping. Yes, here in this room. We glanced nervously at the unfiled piles of papers and books. What, I asked, if the letter containing the secret were lost, or destroyed, say by fire? Courteously, the bishop reminded me that Lucy could write it down again.

Then, with the help of an English-speaking assistant to the bishop, we learned that the bishop actually had permission to open that Secret and read it at any time. Lucy knew she was no longer bound to secrecy. But, on the other hand, while Mary had let her know the third message could now be revealed, she hadn't specifically said it should, or must. Without special directive from heaven to make the message public, the bishop had decided to wait, and together he and Lucy set up the 1960 date.

If there were any hurry, he explained, heaven would have said so. He didn't care to take immediate action on his own initiative.

His fatherly informality had put us all at ease. Now I couldn't help myself.

"Your Excellency," I said, "if I were you I would open that secret right now."

With impassive faces the chain of interpreters passed that remark along to his excellency. His excellency smiled, a beauteous wide smile, and replied. I watched his answer travel the interlingual route, leaving a wake of smiles. At last it reached me.

"His excellency says: 'My dear child, that is why they don't make women bishops!'"

And the Secret, though opened in 1960, and reportedly given to the Pope, was never made public at all. Presumably because men were handling it.

There is now a new bishop of Leiria, and the one who put me so kindly in my place is dead. My thoughts follow him affectionately whenever I catch myself being an upstart female, making the clergy cope with me.

On the whole, bishops who've been put on the spot coping with me have been remarkably kind. Another bishop settled the problem of my feeling ill at ease over sounding off in the Church once and for all. In this age of renewal, there's naturally talk of anti-clericalism. We, who share the priesthood of the laity, sometimes feel, quite accurately, that we're having problems dealing with priests who are anachronistic, intransigent or just humanly ornery. Years ago at a cocktail party Martin and I founded the Anti-Clerical Society, and Father J. Franklin Ewing, the Jesuit expert on evolution, volunteered as charter member and chaplain. We have fun thinking about such nonsense. Yet any layman, if he thinks about it, realizes that priests must sometimes wish there were an Anti-Laical Society, and in an equivalent spirit of frustration must conspire about ways to cope with us.

At a national convention of the Confraternity of Christian Doctrine held in Buffalo, Martin and I were both to speak. He was to speak on the Christian meaning of sex. I was to talk on the Bible. Between us, we felt, we had the makings of a bestseller.

The convention was crammed with fermenters from all over the nation, and the intellectual excitement made it almost difficult to breathe. Martin's speech went well, and we met that pioneer of Christian sex education, Father Sattler, and I got to meet Sister Madaleva and a pride of other literary lions. Everything was wonderful until time for the panel on which I was to speak.

When I looked at the other speakers, I quailed. Every one of them had a string of degrees. Every one wore a Roman collar or a habit. And again I was wearing a maternity dress. Which is sort of a habit.

I turned to Bishop Waters, moderator of the panel, and with all the decorum I could muster explained that I was going to quit, right now. I was going to sit and listen to all these experts, but never get up and talk.

"But you are an expert," he said. "You just don't know the proper definition of an expert. You qualify, very well."

"Oh?" I asked hopefully.

"An expert," the bishop said solemnly, "is a dope away from home. Now go out there and be an expert, and stop this nonsense."

Never again will I fret over my qualifications to sound off or to cope. My qualifications as an expert have episcopal approval.

25

Holy Cunning

Everything always happens at once, for us or to us. On a small scale, if it's five-thirty and dinner's cooking and a baby's being fed, then that's when the repairman comes for the dishwasher, the phone rings with an important soul hoping to speak to my husband, and kids drop the phone receiver on the floor, a boy comes in with a dogbite, and a missionary priest drops by for supper. If the dryer conks out that'll be the week we're having flu and painting the livingroom, and likely enough there'll be a deadline on a column for me, a political hassle for Martin, and the PTA'll need brownies.

We live in a state of blithering excitement, and at least it's not dull.

As 1954 turned sneakily into 1955 we were on a merry-go-round. Tony, who had definitely grown out of being a kid brother and was now Fulton Oursler, Jr. had married Noel and set up housekeeping. Martin and I had been house-hunting because the fourth baby was on the way. And I'd finished a book for children. For years I seemed incapable of writing a book without also having a baby.

Two days after Tony and Noel's wedding our new little Fulton Thomas was born, named for his grandfather and for Bishop Thomas McDonnell. Once he was baptized there was just time for Christmas shopping before the movers came with estimates.

We'd found a home, and early in January we settled into a simply huge new house in the country. At least, it was huge then, with four bedrooms, living room, dining room, kitchen and study, and only four children. Over the years it seems to have shrunk.

But there it stood, pristine and homey in its acre of unlandscaped frozen mud, our introduction to suburbia. And while we explored our new parish of St. Cecilia, and kindergartens and shopping centers, bought sleds and hid from storm-window salesmen, Mother suddenly took off for Formosa.

Ever since those Shanghai days in the thirties our family had nurtured the friendship of Mme. Chiang Kai-shek by mail and by reunions on her occasional visits to this country. Now Madame Chiang, a deeply spiritual woman, had described to Mother her adventures in faith. In China's darkest hours she had understood the need—and the way—to pray for her enemies. Her life now was swept up in a Christian current. Her enthusiasm had kindled others, so that now there were in Formosa strong fires of faith in action, serious groups of lay Christians meeting for prayer and study.

"Many Christians of the present generation," wrote Madame Chiang, "have become confused, and have lacked the spiritual fire to insist on a better world." She added, "Civilization will advance in proportion to the personal concern, enthusiasm and faith through prayer that we soak into it. Then will be sure victory."

My mother was going to Taiwan to help Madame Chiang set down her message of courage and faith in book form. Mother's own life, since my father's death, had been a daily manifesto of faith. Crippled with emphysema, lungs scarred by pneumonias and hindered by asthma, she required sprays and oxygen tanks daily. Her heart wasn't strong. Her two years of widowhood had been difficult in many ways, ridden with lawsuits, financial emergencies, acute loneliness, and grief.

A joyful woman, filled with hope, she was always generating warm plans for the future. Yet I've never known anyone to meet more disappointment. Her every project for the development of my father's literary estate met with curious hurdles, with delays, with schemes against her and with failures. In her own right she conceived the ideas for several television series, including one based on our "Genius for Living" column, and one a combination of fashion, merchandising, New York history, general documentary and current interest, to be called "Fifth Avenue." They didn't click. She worked on a novel, her first in many years, whose heroine, Dorcas, died for a few moments and was restored to life by medical skill. The novel wouldn't, apparently, let itself be written. She wrote and sold magazine articles to major markets, only to wait in vain to see them published, a frustration with which only writers perhaps can sympathize, knowing cash payment isn't enough.

She had her successes, too. She succeeded in having published a collection of my father's articles, called *Lights Along the Shore*. In the years since she had become editor, the circulation of *Guideposts* had jumped from 25,000 to 300,000, and unquestionably her work there had left lasting impact. So firm was her reputation that the New York *Herald Tribune* approached her about the possibility of serving as their religious editor.

Less significant to others, but an accomplishment she was justly proud of, was the publication of thousands of copies of a small prayer she wrote, the Prayer of a Wife and Mother to St. Raphael, Archangel. Not even my father ever had the *imprimatur* put on a prayer!

She prayed constantly. And she prayed about the acute sadness she knew in those two years.

In the midst of all this she decided to go to Formosa. As the doctor said, it was patently ridiculous for her to make the trip. She went, oxygen and all, scarcely worrying about the discomforts and dangers of the journey, because she wanted to see Mme. Chiang's book in print, hoping that testament of faith might inspire others in true work for peace. All her married life she'd accustomed herself to accept my father's direction, plans, initiative. Left alone, she'd found it difficult to remember how to dominate herself. But this woman who had triumphed over alcoholism and was living proof of the power of grace, hadn't lost her zest for seizing the moment, or her belief that if you love God everything comes out all right. She returned from the East tired but triumphant.

Some time before, Martin had left the district attorney's office. His private practice was absorbing time and attention. I was sketching out *The Book of God*, a retelling of the Old Testament for young people. And then, so swiftly that I almost burned the manuscript I'd just started, out came the maternity dresses again.

And, as if that weren't enough, I nearly lost my faith. Or thought I would.

"Irish twins," they call them, when you have two babies less than a year apart. I've written a novel about a young Catholic couple facing a crisis over having too many babies, and their story, *Water in the Wine*, isn't my story, and the heroine of that book, Jane, isn't I. Jane was tempted to the sin of practicing artificial birth control. I wasn't. But the knowledge that I was again with child threw me into confronting temptation against faith.

Everyone with half a mind has to battle to keep faith. Some maintain a conspiracy of silence about these battles, as if the nearness of disbelief were a shameful thing, which only makes it harder for them and for others to come through whole. Once I scandalized a teaching nun by talking freely with our fifth-grader about doubts. In catechism he learned that one of the Spiritual Works of Mercy is to "counsel the doubtful." He knew there were atheists, pagans, agnostics in the world. But no Christian ever doubts the catechism or creed, he said primly. Wrong, said I, we all have doubts sometimes. If we didn't, how would we know we had faith? When he was sure I was leveling with him, his face relaxed in an almost incredulous smile of relief.

Being a sensible fellow, he had more than once found the thought occurring to him during Mass that perhaps nothing at all really happened to the bread and wine. Maybe all he'd been taught by us was a pleasant but far-fetched tale. Being a cautious fellow, he'd decided not to mention these doubts to anyone, even after they passed.

"I thought no one else ever had thoughts like that," he said.

Many experienced teachers believe it's wrong to mention the possibility of doubts to people, no matter how old they are. To me it seems that silence is the best rooting medium for the more virulent forms of disbelief. Let a youngster get the idea that no one else has been smart enough to have questions or misgivings about a doctrine, and he may decide that he's smarter than anyone else, too smart to remain in the Church.

You don't have a virtue of any kind until you've had the chance not to have it. You don't have hope as a virtue until you've had something to despair over. You have not charity unless you've fought the temptation to un-love in your own soul. Faith, which is a gift, is also a virtue, to be occasionally practiced against strong odds. As I see it, God makes sure we each privately get the chance to develop and test these virtues over and over again.

The points of crisis aren't always dramatic, and, like the straw on the poor camel's back, are usually indistinguishable from a million other incidents.

Mine came, as I said, because an Irish twin was coming. Yet it wasn't the question of birth control that got me. And it wasn't that I didn't want this particular child. I knew intellectually my way around all the teachings about love, marriage and babies. And I wasn't emotionally rejecting the unborn child, or anything nice and psychological like that. Pregnancy wasn't the efficient cause of my plunge into the mêlée of darkness. It was merely the occasion. The pattern of soul-life's growth is as well-charted and normed as the patterns of growth in children. It was time for me to leave the pleasant well-lit comfort of infancy and walk by myself in the dark for a while. Only nobody had ever told me about such patterns then. I'd read about what mystics called the dark night of the soul, but what I'd read convinced me this was a rare experience reserved to those who were markedly holy, and so had nothing to do with me. Yet there was a darkness. And, for several months, no guide.

How does it begin, this walk in the dark? It is painful even to remember. It begins with pain, overflowing from the spirit, pervading you. Because you cannot localize the pain of the soul, cannot finger or soothe it, and most of all because in our social climate it is utterly embarrassing to talk about it, the sufferer ordinarily looks for other explanations.

At first I avoided the phantom of anti-faith. Nothing in life seemed worth doing, yet I drove myself to small busy-nesses because I was afraid. An instant's silence, a time of not-thinking a time to try to pray, these would open the window to an almost tangible presence, a presence which, like the high-pitched whine of an insect, did not abate and could not be escaped. A presence that seemed to try to grab me and force me to look at the world with its eyes, and see it godless and lifeless. Understand me, please. I did not see a phantom, nor think there was one to be seen. Rather I was trying not to admit a thought-presence that was trying to be an obsession. When I tried to explain that to myself, I decided I really was insane.

At last I spoke to a priest, Father John McGrath. I attempted, inadequately, to tell him what ailed me. With rare humility, he insisted he couldn't help me but would give me introduction to someone who could. The someone was a Franciscan from Ireland, Father Marius McAuliffe, who had worked all over the world and now was at the monastery in New Canaan, just down the street from our home. A man deceptively given to small jokes, praise of Ireland, and a pipe, Father Marius was in this country assigned to teach seminarians mystical theology, a subject until recently ignored by self-respecting seminaries. Years before, as a young man beginning his career as a priest, he'd fallen so ill that he had been anointed and left to die. He believes Our Lady herself gave him back his life, and he dedicated it to her service. Between teaching at a Franciscan seminary, preaching missions and novenas, he had time to spend on the needy in spirit.

From the edifying tales I'd heard of him, and from what I knew of myself, I half-expected we'd hate each other. I went back time and time again, knowing that through this man I heard the voice of total sanity, the view of an out-of-joint world, seen in the light of faith, that made sense.

A man of many faces, a serious student of psychiatry as well as of spirituality, he used with me the face of a peasant, an anti-intellectual, deliberately irritating me.

"I've written books," he said, showing me some published volumes. "That was before I knew better. One day I burned all my unpublished stuff and promised myself never to waste time on that nonsense again."

And, "You think too much," he said. "Having a mind can be a terrible cross."

And, "I hope I can make you a child again," he said. "A child doesn't pretend to be an intellectual. A child doesn't think too much. And a child loves himself enough to let others, including God, love him."

"Look, Father," I explained, "my whole life has been centered on growing up . . ."

"That's a pity."

". . . and on learning to think, and to write. I don't want to be a child, or an idiot, and I'm sure God didn't intend me to be. I'll have to save my soul the way I am."

"You can't do it." He puffed on his pipe.

"But I've got to." How often he was to exasperate me before I understood. "That's what life is for. The one thing I have to do is find out how to save my soul."

"You can't save your soul. Only Christ can. And you're not giving him a chance." He chuckled.

"You're just playing with words, Father. Of course, Christ saves us, but the old argument about faith and works just . . ."

"Some people have to be told to use their heads, study, and split hairs, but you're not one of them. You do that naturally. You have to be told to put your head to sleep and listen to your heart. Listen to yourself now. You know, way inside, that you'll never in a hundred years make yourself a saint. But you're ashamed to let God catch you out. You don't even want the Lord to know you're in need of redeeming, so you're trying to keep the door closed on him till you smarten up a bit. Like a woman cleaning house before the cleaning woman comes. Or a man who waits till he's less sick and disgusting before calling a doctor to tend his gangrene."

"But everyone tells us to save our souls, cultivate virtues, fight our faults. We can't just sit back and let God make us holy. You sound, forgive me, like a heretic, Father."

"It won't be the first time." He smiled. "You'll have to trust me. I'm not really preaching quietism, or salvation through faith without works, or any of that. I'm simply telling you what you need to know. We're all of us a bit off balance one way or the other. There are people who must be urged to know and serve God, and there are those who must find out how to love him instead. If we who give counsel can't tell the difference between kinds of people, and if we tell everyone the same thing, we're not very good shepherds, are we."

At home everything was outwardly as always. The laundry, the new book to be written, evenings with friends, the old maternity bathing suit, the children, and Martin being the same amazingly patient husband and father. The drama was all hidden inside, and life went on. I could not pray. Yet I could not look out the window, or pause with a cup in my hand, without thinking of God. And the thought of God came always in reverse: not "God is, thank God" —but "Maybe God isn't, so beware."

The temptation to suicide must be somewhat like this. To me then it seemed the simplest, most efficient way out would be to say once and for all: "You're right, it's nonsense, there is no God. No Christ. No trinity. No nothing." Like a man near derangement from pain I craved surcease, surrender. To fight this I'd compel myself to repeat the Apostles' Creed, word by grudging word.

"It doesn't make sense," I told Father Marius. "I know inside me that I don't doubt. If I really weren't sure about God I'd want to follow up those ideas and take them seriously. But if I don't really wonder whether to give up religion, why do I feel like this?"

"See? You're not even a very clever thinker after all." He winked. "How about temptations in the flesh, you understand them?" You know that if a man or woman is sexually aroused or attracted by someone else, that doesn't automatically mean he or she wants to be? A young boy haunted by impure thoughts isn't impure, he is tempted, right? If you'd really lost interest in God, you wouldn't be this intensely distressed. The devil just wants to batter down the citadel of your will, and God's quite willing to let him try, so you can grow stronger."

Through the months this priest's counsel ran like an antiphon. He would digress, to tell of the old days at Adam and Eve's in Dublin, of nuns he'd chaplained in Australia, of his indignation at the loose upbringing American parents gave young girls. At times he could be positively boring when he described the lyrical and moral perfections of life in Ireland. But I began to discern the wisdom hid with holy cunning under his gibes at intellectuals. This man at this time was the one intellectual who could help me.

One day I told a friend a bit about my talks with him.

"Oh, my God, you've gone and gotten yourself a spiritual director! How snobbish can you get, my dear?"

Until a year before, the only folks I knew of who had a spiritual director were either dead and canonized, or living and odd. It hadn't occurred to me that Father Marius was being my spiritual director because that was something I didn't want to have.

"It sounds as if I'm taking myself much too seriously," I protested to him.

"Stuff and nonsense. 'Tis the old American heresy at work. Scared stiff of taking God seriously. In this country priests are kept so busy raising money and building what they call plants that they've no time for souls and spirits. So people get to thinking themselves addled for wanting to be holy.

"The ideal thing would be for everyone to have a spiritual director, at least for some time in their lives. But there aren't enough priests, so God takes care of seeing two people meet at the right time. If it makes you nervous, don't call me a spiritual director. I'm just an old Irish priest who makes you mad. Fair enough?"

Slowly he led me to understand some things which ailed me.
I'd heard Christ's words: "Be you perfect." I hadn't been able to
make myself perfect, and thought it was up to me to do it all by
myself, and so I was in a mess. We began there. We went on to
unfamiliar lessons: penetrating a prayer by Cardinal Merry del Val
called the Litany of Humility, the saying of which goes like a chalk-
screech against the grain of the self-sufficient spirit; a willingness to
pray without written prayers, without even trying to say anything,
but rather waiting, being present, opening oneself to God; a reading of books which altered my life, Boylan's *This Tremendous
Lover,* and *The Virtue of Trust,* by the Jesuit de Jaegher.

One thought in de Jaegher's book startled me. When God asks
you, by circumstance and providence, to take on a certain task, said
Father de Jaegher, he doesn't ask or guarantee that you succeed.
Obvious, perhaps. Yet I had somehow absorbed the notion that if I
were doing what God wanted, I'd naturally do it well as long as I
tried hard. He wanted me to be Martin's wife. To be mother of our
four and a half children. To write. Ergo, I should be a charming,
stable, infinitely loving wife; a wise, helpful, patient, happy
mother; and a good writer. The writing didn't seem to me to be
going too badly. But as a valiant woman, homemaker, heart-of-the-
family, I was edgy, inconsistent, an imperfect flop whose lungpower
was beginning to equal a fishwife's.

"God didn't ask you to succeed. He invited you to try your
best," said my guide. "Failure can be a real advantage. You tell me
about your friend with the one child who's always calm and
patient. Poor soul, she doesn't know yet whether she has a bad
temper or not. God put you in a situation where you know darn
well you have one. Good for the humility."

As we edged slowly forward, the darkness lifted a bit. Then, as
if to reassure me I didn't have time for exaggerated introspection,
into our lives came one of the most unusual houseguests we ever
had, Father Maggioni, IMC. Martin and I had met him in the
Consolata house at Fatima where, in black beret and shiny glasses,

he'd graciously been our guide. Now we could repay his hospitality. He needed a place to stay until arrangements were completed for his return to Europe.

He camped in our living room, a graceful unobtrusive new member of the family, exhausted from his travels, glad for the chance to be among children. The first evening we offered him a drink. He explained that personally he never touched spirits. The next morning after he said Mass I set a specially elegant breakfast for him: the sterling silver, apple juice in a delicate glass, toast wrapped in those little embroidered linen things nuns sell to raise money. He enjoyed it, but he left the juice in discreet silence. Not for a while did we learn that he thought the liquid in that elegant glass must be sherry. He hadn't want to seem rude by letting us know he knew we were debauched enough to have sherry for breakfast.

By this time we were fairly unself-conscious about having priests in the house, and friends no longer felt they must put on Rosary-Altar manners before coming to the door. Yet this time I heard a stranger refer to me as "that woman who comes to daily Mass and brings her own priest," which, since it sounds a bit like bringing your own bottle, tickles me.

The knack of holy cunning we learned from Father Maggioni. Because he'd spent several years in Fatima, he was naturally eager to spread devotion to Our Lady of Fatima, encourage people to pray the rosary, and offer Masses and meditation, as Our Lady asked, on the first Saturday of each month.

"In your parish you don't have special First Saturday Masses," observed Father Maggioni. "You make a fuss over First Fridays for the Sacred Heart of Jesus. Why not for the Saturdays and the Immaculate Heart of Mary?"

Our pastor then was a superbly genial and gently spiritual soul, Father Myron Miller, who was caught up in the rat race of having to spend a million bucks to build a new church and school because of the beanstalk growth of his suburban parish. I truly loved Father Miller, and over the years benefited greatly from his holy shepherding. But he wasn't at all anxious to have First Saturday Masses for Fatima. He wanted Martin and me to lecture about Fatima to parish groups, and we did. He urged people to read our book. But no dice on First Saturdays.

"First things first," he'd say to me. "Saturday's the one morning most people can get to a weekday Mass. People want Masses offered for their dead. They prefer Saturdays. First things first."

This I explained to Father Maggioni. "I did my best," I said. "He's the pastor. You can't buck city hall."

Once that idiom was made clear, Father Maggioni smiled. "You can always buck city hall," he said. "All you need is holy cunning. Once a famous saint wanted to start an order of nuns who wouldn't stay cloistered, but would go out to work in the world among the sick and poor. What you call this city hall said all nuns must be cloistered and stay put. So he started his group, and called it an Institute, not a sisterhood. And he told the women not to call themselves nuns. So everything worked fine. That is holy cunning. Find out what the first things are that must be first, and work around them."

So I did. And I said to myself that if I were a pastor hard-pressed, getting old before my time with the horrid business of fund-raising, contracting, and paying bills, I'd not blame myself for feeling that assistant priests needed all the stipends they could get. So I checked our calendar for the dates of each First Saturday in the coming year. Then I went to Father Miller and said I wanted to arrange for a Mass to be offered on such and such a date. The date was still open, so I reserved it, and gave in my stipend. Then I took the next month's date, and so on. Gravely Father Miller recorded that I wanted a Votive Mass of Our Lady said instead of a requiem on these dates, for which I'd make the usual offering. And that was how it came about that we had First Saturday Masses in our parish, by putting first things first. And instead of getting mad or frustrated by obstacles, I'd learned the knack of holy cunning, which is as important as a sense of humor in this hybrid divine-human organism called the Church.

But holy cunning is not a one-way street. Heaven too is crafty. A good part of the fun in eternity will be looking back at the drama of life from behind scenes, seeing how effects were staged. Was it because of the Masses I wangled that the darkness lifted? Probably not. Everyone was helping me pull through: husband, children, priest. Perhaps the children most of all, irresistible and amazing, endearing and annoyingly alive. They gathered fireflies in milk bottles to shine in darkened rooms. They fished in the creek, skinned their knees, stepped on rusty nails, ate jar after jar of peanut butter, fought, sang and giggled. It is happily difficult to remain self-centered in a house full of youngsters. If you're too sane, they're bound to drive you mad. But if you're a bit crazy to start with, they'll not give you time to go the rest of the way.

Along about August I was reminded that I was meant to be writing an adaptation of the Old Testament for young people. The research was done, and the work wasn't, because I'd been wandering for months in a dual world in and out of time, between the diapers and my visits with Father Marius. I wasn't sure the publishers had mastered the art of serenity, and we needed the payment for the finished manuscript, so with holy cunning, childlike humility, and a dab of worldly desperation, I answered their queries by saying that of course the book was nearly done, and sat down to begin it.

Somehow, in one month of thirty-one days, I wrote the manuscript of *The Book of God,* from the Garden of Eden to the last of the prophets, one of the longest scripts I'd ever done. When the work was finished, and the traditional family celebration of "Mom's finished a book" had been held with double chocolate frosteds and Scotch, the first golden coins fell from the birches, and the darkness of my second world had lifted.

On All Souls Day, November 2, 1955, the fifth Armstrong was born, a handsome big boy we named Caedmon.

We had discovered Saint Caedmon back in the days when I was working on the lives of saints, and had privately designated him patron of all Bible-popularizers, invoking him whenever I got all balled up writing a book. Caedmon had been, according to the legend, a laborer in the famed abbey of Whitby, when St. Hilda was abbess. In those days it was the custom for all to gather in the great dining hall after meals and pass the harp around and sing ballads. But Caedmon was the kind of dope who couldn't make up a verse to any ballad, couldn't even recite or sing something everyone else knew. So he'd go back to the hayloft where he slept, a patient, lonely, humble man. Then one night an angel appeared to him and said:

"Caedmon, sing me a song of creation!"

Caedmon explained to the angel that he had the wrong guy, but the angel insisted. Obediently, Caedmon opened his mouth, and out came verse after verse of the story of Genesis in minstrelsy. Next morning Caedmon went to St. Hilda, told her what happened, and then spent the rest of his life putting Bible stories into ballad form, making them accessible to people who couldn't read or write, but whose popular literature was sung to a harp. Today Caedmon's work is in the beginning of most reputable texts of English poetry.

To Bishop McDonnell we explained that we wanted to give the baby a nice middle name, so that in case he grew up just hating having an unusual one like Caedmon, he'd have something to fall back on. We asked him to suggest a name.

After grave consideration he said, "Call him Eugene."

"Eugene?"

"After the Pope," explained the bishop. "Eugene Pacelli he was, before he was Pius XII."

That seemed a pleasant idea, so we named the child Caedmon Eugene. A few days later the bishop's sisters visited me in the hospital, and asked what the baby was named. I told them, explaining about the Caedmon part.

"But his middle name is Eugene?" they repeated.

"Yes. Your brother suggested it," I began, intending to go on about the Pope. But they interrupted me.

"Isn't that the nicest thing you could have done! For so very long we wanted a baby named Eugene. That was our dear father's name, and since we never married and had children, it seemed we'd never get to see anyone named after him. Now you've done it for us. How thoughtful! Wasn't it like our brother to suggest that!"

Ah yes. And with holy cunning I kept from laughing, too.

26

"Bless Me, Bless Me . . ."

I'd come into New York to have this baby, not because I mistrusted Stamford hospitals, but because it's hard to separate a woman from her obstetrician. Besides, since Martin worked in New York, and his mother and mine both lived there, it was more convenient all around. By now it was old home week for me at Harkness Pavilion. Then one morning Mother set out to come to see me and never got there.

She was standing in the lobby of her apartment hotel. She was turning from the desk when a little boy who had been wildly playing around in the lobby ran into her. She lost her balance on her high heels and fell. Somehow she got back up to her apartment and into bed. She insisted nothing serious was wrong. But somehow I knew then this was no passing thing. I wept for hours. Everyone said it was just post-baby blues.

Usually each baby in a large family is better behaved and easier to handle than the last, as if heaven takes pity and lets mothers get more sleep as the years go by. Caedmon Eugene was a good baby. The doctors kept insisting my mother was getting along well, so I did what came to hand and tried not to worry. We brought Caedmon home, and I began getting back in the swing with Marty and Michael and Cathy and Fulton, finding those little things like potato peelers and knee socks that always are mislaid when a mother's not home, and getting my strength back. But when Caedmon was two weeks old I realized Mother was not doing well at all. Then began a blurred nightmare of commuting to New York as a child to comfort my own mother, and back to Stamford at night to reverse the roles and comfort my children.

Complications were setting in with her circulatory and respiratory systems. Certain drugs given to ease the pain had a frightening effect. Most alcoholics are unable to tolerate barbiturates, and for Mother a phenobarbitol pill, or even a substitute for barbiturates, would have many of the same results as a double shot of whisky. After two such experiences she decided it was better to put up with pain and keep her clarity of thought.

Tony and Noel also had a new baby, their first, dainty little Theresa, a month older than Caedmon. All of us were constantly in and out of the apartment, at first believing, as the doctors expected, that we were cheering Mother in her convalescence. But as weeks passed, we knew death was coming. The first copy of *The Sure Victory*, the Mme. Chiang book, arrived. Mother had it set up where she could see it, and called it her valedictory.

Some people said to us later they thought Mother hadn't wanted to live. Yet for a month before her fall the apartment had been overrun with workmen as rugs were laid, paint and wallpaper applied, bookcases built. Redecoration had been completed just in time for her to lie in bed. She had intended to live, even though she may not have cared to face more years of widowhood.

Many writers find it easier to speak from the heart to God by writing out our private prayers. Most of us tear up these meditations lest someone, finding them, be embarrassed, or else we cache them somewhere, and then forget where we put them. One of Mother's I found under her typewriter where she'd tucked it three months before, in the early fall, when, after a time of discouragement, she had turned again to work.

She had asked the Lord to let her write as never before, to show her what to write. She asked for happy work to do, for strength, and quiet time to think. She ended:

Forgive me my sins, of omission and of weakness.
Bless me, bless me, bless me.

Yet she was ready to die now. Resigned is the word people often use, but Mother wasn't resigned, wasn't making the best of a bad bargain. She believed in heaven. Anyone who really believes in heaven is too excited to be resigned to the prospect of going there.

Phlebitis, bronchitis, heart weakness, pneumonia. One night she was so weak the doctor didn't expect her to last till morning. She said good-bye to us all. But she woke up in the morning. And do you know, I never saw anyone more sweetly but definitely disappointed? She had had her face all fixed for heaven, she said, and now she still had to wait some more.

"I'm sorry to be taking so long about it," she apologized. Then seriously she mused, "I wonder who I shall see first after death?"

I couldn't hide the tears in my eyes. After a moment I spoke. "Did you know," I said lightly, "that Father Marius when he came to see you said your way of preparing for death was edifying?"

"Edifying?" She blinked. "Fancy that now. After all these muddled years, I'm edifying at last."

These weeks wore a film of unreality. Sudden death, such as my father's, is more kind. For those who love the one who is going, the waiting time for death is made more difficult because ordinary tasks seem stupid in relation to imminent entrance into eternity. Yet ordinary tasks must be done. We had then a wonderful woman, Mrs. Lotte Bauer, who came to help us, an incredible smiling bundle of energy, who cleaned and tended babies and big children, and made gorgeous German pancakes. But there are still things you must do yourself, if you are to feel rooted in your own home. And I'd ask Lotte, or neighbors who kindly babysat at night, to try to leave little Caedmon's last bottle for me to give, so I could hold that tiny package of life when I came away from the room where life was ebbing.

I came home and played with Fulton in his playpen, and Cathy who was building vast villages of blocks, and looked at the drawings Mike brought home from kindergarten, and called for Marty when school ended for first-graders. Then the phone rang, and the doctor summoned us back to New York.

Soon the woman who was my mother lay under an oxygen tent while life and death struggled within the body. The bed that had been my father's was gone from the room. And I thought of what it must be to know widowhood, to die without the one you loved most, but to be certain that you will find him in Christ on the other side of death. My mother and father, in season and out, had lived a love story that plumbed depths and remounted the heights. In her journal Mother had placed a few sheets from a pad of pink paper, the one poem of her mature life, untitled reflections of a woman left alone, which I would find years later.

No one wants to enter me now
And it is as well.
I have been populated with love
So many times for so many years.
He used to quote so often
   Come live with me and be my love . . .
And whisper
   And we will all the pleasures prove.
One, only one, who lived with me.
Two dear ones who lived in me.
Every so often it dazes to be unpossessed.

At times it becomes a spell of deep chill
And the baffling dusk of day's end when nothing is clear
And that spell is a fungus hard to throw off.

What is most keen
Is the lack of an arm around you,
An arm about your shoulder,
Arms that reach and catch you close
Holding you and holding to you.

A hand that pressures comfort and courage,
That speaks with mute pride,
Or the playful hand; and the tender pushing back the hair.
The hand that reaches out and locks one's own
Between the beds—the last waking moments.

Martin and I, Tony and his Noel, prayed and sat and waited, somewhere outside of time, in a courtyard of suspension and powerless love. But I think that someone reached out and held her hand the last waking moments.

She died. It was finished. And when what had to be done was done, we walked out into the brilliant splendor of a New York Christmas. I'd forgotten it was nearly time for Santa Claus. We walked past F. A. O. Schwarz toy store to reach the parking lot. The window was filled with gorgeously exaggerated Steiff stuffed animals, a giraffe taller than I, a smiling donkey. I did not even know the date. It was December 16. Nine days till Christmas. Nine days makes a novena. And at home are five children whose grandmother wouldn't want her death to interfere with their Christmas joy. She lived Christmas, centered months on planning for it, savoring every happy surprise she could contrive to give others. She'd die if she thought—no, she wouldn't. She had died. And I must make Christmas come true. Her bedroom closet was stuffed with presents for us and for the children. She'd said they must be opened in gladness.

We drove home in silence.

I welcomed the hugs and kisses of the children. But one of our children, one I'd thought old enough to care, didn't even turn from the television to say hello. My feelings were hurt, and I grew angry. He answered my questions in monosyllables. Yes, Father Miller had told him my mother died. Yes, he understood. Sure, he felt bad about it.

It can be a shock, the first time you discover your children are human, with the same inhibitions and perplexities you have. He was old enough to care. Just old enough to care so much that he didn't know what the heck to say or do. And, by what some might call chance, at that moment I remembered a time when I was little, and my mother had turned on me with hurt and anger, asking if I didn't care. I couldn't explain to her then that I cared so deeply that I was numb and paralyzed. I could only stare at her with dead eyes, and my child stared at me now. Remembering, I put out my arms, and the child came to me, and numbness melted. And I wondered then, as often since, if in the chains of generations, atonement is not often made in just this way. Mother hadn't always understood me, and I'd hurt her because she didn't understand me, but now that she is gone I find it easier to understand and not be hurt by nor hurt those who call me Mother.

For the past week neighbors had come to help out in my absence, to cheer up the children, to do what they could. A friend had offered to take the little ones to see Santa Claus. One had refused. I'd been told of that, but there hadn't been time to try to decipher why. Now suddenly I understood. He'd been too unhappy to go.

"But today I went," he said seriously. "I said I wanted to go, so she took me. And I got in line and I saw him."

"What did you ask for?"

"I didn't ask for anything. I just told him your mother died. I figured he ought to know."

God bless the department store Santa who received that confidence with the dignity it deserved.

27

Sister Teresa

I became a sister in religion a bit irregularly, without preparation, as an old married woman with five kids. I knelt on the library floor

in the friary and Father Marius made me a novice in the Third
Order of St. Francis.

I'd first heard of the order from that Franciscan scholar and
director of secular institutes, Father Stephen Hartdegen, while we
were all at the Confraternity Convention in Buffalo. Martin and I
had played hookey one afternoon to visit Niagara Falls with a number of priests, including Father Stephen. Because of my inborn over-
powering love of water in motion, in ocean or river or fall, Niagara
drew me like a magnet. Father Stephen has the same addiction, and
more courage. He was leaping from rock to crag along the river
above the falls. And, shouting over the roar of the waters he told
me that in a way this spot reminded him of Alvernia, where St.
Francis received the stigmata. The setting is radically different, but
the feeling of being close to the whirlpool of creation is the same.

"How come you're not a tertiary?" cried Father Stephen.

I was holding Martin's hand, trying desperately to follow him
over the crashing white river, while Father Stephen, stunned at my
ignorance, explained what a tertiary was. Martin, having been
trained by the Marist Brothers and the Benedictines, wasn't about
to take on the Franciscan mystique as well. But I listened
fascinated, while, holding to a tree on the bank above the green
current further upstream, Father Stephen shouted out a word-pic-
ture of Franciscanism. He told of the Christ-centered way of loving
God and of understanding the universe, which is the heart of St.
Francis' teaching, and told of the Third Order for lay people which
the beggar-saint founded, as if this were the most natural place in
the world for a lesson. In a way it was.

It was years later that Father Marius threw the same question
at me, "How come you're not a tertiary?"

Not many people know what it means to be a tertiary, a member of the Third Order of St. Francis, and those who have at least
heard of the outfit usually have it pegged wrong. The Happy Death
Society, some used to call it, because for a while mostly old ladies
belonged to it in this country. The Holier-than-Thou Society was
what I suspected it might be. An admirable but impossible group of

souls who should have been in a convent or monastery and were making do with second-best. It's not that at all.

St. Francis of Assisi started it. And it's a funny thing about him. Before I entered the Church I never thought of St. Francis as a Catholic. I loved him, I'd read *The Little Flowers of St. Francis*, that charming quaint collection of biographical legends, knew about Francis and the wolf, Francis and the birds. Vaguely I thought of St. Francis as being, at least in spirit, the first Protestant. A rebel, an *authentic* soul, whom even Pope and cardinals couldn't stifle. Well, reformer he was, but one who bored from within with the drill of loyal love.

In his last testament he exacted three things of his followers: love, faith and submission to Church and clergy. He lived in a time when the Church was not all she should be, a time when sincere souls complained bitterly of abuses of faith and morals, when many priests gave scandal. Yet in his own writings, few as they are, is constant testimony of the saint's intense insistence on remaining an ardent son of the Church, and having all who followed him give honor and respect to all priests, admirable in conduct or not. A realist, Francis was a man chosen by God to "rebuild" the Church, in a movement with the same *aggiornaménto* spirit today permeating the Church. His forthright, almost primitive adherence to the Gospels as a rule of life, his choice of poverty as a bride, his gaiety, his delight in God and life, drew hundreds to follow him. Francis went to the Pope to have his first order, for friars, and his second order, for nuns, approved, along with his way of life. The Pope was less than impressed. He found Francis uncouth, ridiculous, mad and a bit smelly, and said so. Francis was not moved to bitterness or rebellion. Patiently he waited, unwilling to continue without formal approval. And God sent the Pope a dream in which the little troubador beggar from Assisi kept the Church from collapse and ruin. So the Pope sent for Francis and gave him approval.

He started the third order for people who instead of the vocation to altar, monastery or convent, had the vocation to live for

God in the world. For the married and the single, young and old, he established the first religious order in history for the laity, recognizing the dignity and glory of all baptized souls.

Third orders—for there are now third orders other than that of St. Francis—are genuine religious orders, quite different from pious societies such as the Holy Name, or the Knights of Columbus. The Third Order of St. Francis is a religious order in which the world is the cloister for its brothers and sisters. Tertiaries wear a religious habit, a scapular around the neck and over the shoulders, a small white cord knotted around the waist. This is worn under normal clothes. The cord isn't disciplinary or uncomfortable; thin and soft, it serves merely as an unobtrusive reminder to the tertiary of membership in a religious order. The fact that the habit is unseen has led some of us to call the order Franciscans Anonymous. Outwardly we're the same as we've always been. The change in us is where it cannot be seen.

Father Marius gave me my habit, and with it a new name to mark my new life in religion. He named me Sister Teresa, after the saint from Avila whose feast is on my birthday. Frankly, I was scared to let people know I'd joined the order. Father Marius gave me a book called *The Tertionaries' Companion*, and on the flyleaf in the proper place he inscribed the date of my reception as a novice, and my name in religion. I hung on to that book for dear life, not out of piety, but out of a horror that someone might find it, read the inscription, and embarrass me forever.

Of course, Martin knew my deep dark secret, because a wife needs her husband's permission to enter the order.

"If I wanted to be mean, I'd say at last an impossible dream came true," he said. "Now I'm married to a nun. Sister Teresa is the mother of my children."

The children grew up knowing I was a Sister Teresa over at the friary, but because they also knew Sister Maria who has three kids, Sister Philomena with her nine, and Brother Pius and Sister Francis who together have eight, they didn't think it odd. They came with me to the friary, and some intend to become tertiaries themselves when they're old enough. Gradually I overcame self-consciousness.

Like all religious orders, ours has a time of postulancy and novitiate before profession. We take no vows, make no promises that bind under pain of sin. St. Francis felt there were enough ways to commit sin already without his adding any more. The first and second orders take vows of poverty, chastity and obedience. We don't. We do promise before heaven to live according to our rule, which is based on the Gospel, and spells out for us the need to practice the spirit of poverty, the spirit of chastity and the spirit of obedience in our own walks of life. Chastity, poverty and obedience in marriage, or in the single life in the world, are naturally different from the same virtues as practiced in priesthood or cloister, but supernaturally they are the same.

Our rule requires and gives us the privilege of reciting a daily office. The office, the work, of a priest is primarily to praise God. Every Christian's work is to offer the sacrifice of praise to God. The Church assigns priests a particular office, or breviary, a collection of psalms and other prayers to be said daily in the name of the whole Church. The tertiary's office has the same purpose. We pray daily the name of all God's children, a work of praise.

Like all religious orders, ours is formed with a community life. Professed members are grouped into local fraternities, meeting monthly for prayer, conferences and recreation. Each fraternity has a prefect and other officers, including a master or mistress of novices. Fraternities are gathered into provinces, and into one large North American Federation. We number about 125,000 in this country, several million around the globe. And our history is studded with famed names, from Christopher Columbus and Michelangelo to modern scientists and U.N. diplomats.

I'd come into the order by the back door, so to speak, when Father Marius received me privately. For my novitiate I went where I belonged, to the fraternity. There for a year and a day at monthly meetings and classes I was to study the Franciscan way of life. There are differences in spirituality, varied approaches to the one God, and the Franciscan way is not the same as, say, the Benedictine, or Augustinian, Dominican, or Jesuit. Someone once observed that Franciscans are notoriously inefficient and happy-go-lucky slobs, but nice. Uncouth the definition is, but it does rather suit, and by its standards I felt right at home. On another level, it can be said the Franciscan way is to start with love of God as more important than anything else. A more intellectual order may say in effect: "I must know God and study him, so that I may love him." A more liturgically oriented order may say in effect: "I must praise and worship God, and thereby I will come to know him and grow in love." Another may be based on the approach: "I must do God's work, and thereby I will know and love and praise him." But the Franciscan says: "I must love God. The more completely I love him, the more I will know, serve and praise." It's a matter of temperament and vocation, this subtle distinction between ways to God. The way of love makes most sense to me.

How do you apply Franciscan Gospel standards to suburbia? How do you answer questions that aren't in catechisms but that do come up in discussion, such as: "Can a would-be saint honestly wear blue eyeshadow or is that too frivolous?" and "Suppose I could afford one, would it be against the spirit of poverty to have a Cadillac?"

There are no cut-and-dried answers. The one guide is to live according to your station in life, with moderation, gently letting God lead you. The patron saints of our order are a king and queen, King St. Louis of France, Queen St. Elizabeth of Hungary. If you're a king, you must wear a crown. If you're a queen you do the same, and then if, like Elizabeth, you are kicked out of your castle after your royal husband dies, and you're left in poverty, you live in poverty. If you're poor you're to be poor for love of God, without despair or indolence or bitterness. If you're rich, you're not supposed to become eccentric and go around in rags, but rather to learn to live with, and detached from, riches, using them for the glory of God. Which may or may not mean having a Cadillac.

The spirit of St. Francis is focused on Christ, on God-man, on incarnation. If you truly believe God became a human being so that human beings could share God's life, you never again see the world the same way, in the present, or in history, or in planning for the future. Here was a way that didn't flee the world but embraced it to make it holy in Christ. Here was a way that saw in the fact of incarnation the staggering beauty of all human life when transformed with grace, the importance of small tasks, small tears, small joys. The Franciscan centers his view on the manger, the cross, the eucharist: the three great involvements of God with the world.

As far as I'm concerned, Francis is the unique patron saint of all lay apostles, by which I mean all the plain people of the Catholic Church. And we sure need a patron saint today.

Never since the first fifty years has there been a more exciting time to be in the Church. The Holy Spirit today works in new ferment through this mystical body. The truth, which never changes and will never change, is being recast in new dimension. One is tempted to say that the life of the spiritual organism called the Church is now coming of age, now having its confirmation. There have been renewals before, and there will be again. Yet, though we can't consider this a once-and-for-all perfecting of the Church, those of us who live in this time are grateful. Blessed, challenged, excited—and at times, confused.

When you enter the Church you understand that the laity are, as Scripture says, a priestly people, a kingly people, a holy people, co-workers with the ordained in sanctifying the world. When you enter and study the Church you learn it's incorrect to think that Catholics are a bunch of sheep bossed around by the clergy.

But then you see that in plain fact and practice many of the older clergy are convinced that the faithful, a dreary lot, should be sheep to be bossed and sheared and saved against their own stupid instincts. Because they were trained by priests who dealt with immigrant Catholics not well-educated secularly or religiously, or because they themselves have had experiences with a laity not aware of the dignity and responsibility of Christians, they're leary of the new age. If they haven't known laymen with competence in any field, they find it hard to believe such competence exists. So they dig in their heels and stand their ground. The resulting conflict can be depressing for both sides.

When Martin and I, like every other lay couple in the Church today, came up against this kind of conflict, I found St. Francis the one guide to peace of mind. His example, and the advice of priests and laymen who consciously or not bear his spirit into the milieu of American Catholicism, has kept me sane.

"Don't ask. Just do," one priest said to me when I came to him in discouragement. My problem then was that I was involved in a lay society with definite purposes and an intelligent membership that was stymied by a priest who couldn't stand lay societies and had been made chaplain of ours. We couldn't accomplish even the smallest thing because he couldn't or wouldn't get around to making decisions.

"But if I don't ask and just do, what happens to the spirit of obedience?" I asked.

"You don't disobey if you don't ask. If you have a competent, wise chaplain or director, by all means you should ask and obey. If you're forbidden expressly, by even an unwise, incompetent chaplain or director, you must obey. But in practicality and grace, you don't have to ask if you know you'd only be asking for trouble." He smiled. "And as a human being you can understand that often the director would just as soon not be bothered, and will be grateful if you go ahead on your own responsibility, so he'll have to step in only if you go astray."

Don't ask, just do. That advice could smack of heresy, of individualism, of presumption, of—horror of horrors—Protestantism. It could really lead to ruin if it were misunderstood. But St. Augustine long ago said, "Love God, and then do what you will." Following that advice we may make mistakes, we may fool ourselves about how much we love God and how much we love having our own way. But it seems to me the plain people of God have to be willing today to take that risk.

And there are many priests, from parish to the See of Peter, who are calling us to that maturity. Their voices outnumber those who are still afraid to trust the sincerity of our love for Christ. There's a new breed of priest, some young, some white-haired and young only in the vibrancy of grace, who breathe the new spirit. Some of them are having their own troubles with the conservative wing, as leaven may be said to struggle till the whole be leavened.

St. Paul called himself a fool for Christ. St. Francis was willing, even anxious, to make a fool of himself if thereby he could show God's power and glory. Enthusiasm, love of God and of man, are bound to look ridiculous. In total abandonment to the moment in Christ, natural pride stands aside long enough to let you make glorious mistakes and achieve more glorious victories. If we're afraid to be inefficient, mistaken, laughed at, or properly rebuked along the way, we won't be much of a Christian community. A fool for Christ is in tune with the world as well as with eternity, a man who catches up the Word of God and utters it in the tongue of today.

The surest way to meet one of these priests of relevance, one of these wise fools for Christ, is to speak out from the heart and draw down on yourself the wrath of those other good earnest priests who don't happen to speak the language of today.

I did that, in innocence. And the drawing down of wrath was a ghastly experience, but immensely valuable. I wrote an article, and what resulted was a coming-of-age ritual, a trial by fire. My opinions and suggestions on a certain minor topic, printed in a magazine for priests only, stirred up a hornet's nest. What made the most trouble was not what I said, but that *I* said it. A *woman*. A *laywoman*. Woe and begorrah and heaven help us, things had come to a terrible pass if such a creature dared say anything.

But at the same time, precisely because I made so many clergy-men openly and loudly cross, I acquired new priestly friends, all of them fools for Christ. Young Father Bill Joyce of the Holy Ghost Fathers wrote to me because he was afraid I might have my faith shaken if I thought all priests wanted to silence all women. Father

Bernard Foschini, immersed in raising funds for Far Eastern Missions, took time to be concerned. Father Bruce Molinas, young Biblical scholar and foreign missionary; Father Lawrence, Byzantine Franciscan, musician, painter, liturgist and argumentician; and many more whom I've never yet met in person, took the time and trouble to write me.

Since then Martin and I have known other discouraging instances when our ideas or work we thought important suffered from friction between people and clergy. It happens to everyone. We've mellowed a bit, grown more patient, grown able to laugh, learned not to give up. We've decided there are going to be a lot of people in heaven who earned their way there by putting up with us. At our worst, we're good for something. Outsiders sometimes ask me why I stay in the Catholic Church where, as they see it, even today pomposities and protocol can stifle Christian action. My answer is that it would be ridiculous to pick up your marbles and go home, especially when you're home already.

Pax et bonum, "Peace and good." That's the third order byword. And being an "instrument of peace" is no simple task. The order and the rule keeps patiently yanking tertiaries out of comfortable ruts and turning us back to the full responsibility of trying to live by the Gospel. Trying to teach us humility, awareness of who and what we are. And simplicity. And love. An almost endless task, to learn these basic truths. The Franciscan has to pray for the grace to like the most unlikeable, forgive the unpardonable, love the unloveable. As that greatly gentle man, Philip Scharper, said to me when I was suffering from a particularly uncomfortable verbal attack by a man who gloried in being my enemy: "You know you have to offer up your misery and make it a prayer. The hell of it is that you have to offer it up for your enemy."

The other lesson for Franciscans, an easier one perhaps, is the willingness to see the dear ridiculousness of the human condition. As the years passed I no longer lived in fear that someone would think I was making myself out to be a pseudo-nun. And when I learned that at death tertiaries may choose to be buried in the order's brown monk-like robe, I was tickled silly. I really couldn't wait to see the faces on folks at my funeral when they found me laid out like that.

Eventually I was made mistress of novices at our fraternity, and it was my turn to teach those who were interested in becoming tertiaries. The most ridiculous thing that ever happened to me in my role as Sister Teresa occurred in a seminary of the Holy Ghost Fathers in Norwalk.

I was seated on the teacher's platform in a seminary classroom. I'd been invited to address the students about the problems and joys of being a lay Catholic writer. Being the first woman to invade the lecture program, I was a bit ill at ease.

The priest who introduced my speech was our good friend, Father Melinowski, a keen Scripture scholar, a fool for Christ. He is also an extraordinarily gifted amateur photographer. An expert at communicating deep truths to even shallow minds, he was for some reason also ill at ease this night, and not quite his articulate self. Perhaps he wondered if I'd blunder and make some faux pas which would discredit his program of lay speakers. More probably he wasn't thinking about me at all, for he's a man who juggles a thousand problems and enthusiasms in his mind at once. Anyway, he was laying it on a bit thick during the introduction, and what he said went this way:

"Mrs. Armstrong has not only written all those books I mentioned, but she has seven children and is a busy wife and mother. And she is active in the parish. And more than that. In spite of being a wife and mother, she finds time to be the mistress of—"

Incredibly, he stopped. Silence. A roomful of seminarians stared.

"Mistress of—" he repeated, distinctly. He looked calm. I wasn't. I couldn't stand it another second.

"Father," I croaked, "for heaven's sake finish that sentence, quick!"

He visibly recalled his mind from some far-off island.

"She's Mistress of Novices in the Third Order of St. Francis," he said, "and does a very good job."

It was the best intro I ever had.

28

See the Christian Family. O See!

One hardship of being a sincere Christian, is facing up to what people expect of you. The only way to cope with that is to keep laughing.

When I speak of others' opinions as a hardship, I'm not speaking of people who hate Catholics, or enjoy making them squirm, discriminating against them. No one's ever done that to me, at least as far as I know. I figure most people who would dislike me for being a "dirty Catholic" probably think of the Church with the same honest misconceptions I once had, and I can't get mad about that. Some people hate me, as one among many Catholics, because of some harm or injustice they think the Church did them. I keep trying to decide that lets me qualify for the beatitude about when one is persecuted for Christ's name's sake, but since I'm not really very persecuted, and since my own sake has had something to do with these people's disliking me, I'm afraid I don't rate.

Nor do I object to the attitudes of friends who are not Catholics. Non-Catholics often expect more of Catholics than of anyone else. They may swear like chorus girls themselves, but they're noticeably upset when someone like me comes out with a "damn" or a "hell." They think I should know better. They're right. I do know better. But the habit of using certain idioms is a persnickety thing to break, and I'm using my spare energy to break other much worse habits. I trust God knows I don't mean them literally. Besides, times are changing. When our boys came home and said young Father X said that it wasn't cursing to say "damn" or "hell," I shrugged it off as a peccadillo. But when the Cenacle nun told young children it was no sin to curse, assuming that by curse they merely said "Damn it," I began to feel old-fashioned. Sin or not, I promise all those whom I scandalize that someday I'll tidy up my speech.

Non-Catholics are sometimes awfully sweet, worrying about a Catholic's soul. They'll keep peering at you to see if they offend you by a slightly risqué story, or what they fear you might consider an irreverent joke, and you have to be cautious about telling them some of the jokes Catholics enjoy. They want to help you keep the faith, even when they think it irrelevant. I remember once having lunch with one of my editors, who is Jewish, on a Friday. He usually takes me to lunch on Friday, which I'm absolutely certain is a matter of coincidence and not of design. This particular Friday, however, Catholics were dispensed from the obligation to abstain from meat. Not eating meat on Friday is a matter not of faith and morals, but of Church discipline. Men made the rule, and men can change it. This was the day after Thanksgiving, and our bishop let us off for the day because it would be a shame to waste all those good turkey leftovers, families would be celebrating and so on. So I looked at the menu happily and chose roast beef. The editor said the lobster looked nice. So did the shrimp. Maybe deviled crab? "Roast beef," said I blissfully. I put away the menu and for the first time looked at his face. He was upset. What on earth was the matter? Surely he didn't thing I'd ordered something too expensive? Even scrambled eggs at this restaurant cost a fortune.

"Are you sure you want roast beef? There's a lot of fish on the menu," he said tactfully. I blinked. "It's Friday!" he cried in desperation.

So I explained about the bishop's dispensation, which he

thought was an astonishingly intelligent and relevant sign in the Church, and he relaxed. Poor dear, he really wanted to save me from committing a sin, and he went to so much trouble. I love him for it.

Maybe the surest path to sanctity would be to walk through a daily audience of non-Catholics with a Catholic label on you. No matter how outdated, dangerous or unintelligent they may think the Church is, they're usually good enough to want individual Catholics to live up to all the Church claims to be. In such company you're easily reminded when your lack of charity is showing.

No, the people who make life unbearable aren't enemies of the Church, or goodhearted servants of God outside the Church, but Catholics with a preconception of what it means to love and serve God, who try to make others fit it. I can't blame them for the preconception. It comes directly from all the sentimental statues that used to clutter our churches, and from all the platitudinous lives of saints Catholic children used to have to swallow, and all the flowery nonsense our creed was wrapped in. Pity the Son of God, who for so long has been pictured in effeminate curls, or as a baby prince in an incredible dress, and who has to overcome these handicaps and save the world in spite of his friends. The real life of Christ, the real lives of saints, would scandalize these earnest pious souls if they ever found out about them.

Almost unconsciously they've built up an idea of the perfect Christian which, in practice, amounts to being a perfect nincompoop. They *feel*—they can't really *think* that way—that the perfect Christian never loses his temper, has no feelings to be hurt, gives generously to the poor and trusts God, but somehow always has enough money, is so busy relying on God that he has no worries at all, has only nice friends, and nice children, and nice ways himself, is clean, orderly, and has progressed so far that he's never tempted and never even wants to do something he shouldn't. And above all, the perfect Christian never has disagreements with anyone. Theirs is a neatly compartmented world, where all motives are clear, and anyone can be judged in an instant.

I don't often get a halo stuck on my head. But occasionally you run into someone who's determined to see you through beatifying glasses. That's a ghastly experience. Our family went through it one hot summer day, emblazoned now forever in our memory.

There was a nun writer I very much wanted to meet, and thanks to the maneuvers of a mutual friend, a woman editor, Sister phoned one day to say she could come to visit.

"But, may I bring Mother Superior with me? We may not travel without a companion, even from New York to Stamford. I'm staying at a convent other than my own in order to take some summer courses, and when Mother Superior here heard I was going to visit you she said she'd be pleased to accompany me."

Poor Mother Superior. Poor nun writer, whom I shall here call Sister Patricia. And poor us.

They were to come on Saturday. Saturday morning early a friend called to ask if I could possibly watch little Joey for the day because little Joey was having a tantrum about a particular babysitter who was watching the rest of the family. So I piled our gang in the station wagon, picked up Sister Patricia and Mother Superior at the railroad station, and went to fetch Joey, who was five, and possessed, I knew, of a large set of lungs.

When I explained what we were doing Sister Patricia just nodded matter-of-factly. But Mother Superior smiled and caught her breath at the same time, which is a difficult trick. "This is the real Christian family in action," she said. "How wonderful!"

I looked at Sister Patricia, but Sister Patricia was looking at her hands. Then I looked at Mother Superior, and sure enough, she meant exactly what she said.

"It's not really a Christian Family Movement job," I said. "I don't belong to CFM, though Joey's mother, Betty, does. It's just something you have to do, or want to do, because Betty's done things for me. She once moved in with her husband and all her kids to take care of my crew when I had a baby."

"See how humbly these modern mothers underplay their roles, Sister," said Mother Superior.

Joey was all smiles about coming to our house and escaping the babysitting ogress until he saw the two nuns, and then he began to scream. Betty made polite noises at the nuns, and naturally impolite ones to Joey, smiled, and finally shoved him in over the tailgate, and off we went, quick. There was no conversation till we reached home, because Joey was using up all the available air.

Our own kids were sort of desperate, and so as we pulled into the driveway they volunteered to watch Joey, outside. They obviously intended to shut him up their own way.

"See how the children of a Christian family rally round in charity," said Mother Superior.

Martin came round from the porch in his khakis and his old shirt. He and our good friend "Nick" Nichol had been planning for some time that this Saturday they would screen in our porch, and they were not going to be thrown off by any guests.

"I hope the good Sisters will understand," Martin said now, smiling.

The day was already hot and sticky. Heavy clouds moved listlessly overhead.

"Such a good man," said Mother Superior, "working hard all week and giving his day off to making a more comfortable home for his family."

Martin nodded, visibly relieved not to be thought rude. Nick joined us, dressed like Martin in beat-up workpants and an already sweat-soaked shirt. We introduced him.

"Nick's our godson," said Martin. He didn't know, because of course I'd had no chance to warn him, that we should have kept that detail quiet.

"Your godson!" Mother Superior clapped her little hands together. "How wonderful! An adult convert?"

Nick, who's a big hunting-fishing-type man, a few years older than we are, nodded.

"Imagine! And could there be anything more edifying than to meet the head of a Christian family and his godson screening in a porch!"

Martin rolled his eyes, and I managed to let him know he was the head of the Christian family Mother was speaking of, and the day was off to a great start. Joey kept running away looking for his Mommy, and Cathy and Mike and Marty would go bring him back by the scruff of his playshirt, and he'd howl, and they'd give him cookies and lollipops, and that happened three times. I settled the nuns on aluminum and webbing furniture on the front lawn. Sister Patricia and I had just begun to talk about writing when the clouds let loose a few raindrops, so we turned the furniture upside down and hurried into the living room. There, even with the fans going, it was unspeakably hot, and noisy because not only could we hear Joey, but little Fulton and Caedmon didn't want to be put in the playpen and so they howled too. Then the sun would come out, and we'd scurry outside and try again. And that happened three times.

By this time Mother Superior was not only convinced that she was in the midst of a C.F., but she wore a slightly daring smile as if she'd stumbled unknowingly into Greenwich Village, the Left Bank, and Father Feeney's band of excommunicates up in Boston. In spite of all, Sister Patricia and I had managed to do a bit of talking. We'd talked of literature and trash, and exotic pieces Mother Superior hadn't read, such as *The Cypresses Believe in God,* and Graham Greene. And, by chance, every time we did mention something she'd read it was to speak of it in disparaging tones. Then Sister Patricia mentioned the article of mine which had stirred up the hornet's nest, and we got off into a discussion of the reader reaction. Mother Superior sat on the edge of that wobbly aluminum chair, scared to death. Joey's howls ceased, leaving us only with the hammering of the Christian men on the porch, and minor noises as Caedmon tried to swallow his fist.

"You have to be willing to take abuse," said Sister Patricia. "You can't stop saying what's right just because some of the clergy don't like it. Why I—"

Mother Superior appeared to be feeling the heat. I went for iced tea and came back to find that Sister Patricia had worked wonders by simply supplying Mother Superior with a lapful of my less daring works, such as *Stories from the Life of Jesus.* Mother found the *imprimaturs,* drank her iced tea and was almost relaxed by the time the next rain fell.

We went back to the living room. I'd closed the windows there to keep out some of the noise of the porch-screen business, but by now any noise seemed better than the heat, so I opened them. Sister Patricia was trying to warn me that it'd be better not to talk shop for a while, and she suggested tactfully that Mother Superior might perhaps enjoy a little nap in the afternoon. If it would only clear up she could rest under the trees.

I made final preparations of the luncheon I'd had almost ready, laid out plates of peanut butter sandwiches for the children in the kitchen, and then there was nothing to do but sit. So Mother Superior began telling us about the nature of Christian families, and everything she said was quite right, but also unbearable.

"And living in this way, in charity and peace, there comes a real glow of purity," said Mother Superior.

"Yes, Mother," said Sister Patricia quietly.

"Yes," said I, not knowing whether it seemed prideful to agree, and not caring.

There was nothing else to say. We sat in purity. We could hear the paper napkins crackling in the kitchen as children wiped their mouths. They were too oppressed to fight. The coffee pot was percolating. Sister's stomach gurgled. The men hammered and grunted. Then it happened.

In a loud clear big voice, Nick said, "Oh ————!"

A simple word. One every child knows, and sees painted on bus stop signs and speed-limit signs and in public bathrooms. It fit. And it came out with endearing naturalness, and came spinning through the open window and hung in the heavy living room air. Oh, it was beautiful.

As if she could make it seem irrelevant, Mother Superior closed her mouth, opened it again, and said: "Oh, by the way," and began telling us about children who turn up in the school which her order runs, children who use the foulest language.

"When the Sisters speak to the parents about it, the parents always protest that they can't imagine where the children have heard these words, unless it be at school. But we know they don't hear those words in our school. And we do know where they do hear them. It's hard to judge a family on outward appearances."

Ah. So we had lunch decorously. Martin and Nick had had such a good laugh together that they made fine conversation, and Mother Superior's silence went so unnoticed that soon she was able to take an interest in life again.

Come what may, Sister Patricia and I were resolved we'd have a good dose of shoptalk that afternoon. The weather cleared, Joey went to sleep under the oak tree, our babies napped, the electric drill screamed up on the porch drowning out the men's voices, and Mother Superior nodded in the chaise longue. Sister Patricia and I dissected the latest trends in Catholic literary criticism, took care of Dan Herr and a few other upstarts, debated what ailed Catholic fiction, rehashed the merits and lack of same in *America* and *Commonweal,* and latched on to the fascinating problem of dealing with Catholic editors, who, being priests, offer special challenges to diplomacy and manners.

"The trouble with the Catholic press," said Sister.

"The trouble with the Catholic press," said I. Finally we came up with what we thought was the clincher.

"The trouble is that too often the wrong men edit the Catholic press. Orders assign a man to edit a magazine with less thought than they give to choosing a monastery porter. The man who's saddled with the job half the time doesn't know the first thing about editing, and doesn't want to know. With the best will in the world, he does a horrid job. The Catholic press doesn't pay enough to attract good writers and . . ."

Poor Mother Superior. She had hoped Nick's slip had been only a passing thing, that there'd be no other flaws in the picture of the Christian writer and the C.F. But criticism of the clergy, criticism of the Catholic press, smacked of heresy, and while she could let me go to perdition if I insisted, she was temporarily responsible for Sister Patricia's spiritual health. Wearily she rallied herself to deliver a sermon on humility, and on not judging, and then proceeded to extol the pious magazines.

Suddenly Mike ran up and whispered in my ear. Out of the corner of my eye I saw that there was indeed a car in the driveway. I excused myself and went to the kitchen. There stood Father Luke Ciampi, O.F.M., a modern black-suited Franciscan who could have modeled in costume for Friar Tuck. In his hand was his traditional giant box of Italian pastries. Editor of *Padre* magazine he was then, and an assistant pastor who had singlehandedly in his spare time designed, built, paved and equipped a small recreation park for his younger parishioners in the Bronx. Another Christian fool. He had every intention of hiding out in the kitchen until the good Sisters were gone.

"But we only get to see you once or twice a year. And one of the nuns is Sister Patricia, the writer."

"I know her. I like her. Let's go."

"But first, I'd better brief you." I rehearsed the events of the day, and he laughed so loud over Nick's outburst that there was no more hope of pretending he wasn't here.

"I want to talk to Sister Patricia," I said, "and I can't, because Mother Superior keeps wanting to make me part of a Christian family. You have to come and do something."

"Divine Providence sent me," he said, clasping his hands over his stomach and lowering his eyes modestly. "Get me a drink. A drink that looks like a drink and cannot be mistaken for iced tea or lemonade." He removed his jacket and his rabat. He was wearing a ribbed cotton white sweatshirt with long sleeves, and the shirt was totally body-conforming, and most beneficently out of style and conservative at the same time. Drink in hand, he set out forthrightly for the lawn.

Mother Superior's eyes widened. Sister Patricia stood up, joy shining on her hot cheeks. "Father Luke!"

"Father?" asked Mother Superior weakly, struggling with the folding chaise longue which would not let her rise.

"Sit, Mother, pray. What were you talking about before I came?" Father Luke asked, once the pleasantries subsided. "I should like to not disturb anything. So we may continue where you left off."

"About what was wrong with the Catholic press," said Sister Patricia demurely.

"I'll tell you what's wrong with the Catholic press," Father Luke boomed from the depths of his massive chest, and his shirt moved in echo. "Religious superiors!"

And smiling earnestly at Mother Superior he proceeded to hold forth on a theory that may or may not have been dear to his heart, but that he felt to be appropriate at the time. In a tour de force he accused religious superiors of being unaware of the true importance of the press, of prostituting it as a fund-raising medium, of being unable to understand writers and editors who need money and time, of being afraid of anything new or fine.

"Heaven save us from religious superiors!" he cried. "Don't you agree, Mother?"

"Yes, Father, oh yes, Father," said Mother Superior, who seemed to be wondering what Father's own superior would have thought of that sweatshirt.

The sun settled slowly in the west, and Mother Superior settled back in her chair to offer up the most difficult and dismaying afternoon of her life. But Father Luke and Sister Patricia and I had a good talk, and the children seemed to know it was safe to be themselves again, so they had a glorious time being naughty and began carrying frogs and slimy things from the brook to "show" Mother Superior. Even the men on the porch, having long since finished their job, decided it was safe to stop pretending to be busy and emerged to join Father Luke in a drink.

At last Mother Superior insisted it was time to catch the train. She gathered the children around and bade them farewell and forgave them for the frogs, and seemed to recapture some of her faith in the essential feasibility of a C.F. She even smiled graciously on

Nick. Then, doling out one holy card each to the children, she climbed into the station wagon.

One of our little boys ran over and stood on tiptoe at the car window.

"Sister," he said, "do you know what I want to be when I grow up?"

Ah, poor Mother Superior. "What do you want to be, little man?"

"A Jew."

I started the car motor.

"Don't you want to know why, Sister?" continued my dear little man.

"Why?" asked Mother Superior, more of God and about the whole day, than of the boy and his ambition to become a Jew. "Why?"

"Because the little girl down the street and I want to get married and she can't marry anyone but a Jew, her father said."

"Go tell her she's got to be a Christian to marry you," said Mother Superior with asperity.

"Hey, that's an idea! You're real smart, aren't you, Sister?" His eyes actually were innocent, and they gleamed with admiration, which even Mother Superior could not mistake for malice or boldness.

I blessed him silently, and put an end to small talk by taking off for the station.

"I want to be a Jew," Mother Superior murmured from time to time. "And it never occurred to him she could convert."

At the station she thanked me with enthusiasm and grace that I couldn't help but applaud for a charming visit. And when the train left I got into the car and slammed the door and sped unapostolically home, and for the next two hours we were all as uncouth as we knew how.

There's a story about a saint whose ability to work miracles and whose general holiness was so renowned that a group of important people came to get a look at him. The saint, hearing them approach, ran out of the house and down the street to a playground, climbed on a seesaw, and began making an absolute idiot of himself. At one time the story made no sense to me. But now and again, I can see how he must have felt.

29

In My House Are Many Fathers

In my Father's house are many mansions, but in our house are many fathers, for we have, without quite knowing how, been privileged to count priests as our true and relaxed friends. Parish priests have to be careful about fraternizing with the laity, and some of them worry about being taken over, but fathers in various orders needn't concern themselves so much with those problems.

Because our priest friends are the kind who can decide to be our friends, they are obviously the kind of men who can put up with anything. They do not expect to be treated as guests. They do not behave as guests. They come when they can, always tactfully without warning, so they don't rob us of excuses for being in our usual state of confusion. They pick their way through children and noise, and stay for an hour, a couple of days, or longer. One stayed three months.

Unfortunately, this easygoing relationship is not common in most houses, because most families are better-organized than ours, and therefore are able to be more polite and hospitable to the clergy, and formality is the foe of genuine Christian friendship. Priests particularly get their fill of formality and ritual, and secretly yearn for a place to hang up their collar and feel at home. All unconsciously and naïvely we discovered this by being ourselves. I keep thanking all the saints for arranging things this way.

Of course, some people feel sorry for us, imagining that we are dreadfully imposed on, and others assume we must be status-seekers. They don't understand. I suppose ever since the days when the Master used to drop in on Mary, Martha and Lazarus, Christ in the house has caused some eyebrows to go up.

Once a young and rather handsome priest from Portugal, with the profile of a Pharaoh and a poignant voice for Gregorian chant and folksong, stayed with us. Father Aventino was newly ordained and entitled to a vacation. He had no relatives in the United States. The Consolata Foreign Mission Society superiors, who knew us well, asked if we'd let him stay with us, and just relax in the fresh air for a while. We were delighted. He was, like most brand-new priests, still likely to sound off with small dissertations and useless answers to examination questions fifty times a day. He was, like all brand-new priests, still so totally aware of the immense thing which had happened to him at ordination that grace played around him like an aureole. He was also young, and full of fun and ideals. He was an amateur pianist, a great hand with the lawnmower and with a baseball, and the one thing he'd wanted all his life was a BB gun. So we bought him khakis, T shirts and a BB gun. He borrowed a pith helmet from our young adventurers. Each morning he would offer Mass with solemn beauty at St. Cecilia's, come home, change and spend hours high in the trees in the then undeveloped acreage next to ours. The squirrels were ruining our tomatoes, which gave him a fine reason to develop skill as a sharpshooter.

A Jewish family moved in down the road. As usual, our children went to welcome newcomers and talk their ears off. A few days later, as I sprayed the roses, I noticed the man and wife lingering on the road by our split-rail fence hoping to run into me casually. Casually, I went over. After a bit of chitchat they got to the point.

"Cathy and Fulton are such little charmers, and so well-spoken. But they said something we must admit intrigues and puzzles us. Children do say the darnedest things, don't they?"

"They do."

"They keep telling us about a man who sleeps in your living room, and they call the man Father but they insist he's not their Daddy. They say he's a police?"

"Ah," I said, relieved that the problem was so simple. And I explained that there was no scandal. I explained about the priest, who of course was called Father, who slept in our living room because we had no guest room. And this did put these nice people's minds to rest, and they said they'd noticed that children had trouble with their "r's" and "l's," and of course priest would sound like p'lice, and they laughed and were duly impressed by the priest in the house. They even said it would be pleasant for our children to play with their child, and everything was going beautifully. And just then our tribe, which had come out to the fence to hear what was going on, let out a shriek of greeting:

"Father!"

I followed the neighbors' gaze. Down from the treetops on the next lot came a handsome dark young man in slightly scuffed khakis carrying a BB gun. No Roman collar. And that pith helmet. As the Armstrong innocents pelted across the grass to swarm over him, our new neighbors, eyebrows elevated, left.

Honi soit qui mal y pense, and bad cess to them, as the Irish babysitter used to say. I never saw them again.

And at the Bronx Zoo. Ah, the zoo, to which Father Aventino very much wanted to go, so he could see the African Plains exhibit in case he ever achieved his dream of being sent to work in Kenya. Father wanted to take the whole neighborhood along, so there we were, me in my maternity skirt, Father in civvies, lithe and young, surrounded by thirteen ambulatory children and one in a stroller. We boarded the tractor train at the zoo. The conductor asked for tickets. One by one the children said, "Father will pay." By the time the conductor, counting on his fingers, reached me, he rolled nervous eyes at Father Aventino and asked me if my husband were paying for me, too. Whereupon, of course, one of my own children had to explain loudly,

"Father isn't married to Mommy, silly!"

Are we too casual about priests? The only thing about the fathers in our house that worries me is that our little ones are so used to having priests wander through and make themselves at home like a batch of uncles that when they see a Roman collar I'm afraid they automatically expect a bit of Indian wrestling, or at least a movie. We're always seeing movies in our living room about mission work, in No-Priest-Land-USA, which to Glenmary priests is mostly the American South, or in Brazil, or Colombia, or Kenya. If we're not seeing the movies we're writing scripts for them, viewing the uncut footage over and over ninety times.

We have one priest friend, Father Francis, who takes youngsters by the carload to amusement parks, which is nothing new evidently, for Martin remembers as a boy going to Steeplechase with Father Neal Boyton, S.J., who swore one of the best places to say his breviary was in solitary splendor on a Ferris wheel. Father Theodore is adept at elaborate deceptions, disguises and fictions, and has more than once convinced our boys and others that he was a detective about to arrest them for prowling the friary apple orchard. Father Paul calls up and gives phony names, so that our toddlers answer the phone and tell me Santa Claus is calling from the North Pole.

But I suspect that children who have played with priests may grow up with more respect for the priesthood, more chance of vocation. I remember once when Father Peter Mongiano came for a summer day. I was painting furniture for the children's rooms, and he hoped I might help translate a small prayer book from Church English into the vernacular of modern America. So he painted the furniture while I worked. And he played hide-and-seek with the little ones. He spent the night. In the morning we all went to St. Cecilia's for Mass. When Father walked out to the altar in his vestments one of our boys, then only five, turned to me and demanded:

"Is that the same man who is at our house?"

Against such a background the unique dignity of priesthood

has real meaning, for children and for adults. And perhaps boys as they grow to manhood may have more respect for men who, like their Master, say, "Let the little children come to me."

The older boys, outgrowing purely animal nature and becoming slightly intelligent human beings, find the intellectual challenge of these priests as stimulating as we do. Father Lawrence, the Franciscan who likes chocolate ice cream, and painted the picture of St. Francis in our hall, has become for them an apostle for the understanding of theology, and for making teen-age sense out of morals. Father Joe Debergh, O.M.I., who came to share with us his knowledge of the shrine of Beauraing in his native Belgium, quickened their interest in understanding more of Europe, which till then they'd unconsciously assumed consisted merely of Italy, Portugal and Paris. Father Bill Joyce, on rare leaves from work in a Southern parish, startles them with his presentation of race problems. And for our own parish priests, for Father Heffernan our pastor, Father Botton, the curate who taught them to be altar boys and chaplains our choir, and Father Brett, young liturgical firebrand, they preserve admiration and respect.

One priest more than any other shaped our lives, Father John de Marchi, I.M.C., the same who helped brief us on Fatima. He is, I think, the closest and dearest friend any one of us has had. When we met him he was superior of the Consolatas in this country. He had built a seminary in Fatima, then come to the United States with no money and little English to set up a base of operations for the Society in Washington, D.C. He learned English, made friends and a little money, had a book published, bought two old houses for the Society, began to publish a magazine and to raise funds for missionary work in Africa and South America, and to encourage vocations, and eventually built a seminary near Buffalo, New York to shelter these vocations. Almost singlehanded, in a deceptively quiet whirlwind, he accomplished the task of making the Consolatas known and liked in this country where there are already more orders and societies than any Catholic can keep track of.

He drew us into his own world of loving action for Christ. He never exhorted, never preached. But as time passed he gave us all awareness of the world-wide Church, made small mission outposts in Caquetá or Tusamagonga as much a part of our thoughts as the stories in the daily papers. From him and for him the children learned to make the sign of the cross in the rhythmic sing-song hummed accents of Swahili:

"Kwajina la baba, na la mwana, na la mroho mtakatifu, Ameena."

From him too they learned to know Italy, the life of peasants and cities and monasteries, the history and songs and traditions of the faith in Mediterranean climes and Alpine heights.

The spirit of poverty pervaded him, so that being close to him you caught it like a fever. He supported his work completely by lecture fees, offerings for religious services and gifts. And he never thought to spend a penny on himself. Often we'd surreptitiously mend a frayed jacket, or dig up some buttons to spruce him up when he was on his way to call on a bishop or a rich man. He hated to have things when others did not. We played a game trying to think of something we could give him for Christmas which he would keep for more than a week. Once, when we were particularly strapped for money, we nevertheless bought him the finest fur-lined leather driving gloves we could find. He was always junketing around the country in the Society's car, and the heater didn't work. and his hands showed signs of chilblains. He kept the gloves two days, then gave them to a man he'd known for ten minutes.

"His hands were cold," he explained simply. "And I was so glad you'd picked out such fine gloves for me because it's more fun for me to be able to give something fine too, somehow."

In the years when we were first cementing the bonds of adoption between us, we had much to learn about this Father John who seemed, literally, too good to be true. We noticed that he arrived at our house always in time for a meal. We were honestly happy to have him, and he ate almost nothing, but being human we couldn't help making a remark about it after a while. He'd say he just happened to be passing by, but he'd make a detour of some ninety miles to take potluck and sleep on our lumpy sofa with dogs and noisy children to tease him awake.

"Some people are just plain cheap moochers," we said.

He laughed, because he knew we loved him. But later he said, "All my days I spend begging for Christ's poor, and people give to me money they sacrifice so it can be used for God's work. I know you were joking. But I think, somehow, I must see that you truly understand. I cannot make myself take any of that money and spend it on me, for a hamburger and a cup of coffee, for a hotel bed. It was not for me it was given, somehow. And so I go out of my way a little to be where I do not have to pay, and I am richer because I am thereby being with friends, somehow."

"Somehow." That word cropped out in his conversation always, used as a drop of oil to smooth out the rough spots, to suggest with a bow that he had something to tell us that he felt the Lord wanted us to know.

Of himself, Father John always asked the impossible, knowing that of himself he could do nothing, but with God he could do anything. He spent himself and ignored himself, not in conscious frightening asceticism, but as man forgetting himself in love with someone else. And of us, too, he asked the impossible, and we were able to do it. He asked us to write movie scripts, which was impossible because we didn't have the know-how, let alone the time. But he believed we could do it, and would, somehow. He also believed he could put out a prize-winning film in color with music and Bob Considine to narrate it, the whole package to cost under $5,000 for a half-hour show. And he did it. He asked us to throw a small charity ball on our crabgrass lawn, and let him show his movies and beg for money. Our choir director, Joe Rich, got together a combo and played on the porch, and Father Aventino and the kids strung Chinese lanterns, and it was lovely, and no one stopped being our friend for having been milked for charity. He asked us to sell carved statuettes of animals and Madonnas made by Kikuyus, and I'm the type who won't sell a raffle ticket but prefer to buy the whole book myself. But the statues were sold, some by our porch-fixing godson Nick, who is a supersalesman, and some even by me.

Father John brought into our home tangible awareness of the indwelling of the Trinity, without ever cluttering up our friendship with fancy words. Once, when we spoke about the dearth of spiritual direction in modern life, exploring the reasons for it, he said:

"I have found that the Holy Spirit is the spiritual director for all souls, and the only one we need. We can do without the luxury of having a human voice and mind guide us, if we will let the Spirit blow in us, and be silent, somehow, to hear him."

The Spirit blew him where it would, and in silence he saw what was to be done, and did it enthusiastically. But what we remember most about Father John was his total rejoicing in the goodness of others. He never boasted of himself. But he'd sit for hours telling us about mothers and fathers and children he knew who lived good lives, about young doctors giving up practices to take their families to work in the missions, about a special child he'd met, about a stranger who gave him a seat on a bus. He'd get so very excited and happy about the smallest sign of grace in people that tears would have to be blinked away.

He accepted hardship, illness, pain as normal parts of living for himself, and grew distressed when anyone else suffered even a little. He disciplined himself and admired others who had learned to control themselves, and certainly he expected children to be disciplined in order to be happy. But rules did not obsess or dismay him. Pharisees did. So did the hint that a person might be able to measure out how much to give God.

In September 1958 our beautiful little Clare Ellen was born in St. Joseph's Hospital in Stamford. Father John came to see us there. We were in a small dither because since she was the sixth child we were running out of suitable godparents.

"Too bad you can't be her godfather," I said to Father John. "It would be nice because we all love you so, and then you'd really be part of the family."

"But I can be," said Father John.

Now Martin and I had always understood that priests couldn't be godfathers, but we weren't going to argue because one look at Father John's face as he stared down at Clare silenced us. He wasn't making an idle joke. He intended to be her godfather. We were delighted, if a little nervous.

Tony's wife, Noel, was to be godmother, and at least there was nothing wrong about that from a legal point of view, and a child really needs only one godparent. I think we told Bishop McDonnell about Father John's being the godfather beforehand, and I know we told him about Noel. Anyway, the bishop flew in from Wheeling, West Virginia, to New York City, and with scant time to spare drove up with his sister Anna to perform the baptism. He came to the house, said he'd have to take off right after the ceremony, and greeted everyone jovially, and we all went to St. Cecilia's. Young Father Botton was assisting the bishop, who was vested in his imposing episcopal attire, and asked where the godparents were.

"Here," said Noel.

"Here," said Father John.

The bishop glanced around. I could feel color rising in my face. Martin and I stared at each other and wondered what would happen. Father Botton looked as if he wished he weren't standing right between Father John and the bishop. Here were our two dearest friends in the clergy, and it wasn't the Holy Spirit giving off tongues of fire between them.

"Who is the godfather?" asked the bishop.

"Father John," said Martin.

"I am," said Father John.

"But you can't be, Father," said the bishop courteously. And the look in his eye asked why this priest should place him in the embarrassing position of saying No. And the look in Father John's eye asked why this bishop should assume he would do such a thing.

"You must have permission of your superior," said the bishop. "Only a superior could make an exception so you could do this."

"I am the superior," said Father John.

So Clare Ellen became a child of God, at the hands of Bishop McDonnell, and in the arms of Noel and Father John. The love between Clare and Father John is holy and fine, and he's planning now for the day that she will be grown and he will either witness her marriage or receive her into the Consolata nuns. And she prays for him every night of her life. Perhaps it *was* the Holy Spirit who was striking the sparks around that baptismal font.

Father John taught us, just by being himself, to see everything, somehow, *in conspectu Dei.*

He has now left the United States to work in Kenya. Before he left he went to great trouble to visit us for one last evening. He'd always hoped to be sent to the missions. The thought of being in Kenya in its hour of birth into independence thrilled him. Our older boys, who'd been in on the writing of a film about the Mau Mau, and were well aware of the bloodshed accompanying independence in the Congo, asked Father John if he weren't the least bit frightened.

"Of course," he laughed. "Of course. But only a little while. I am somehow more happy than frightened. It will be the greatest adventure being there when all those you met in our films, the Kikuyu, the Masai, everyone, become free to run their own land."

He'd polished up his Swahili, and was eager to be off. He asked us to pray for him. He promised to pray for us. And though there are still many fathers in our house, somehow it's a little emptier and lonelier now.

30

Things My Children
Taught Me

If I try to set down on paper all the things I do every day and fit
them into an orderly schedule, they just won't fit. Logically, you
can't write books and columns, go lecturing even nearby, do your
housework, be a good wife, belong to church groups, sing in the
choir, read, knit, have fun and take care of seven children, too. But
there's little that's logical about living. And I can explain about
the knitting. Just call me Mme. Defarge. The whole revolution can
explode around me and I sit and knit. Knitting is the only thing I
do that stays done. And the only thing I can do and know I'm
doing right. All you have to do is follow directions, and that's more
than you can do with children. There's nothing like a good intricate sweater pattern to calm the nerves.

I do rather lose track of time. Or it loses track of me. I neglected to tell you chronologically when Clare was born, and I kept
sneaking seven children into this story before Paul was even thought
of, and that's simply because lately I get mixed up about chronolo-
gies. Our handsome, mischievous Paul Louis arrived late in 1959,
and he wasn't coming easily, but he was born on St. Louis' day
with no trouble. That's the least trouble he's ever been, actually.

But to get back to this matter of logic. As I see it, time is
elastic. I am less busy now with seven than I was when we had only
two babies. Efficiency experts notwithstanding, for me it is not best
to measure time, motion and energy. I can't plan my time. Who
knows when a boy will stuff a pussywillow in his ear so far that he
has to go to the doctor? Certain things I know must be done at
certain times, like meals, the laundering of specific clothes, and the

keeping of appointments. But there's no law saying you can't iron at midnight. Or that you must finish chores before doing what seems like more fun. All our children pitch in with K.P. and bed-making, and when they must they mow the lawn, clean the garage and hang up their clothes. But if I worked from dawn to dawn on nothing else I'd never finish all the domestic work in our home. When nine people live together the place is never totally picked up or totally cleaned. And, if there are small ones around, as so far there have always been, then someone's sure to do something messy like pouring blue ink out the window onto shingles Daddy just painted white, or knocking over cereal boxes. So you learn to sort out what's vital, like keeping the house relatively sanitary, being sure each one has a pair of socks and knows he's loved, and let nonessentials go.

One of the first valuable lessons children teach mothers is that you can't be perfect, so you needn't knock yourself out trying. Home is a place for the family and its friends, not a place for demonstrating household cleaning implements. To be sure, orderliness is a sign of sanctity, to a degree. We all need the discipline of taking care of material objects, and the discipline of rules for social living. We need to learn how to help each other and not be obnoxious. But I think there's been more than enough written urging women to do these things. We need more urging not to make a fetish out of shining houses and shining children. I do still yearn for the day when everyone in our family will be civilized, and we can do a bit of gracious living with all those wedding presents now in the attic, and not trip over dirty sneakers or a bottlecap collection. Someday. Meanwhile, I'll settle for living with grace instead of gracious living.

Children teach you not only that it's impossible to be a perfect housekeeper, but also that it's impossible to be perfect at anything. Not everyone really knows this, but mothers of large families do. You cannot be perfectly even-tempered, because at least nineteen times a day someone will do or say something to which you'll react before you think, such as calling his brother an imbecile at the top of his voice, or dropping a set of barbells on the floor, or not being able to find her milk money after you've found it for her four times already. You cannot be perfectly wise because you're called on to make split decisions which would make Solomon quail. Whose turtle is whose after just one of an identical pair got lost? Who started a fight? Who gets the boxtop? Who started a fight? How do you make a big child stop teasing a little one? Who started a fight? How do you make a little child leave a big one alone? And who started another fight?

Eventually you learn a third lesson: no parent can be a perfect parent. Anything you resented in your own parents when you were a child is really nothing next to what your children are going to be able to resent in you. The things you vowed you'd never do to your children you find yourself doing because they're wise, appropriate, or inevitable.

I'm weary of texts on teaching children to be good people, the advice which promises that if you give them a nice environment and are nice yourself, they'll be nice. That's the most unrealistic nonsense in the world. We need more reminders of how much children teach us, if we let them. Everyone knows they teach us to be more aware, more fully alive, never to take things for granted. They teach us to appreciate. But it's what children have taught me about people, including myself, and about God, and about love, that I value most.

I'm not sure, but I think changing diapers led me to my keenest understanding of love. No one in her right mind enjoys diapers. I'd had all sorts of high-falutin' notions about love as being a sort of mutual recognition, based on a sharing of values. Babies and I have little sharing of values when it comes to diapers, except that we both like clean diapers on the same behind. Love really has very little to do with liking, or logic. Its root is in the will, not the head or heart. You will to love someone, and the kind of love which sometimes springs up before you make any decision isn't yet ripe enough to be called love. You may love a baby because it's yours, which it isn't essentially, or because it's cute and cuddly. But you will also love a baby that's ugly, cranky, sick and nasty. You'll love a child no matter what it does. You may not like the kid, particularly at those noisome ages of 2½ or 13, when they're constitutionally unable to be very likeable. But you'll still love him. You'll search for motives, to understand these people you love. You'll see the nylon blouse melt under the iron, and know that the child who ironed it thought she was doing a glorious thing. You'll wear the gaudy pin the child buys, keep the felt-covered soup can that is now a pencil holder, and learn to see that the boy who is being a bully is really scared to death of the report card he must soon bring home, and quite unable to admit that he's scared, so he's mean instead.

You'll learn that firm discipline, chastisement, can be the most difficult, and most necessary expression of your love.

I have a feeling that if Martin and I had only one child, we'd make a good stab at ruining him. Many people do a superb job with an only child. I just think we wouldn't. With seven there isn't time to worry too much over this small fault or that small problem, there isn't time or energy enough to be dominating or possessive. And because we must treat with our seven on seven different levels —from kindergarten drawings to algebra—we're kept from falling into ruts. No two children are alike.

But all have one need in common. The need to give and to receive love. The need to live in an atmosphere of love.

And, contrary to myth, loving is not easy to do. Brotherly love doesn't come naturally, and anyone who thinks it does is in for a rude shock when she faces a batch of children on a rainy day. The human animal must learn to love, and most of us skimmed through youth without really learning. At least I did for a long time. I thought I understood love, but what I really understood was loving what suited me. And that's not only cheating, it's impossible to live with. If we love only the loveable, we can't really love ourselves, whom we know so well. And if we can't do that, we can't begin to love other people or God.

The one full-time vocation of each person is to love. To fulfill that career we must use every ounce of intelligence, strength, heart and grace. St. Paul's Epistle to the Corinthians, chapter thirteen, is the text for parents to study, and the only one I will recommend. I'll never give advice about how to raise children. I don't have the faintest idea how to do it.

I don't know whether, judged objectively, Martin and I are doing a good job or not. But we're doing our best moment to moment, and entrusting the whole family to God. And I don't believe parents may take credit for children who turn out well, nor, in most cases, blame for children who do not.

God created the souls of these children. They were made by him, destined by him to live with his life forever in heaven. They were then entrusted to us as parents by the all-wise God, who is not going to let us thwart his plan for them. The only thwarting can be done by the child himself.

God help us if we deliberately fail to be the best parents we can. God help us if we don't turn to him and ask for help in raising his children. On this we will be judged.

But God help the child who when grown, in full possession of free will, turns and blames his parents for his own failures. Did Judas turn and cry that his father didn't love him, or that he came from a broken home? Do we blame St. Monica for the notorious bad life of her son St. Augustine before his conversion? There are black sheep in every family, and if good family life guaranteed the mental health and holiness of each child, there wouldn't be many confessionals in our modern churches. Jesus Christ came into the world to redeem sinners, and if sinners could be prevented by good parents, who would need God?

Yet every parent's heart trembles with love and the belief that his own children should surpass him in every way. To this end we pray, and teach our children to pray.

Teaching children to pray is like teaching them to have fun. It's only difficult if you don't know how yourself. Children come as naturally to prayer as to smiling. Complicated rigid forms, or over-organized cuteness which adults feel may be appropriate, can be as oppressive to a youngster who wants to pray as expensive contrived entertainment often proves to be for children who want to play. Children, being honest, go right to the heart of anything and anyone.

Our liturgy, our Church's public worship, is shaped and cycled to dramatize God's life, and our own lives, through the seasons. Like most Catholic parents today we've tried to bring liturgy into the home. Our liturgical year begins with Advent in the end of November, the time of waiting for the symbolic coming of the Lord in Christmas, and sometime, really, at the end of the world.

For Advent children make an evergreen wreath with candles, and a Tower of David to recall Old Testament prophecies. Our children not only write letters to Santa Claus, they pray to him. Which sounds awful until you remember that we know he is really St. Nicholas, who, being a real saint in heaven, can in the communion of saints hear us and intercede for us. They don't expect the saintly bishop to come down with a sack of presents, and they are, as they grow older, praying for quite unmaterial things.

In the name of all who prepare for the Second Coming, our children make small sacrifices during Advent, giving up occasional lunch desserts, doing hidden kindnesses for each other—which is much more difficult—accumulating a present of grace for the Savior on his birthday. One year the children started Advent sacrifice by turning over all their Trick-or-Treat loot after Halloween to a Glenmary missioner to bring to the poor. And of course on Christmas morning for breakfast we have a birthday cake.

Does it all go smoothly? It does not. Children can get into snits and tantrums making cutout symbols of the Root of Jesse as easily as if they were making a toy bomb.

Patience, they teach us. We're not transformed over night, or in thirty years, either. Lent is a time of patience. In those forty days preparing for Easter, we do penance for our sins which, though forgiven, still in justice have to be paid for sometime. And that gets us into the problem of knowing what sin is, and isn't. Children, if they haven't been scared by some adult, have a nice sense of sin's nature, and why it must be paid for. I remember when one of our young ones explained:

"If you're very good you go to heaven. If you're very bad, you go to hell. If you're just not quite good enough yet, you go to Lavatory to get cleaned up."

Which is as good a way as any to explain Purgatory. And in the hopes of not having to stop off there, our family sets about making up to God and to each other for any injuries we may have done the spiritual health of all. Adults fast with the Church. But old and young do little extra things, what you might call "taking-on" instead of "giving-up." A little girl of four stole about making her two big brothers' beds for them on the sly. It was penance for them to seem grateful, and remake them as unobtrusively as possible. The boy who hates to do dishes, did them. The year that one lad gave up eating red lollipops but not purple, he asked at dinner table of his next younger brother:

"What did you do for the Lord today?"

"When that guy down the street made me mad I didn't give him a sock in the nose," he replied. "I just spitted."

From children parents learn, as God the Father knows, that it's the intention which matters.

If children are wholehearted and unself-conscious about their faith, they're also so literal-minded that they compel us not to take anything for granted. I remember the time a seven-year-old turned to us in outrage, demanding,

"How dare that man on TV call himself the host?"

This involved us in detective work on the word *host*, which in the past has meant everything from stranger to friend, and now serves in biology to indicate a living being supporting parasites, and, so some say, in the entertainment world indicates a parasite supported by a living cast. *Host* meaning victim or sacrificial offering, with its connotations of food and of hostage and of the reception of friends and strangers, is a word which becomes food for thought when a child's fresh view focuses on it.

So far Catholic truth in America has been dressed in absurd hoopskirt words, bastard anglicizations of Latin phrases, often meaningless to our ears. We as parents have the job of translating the truth to our children, and often to ourselves. And by examining words we find the truth newly.

A little girl of five, praying her rosary, announced proudly that she was going to pray thinking about the mystery of the Pronunciation.

"You mean Annunciation, you stupid idiot," said one of her uncharitable brothers. "Pronunciation has nothin' to do with it."

As a small lesson in charity we all looked into the problem and found that Pronunciation was an apt transliteration. The day when Mary accepted the word of God, and replied to the angel, was the day the Word became flesh, the day the Word of God was uttered, or pronounced, as never before.

Let no one think I think young Armstrongs are heavenly cherubs. They are, as they've often heard me say, of the earth, earthy. But I won't tell you about them and embarrass them. And they won't tell you about me. A family has to stick together in these things. And we all remember the day when an eight-year-old in one of his rare theological moments, having done something wrong, yelled out to the rest of our family:

"You don't need to tell everyone about it! On the Last Day at the Last Judgment everybody will know everything we all did. Until then, just keep quiet, will ya?"

Amen to that, say I. The longer I live, the more I love, the more I understand that if ever I'm perfected and become the person God designed me to be, it'll be with and through and for our seven children. It could be, if we know how to surrender to grace, that the coming of one child could make parents saints. To be a saint is only to make God's ways your ways, his thoughts your thoughts, and let him possess you.

Of all the events and circumstances and achievements of life, I suspect parenthood, where the sublime and the earthy meet in moments of glory and worry, fear and laughter, is the one most meaningful in the life with the Persons who are God. The pity is, we keep looking elsewhere.

Between mothers and priests is a special likeness. When a priest consecrates the host at Mass, he changes the substance of bread and wine into the flesh and blood, soul and divinity, and living presence of God. But a mother, also by God's power, changes the substance of her own body into a child, who will become part of the living Christ. Both changes are purchased by love and sacrifice. And in both we penetrate beyond the world of appearances and touch eternity.

The nine months of forming a child are a nine-month parable of truth, intimate evidence that all of life is a sacrament, a sign under which God conceals his presence and power. We in this modern day, knowing so much of the biology and sociology of birth, can lose sight of its true meaning.

A woman carries life within her. She is not herself, the woman says. And she is right. A life not her own has a lien on hers, has commandeered her. The parable is begun. For does not faith teach that each of us lives only to bring forth other life, Christ life? Many months pass before the mother-to-be can feel movement within her. We may for years have no sign of God's dwelling in our souls.

All the world, says St. Paul, groans in the labor pain of giving birth to Christ. And the woman, carrying the unborn babe, walks as a symbol of all life on earth. Yet, while the deepest transfiguring lessons of soul are worked out in her, beyond words, she is forever in touch with reality. She is both Mary and Martha, like it or not. Being realistic is no problem for a Christian mother at all.

In a big family, life crowds us with detail. There's a vaudeville act in which a man sets plates spinning, each on its own slender pole, then runs from one to the others to keep them moving in balance, all the while setting more in motion. At times this is how I see myself, running from kindergarten to high school, without rhyme or reason. Uptairs a victrola bleats with the twist, and rock and roll, and Mommy's old-fashioned to call it a victrola because it's a record player now, or a disc-whisk. Downstairs someone is singing "The Farmer in the Dell." A tot strolls by with his tool-chest, eyes gleaming with premeditation. The front doorbell rings and a girl's friends have come to practice a great new home-written drama, with incidental music. The back doorbell rings and some boys want to go fishing. The icebox door opens and closes in syncopation. The washer and dryer whirl in the background. A high schooler wants to discuss the international news, a young man wants me to talk over the advisability of investing in a proof set of a small-date penny, the repairman's here for the electric typewriter, and Martin's having a meeting of men here tonight. You must make your meditation where you find it, but if you don't have something to meditate on the whole thing turns into a nightmare.

I'm not sure whether a few years of this teaches one serenity, or whether I've just gotten numb. I do know the sight of blood no longer throws me. I used to get upset when a child needed stitches. Now my problem usually is trying to sound coherent when the emergency room dutifully inquires how the accident happened.

"He dropped a railroad track on his hand," I said once, thinking anyone could understand that.

"One of those little HO tracks did that?" the nurse asked.

"No, a real railroad track," I explained patiently. "The big kind. Must weight 200 pounds, maybe more."

"Where did this happen?"

"In our backyard, of course." Doesn't everyone have a railroad track or two in the backyard? We had one there for a month or so, and the kids brought it there themselves on their little red wagons all in a row, and they picked it up in the woods, and if you can tell me why it was in the woods, I'll tell you why we had it near the apple trees. I made them take it back after the accident, and no one has quite forgiven me yet.

One boy went through a year or so of being constantly injured, through overenthusiasm and a slight inability to locate himself in space. But he gave us a bit of Christian philosophy which does a lot to make life bearable.

One day when he was too young to be cautious, unknown to

me he borrowed someone's two-wheeler and set out for a ride. The hitch was that he'd never learned to ride a bike. He went about thirty feet down our quiet road, lost control, hurtled over a culvert, and plunged with the bike into a tiny brook. The brook babbles around a thousand rocks. The boy landed on his head.

The first I knew of it my neighbor was coming across the yards carrying him in her arms. Without irreverence I must say he looked exactly like a model for Christ taken down from the cross. Limp and pale he lay, arms and feet dangling. I could hardly breathe as I went toward them.

"Here is your son," she said, for what else is there to say?

"Thank you," I said, because it's hard to speak when your heart's in your mouth.

But the boy opened his eyes.

"I'm alive, Mom," he said. "You know how I know? It hurts, and when something hurts you know you're alive."

As it turned out, he was fine. No concussion, no stitches needed. For months everyone called him Rockhead, a name he accepted with grinning pride. Rockhead the Indestructible. It takes mothers longer to recover each time their children are in danger. I usually get the shakes the next day and collapse in a corner. And it does hurt me more than it hurts them, in a different way.

Only now I keep remembering what the boy said, and as long as it hurts I know I'm alive.

"Let the little children come to me," said the Lord whose life we share.

I intended to take them to him. Instead, they're taking me.

31

Possibilities

Most of the time I don't try to understand myself or my life at all, not because I've progressed to a high degree of virtue where I'm humble and forgetful of self, but because I don't have time. I suspect that being a bit rattled, like having wrinkles or varicose veins, is one of the natural results of growing older in the full life. But when I do think, I'm often startled because I find I'm not the same person I used to be. I'm not living the same natural life. I still get scraggly, depressed and tired. And unhappy. But there's the presence of joy under all. Another life has been added to me.

"I am come that you may have life, and that more abundantly," said the Lord.

The life he offers is his own. There's an extra dimension of reality. Now, since I, at least, am not yet perfectly christified, and his life doesn't yet permeate all my natural life, I can't go around aware of the unseen realities all the time. I couldn't yet bear to be. But though I do not look their brilliance full face, I move in the filtered glory of their truth. Which is a state both joyful and humiliating.

The Trinity, who created the whole universe and redeemed it and makes it holy, dwells within me, and in a sense is more me than I am. I know that. Yet here I am, quite capable of wishing I had money to meet bills or build on to our house, or a more interesting way of spending this evening, or a chance to get eight hours straight sleep. The Prince of Peace is nearer to me than I am to myself, and I believe that, yet I still lose my temper at a cranky child, or an enemy, or simply because I have a headache and the washing machine won't work. It's very discouraging. The only one it doesn't discourage is God. The hardest thing about being turned toward God, is knowing how far one still has to go.

"What are you working on now?" people have politely asked me.

"An autobiography," I said, as slowly this book took shape.

Some people sighed and said they supposed every writer had to show off and write about himself sometime. Others took pity on me, for they assumed I must feel I'd gone about as far as I could go, and must feel old, through.

Well, goodness knows I've felt that way often enough. I used to feel ancient, bored and decrepit frequently in my teens, and occasionally in my twenties, and on my thirtieth birthday I felt it so strongly that I sat down and sniffled because there was nothing left in life for me at all.

But, seriously, that's not the way of it all. I feel as if life were a script sketched out, which I'm allowed to see only one page at a time. And I'm eager to see what happens next.

Everything up to now had been so unexpected, the exact opposite of what I thought I wanted. And grace is the incalculable in any equation.

"The possibilities," I explained to one earnest gentleman, "are almost unlimited. I haven't the faintest idea what I'll be, or where."

With tender patience and logic he explained that mine was a charming but unrealistic outlook.

"You've already lived, say, half your life. Lots of possibilities now are out. You can't be not-married, not-a-mother. The pattern is set."

But it's not set. Or at least not so I can see it. Looking back on myself fifteen years ago, I can see that it makes sense that I'd become what I am now. But then I thought I was going another way entirely.

Married I am, and thanks be to God, because my husband is incomparable, and we love each other. Mother I am, but motherhood is not a static thing. The purpose of a mother is to become unnecessary to her children.

What shall I be when they in turn bring life into the world? At the moment it seems to me eminently reasonable and pleasant to think that Martin and I will live quietly, welcoming younger generations when they fly private helicopters or return from jaunts to the moon, and perhaps fortunate enough to rejoice in knowing our sons are priests.

But because that seems so reasonable and pleasant, it probably won't happen. Perhaps we shall become very rich—which I guess would be difficult to live with—or very poor, or wander our way around the globe, or from home to home. Perhaps the fascination of politics which has often reached into our lives—when Martin was in the legislature and when he ran for Mayor—will have led us into the arena again for better or worse.

Even while I was writing this book the unexpected happened. I went back to school, to study for an advanced degree in theology, commuting to graduate school at Fordham University. I find formal study exciting and valuable after all these years, and I do homework along with housework, and try to get the mail with my report card before the children spot it. Perhaps someday I'll be a woman theologian.

Yet I have a hunch none of these guesses of the future will prove accurate. Our lives aren't our own, and so far I've never outguessed God. If the past is any guide, then the future will include something I can't even stand imagining now, but will enjoy then. Like becoming a nun, or a public sort of person constantly before an audience, or being crippled. Or like living in a hot buggy place, or being so far away from the ocean that I'll dry up like a prune.

The truth is I don't want to know what comes next. There will, I'm certain, be tragedy, terror and pain, in proportions at least equal to happiness and peace. That is the way of life, and only in living it each moment do we begin to penetrate the mystery. But I'm not afraid. I have only compassion for those who fear. Nothing, not calamity or war, personal failure or suffering, should frighten us. We have to avoid two equally serious delusions: that of thinking we are gods, and that of thinking there is no God.

I've been told I speak too much about God, that I seem obsessed by God. If I am obsessed by him, I am grateful to him for it. For this is true: that all of life, from my private thoughts to politics and rockets to the moon, makes sense to me only in the knowledge that time is permeated with Christ. In him we all move and have our being. In the eyes of faith there isn't one thing in the day that can't remind us of divine truth. I plant a bulb in November, a dead brown thing buried in earth, knowing it conceals the mystery of life and death. I prune roses, knowing my Lord has said that those he loves he cuts back so they may grow with more vigor. I clean, I oil, I patch, I search for lost things, and the parables echo. Laugh, weep, work, sleep, render unto Caesar, give birth, bury, love, embrace, grow, age, whatever we do can show us the mystery of God's love.

Whatever else it may be, the life we share with each other and with him is not dull.

Deo gratias.

*"The Church is
a house with a
hundred gates;
and no two men enter
at exactly the same angle."*
—G. K. Chesterton

House with a Hundred Gates
by April Oursler Armstrong

In this warm, exuberant autobiography, April Oursler Armstrong tells of life with her famous father, Fulton Oursler, author of *The Greatest Story Ever Told,* and of the adventures which led a family of skeptics to enter the gates at different angles. She writes of her young fumblings toward religious faith against the background of her father's profound and witty skepticism; of her own turning away from God, followed by her father's much-publicized conversion; and of her eventual discovery of the Catholic Church.

With love and skill, she brings to life the hectic, happy household of her childhood when the great and near-great were constant visitors. Her father's work as editor in chief of Macfadden Publications kept him constantly in the midst of the most exciting events of his time, and Mrs. Armstrong vividly recalls herself as a child of seven having breakfast in bed
(continued on back flap)